100 Important Questions About the Bible ... Answered!

"Lee McDonald breaks down a lifetime of research on the formation of the Bible into 100 questions, answered in terms a layman can understand. This book should be read by anyone who accepts the Bible as authoritative in any sense."

—**John J. Collins**, Holmes Professor of Old Testament Emeritus, Yale University

"Lee McDonald drew on his vast storehouse of knowledge in order to create for us a highly attractive and original handbook to the most basic questions that are in our mind when thinking about the Old and New Testaments. I, for one, learned much, and I trust that the scholar and layperson alike will benefit much from the expected and unexpected questions asked and expertly answered about the scriptures. Warmly recommended!"

—**Emanuel Tov**, J. L. Magnes Professor of Biblical Studies, Hebrew University, Jerusalem

"In *100 Important Questions About the Bible . . . Answered!*, scholar-pastor Lee Martin McDonald offers a clear and informed guide to some of the most important but misunderstood questions about the Bible. Drawing on decades of both scholarship and pastoral wisdom, McDonald addresses the formation of the biblical canon, the transmission of its texts, and the nature of scriptural inspiration with both academic integrity and accessible insight. Whether you're a student, pastor, or curious reader, this book provides trustworthy answers rooted in historical evidence and theological depth. A vital resource from a trusted voice."

—**Clare Rothschild**, Professor of Scripture Studies, Lewis University, Illinois

"For many years I have taught a class of 'How We Got the Bible.' Dr. Lee McDonald's new book answers all the questions students typically ask about this process and more. McDonald is already the author of the most comprehensive book on the canonization of scripture, *The Biblical Canon: Its Origin, Transmission, and Authority*. He takes a fair, thorough, moderate, and non-fundamentalist approach to this subject of interest to all readers who take the Bible seriously. The scholar and teacher will also find useful material here, clearly explained."

—**Thomas F. Johnson**, Retired Dean, Portland Seminary, George Fox University

"McDonald's mind is amazingly energetic and brimming with challenging issues. The most important dimension of this valuable book is not any one question. It is the freedom and desire to approach our *sacra scriptura* with an unlimited barrage of questions. Dogmatic answers kill. Lively questions stimulate a living faith."

—**James H. Charlesworth**, President, Foundation on Judaism and Christian Origins

"Lee McDonald translates a lifetime of meticulous study into this winsomely accessible book. He breaks down complex issues related to the centuries-long process of the formation of the canons of the Old and New Testaments into bite-size, question-and-answer, easily digestible pieces. It is as informative in teaching us the questions we may never have thought to have asked as it is in rich and reliable answers."

—**David A. deSilva**, Trustees' Distinguished Professor of New Testament and Greek, Ashland Theological Seminary, Cleveland

"Who decided what goes in the Bible and why? Lee Martin McDonald, the foremost authority on the biblical canon, answers 100 such questions in this essential guide. Drawing on five decades of scholarship, McDonald distills a complex history into a clear question-and-answer format, making his profound knowledge accessible to any curious reader. For anyone asking serious questions about the Bible's origins, this is the ideal starting point."

—**Ken M. Penner**, Professor of Religious Studies, St. Francis Xavier University

"Anyone who *likes* the Bible will *love* this book! In this tour de force, providing a hundred answers to common and critical questions about the Bible, Lee McDonald—the world's leading authority on how the Bible was composed and finalized in its various forms—explains how the Holy Writ was written, and also how to embrace its inspired and inspiring authority. With the addition of striking photo-images of ancient texts, this book stands alone as a state-of-the-art contribution on this important subject. A must-read, for sure!"

—**Paul N. Anderson**, author of *From Crisis to Christ: A Contextual Reading of the New Testament*

100 Important Questions About the Bible... Answered!

―――― *Its Origin, Development, and Inspiration* ――――

Lee Martin McDonald

CASCADE *Books* • Eugene, Oregon

100 IMPORTANT QUESTIONS ABOUT THE BIBLE . . . ANSWERED!
Its Origin, Development, and Inspiration

Copyright © 2025 Lee Martin McDonald. All rights reserved. Except for brief quotations in critical publications or reviews, no part of this book may be reproduced in any manner without prior written permission from the publisher. Write: Permissions, Wipf and Stock Publishers, 199 W. 8th Ave., Suite 3, Eugene, OR 97401.

Cascade Books
An Imprint of Wipf and Stock Publishers
199 W. 8th Ave., Suite 3
Eugene, OR 97401

www.wipfandstock.com

PAPERBACK ISBN: 979-8-3852-4995-4
HARDCOVER ISBN: 979-8-3852-4996-1
EBOOK ISBN: 979-8-3852-4997-8

Cataloguing-in-Publication data:

Names: McDonald, Lee Martin, 1942– [author].

Title: 100 important questions about the Bible . . . answered! : its origin, development, and inspiration / by Lee Martin McDonald.

Description: Eugene, OR: Cascade Books, 2025 | Includes bibliographical references.

Identifiers: ISBN 979-8-3852-4995-4 (paperback) | ISBN 979-8-3852-4996-1 (hardcover) | ISBN 979-8-3852-4997-8 (ebook)

Subjects: LCSH: Bible—Canon—History. | Bible.—Old Testament—Canon. | Bible.—New Testament—Canon. | Apocryphal books—Criticism, interpretation, etc. | Bible—Inspiration.

Classification: BS465 M346 2025 (paperback) | BS465 (ebook)

Scripture quotations are from] New Revised Standard Version Bible, copyright © 1989 National Council of the Churches of Christ in the United States of America. Used by permission. All rights reserved worldwide.

VERSION NUMBER 08/18/25

With sincere appreciation for my dear colleagues
in Christian ministry

Gloria Kott, Kimlyn and Trudy Bender,
Ruth Acosta, and Andy Quient

Thank you for your dedicated service.
It was an honor and a blessing for me to serve God
and the church with you!

Contents

Abbreviations | xv
Introduction | xvii

Chapter 1: **The Origin of the Bible** | 1

1. What is the Bible and when was the term first used?   1
2. What does the word "Scripture" mean and when did it emerge among Jews and Christians?   3
3. What is meant by the term "canon"?   6
4. What is a "biblical canon"?   6
5. When did the formation of the Hebrew Scriptures begin?   8
6. What is the Old Testament and how is it different from the Hebrew Scriptures?   9
7. Were the Hebrew Scriptures complete and fixed in the time of Jesus?   11
8. Was the Hebrew Bible settled for the Jews at a council at Jamnia near the end of the first century CE?   12
9. What is the Septuagint (LXX) and why is it important for understanding the origin of the Bible?   13
10. Why is the book of Sirach important for understanding the formation of the Old Testament?   14
11. What books were in the LXX that were not included in the Hebrew Scriptures?   17

CONTENTS

12. What are the Dead Sea Scrolls and how do they aid in our understanding of the Jewish Scriptures in the time of Jesus?   20
13. Why did the ancient Jews number their sacred Scriptures either as twenty-two or twenty-four books?   23
14. When did lists of the Hebrew Bible books begin to circulate among some Jews and lists of the Old Testament books among the early Christians?   24
15. Were all the books in Hebrew Bible accepted as Scripture by the early Christians? Did they accept more or fewer sacred books than their Jewish siblings?   26
16. What Old Testament Scriptures do all churches now accept?   27
17. Why are the same books in the Hebrew Bible and the Christian Old Testament ordered differently?   28
18. Why is Josephus important for knowing which books were recognized as Scripture in the late first century CE?   30
19. Did some Jews believe that the Spirit of prophecy and the writing of Scripture had departed from Israel following Ezra and Nehemiah?   31
20. Which Jewish and Christian writings were welcomed as authoritative Scripture in the time of Jesus?   32
21. Did the Diaspora Jews and early Christians read the Greek translation of Hebrew Scriptures?   34
22. Do the Old Testaments in early Christian Scripture collections include all the books in the Hebrew Scriptures?   37
23. What are the "unknown" or "lost" books cited in the Old Testament and what influence did they have in ancient Israel?   38
24. When did lists of the Scriptures appear in ancient Judaism and early Christianity?   42
25. What criteria were employed to determine which books to include in the churches' Old Testament?   43

26. Scholars have long acknowledged the many variants or differences in the surviving biblical manuscripts. What do those differences show about the formation of the Bible?   44

Chapter 2: **The Old Testament Apocrypha and Pseudepigrapha** | 46

27. What was meant by the term "apocrypha" in antiquity and currently?   46
28. Are there examples in the New Testament that show familiarity with the apocryphal books in the Septuagint (LXX)?   49
29. What are the pseudepigrapha?"   50
30. How common was the production and use of pseudepigraphal texts in antiquity?   51
31. Did some early Christians welcome Jewish pseudepigraphal books as Scripture?   54
32. What are some of the more popular pseudepigraphal texts welcomed by some Jews and some early Christians?   55
33. Who was Athanasius and what did he say about which Scriptures could be read in churches?   56
34. Do Catholic and Orthodox Churches welcome the apocryphal or deuterocanonical books the same way?   58
35. What books did the ecumenical church councils affirm for reading in churches?   58
36. Why do most Protestants reject the Old Testament apocrypha as Scripture?   59

Chapter 3: **The Formation of the New Testament Canon** | 61

37. What key factors were involved in the formation of the New Testament?   61
38. What are the most important ancient resources for the study of the formation of the New Testament?   62
39. Did the ancient churches accept only the four Gospels or did some also accept other gospels?   63

40. What other gospels were read in some ancient churches? 64

41. What was the status of the Book of Acts when churches began forming their New Testament? 66

42. When were Paul's letters recognized as sacred Scripture? 66

43. Did Paul write the book of Hebrews and when was its scriptural status affirmed? 68

44. If any of Paul's lost letters (1 Cor 5:9; Col 4:16) were found, should they be included in the New Testament? 70

45. Which New Testament writings were most disputed in the early churches? 73

46. Why were some Catholic Epistles (James, 1 and 2 Peter, 2–3 John, Jude) and Revelation disputed well into the fourth century and even later? 76

47. Does Revelation 22:18–19 say that the whole Bible is a divine revelation and inspired? 78

48. Were there other collections of Scriptures in antiquity that included books that are not in the New Testament today? 80

49. Because *1 Clement* was a popular orthodox Christian book and even called Scripture by some Christians, why was it not included in the New Testament? 81

50. What led the ancient churches to see the need for a fixed list of books (a canon) that could be read in churches? 82

51. When did biblical canons begin to emerge in early Christianity? 82

52. What criteria were employed by the ancient churches to determine which books would be included in the New Testament? 83

53. When was the Bible officially closed or was it ever closed? 85

54. When were the final decisions made about the formation of the Bible, that is, when could nothing more could be added or taken away? 88

CONTENTS xi

Chapter 4: **Important Christian Artifacts: Creeds, Canon Lists, Manuscripts, *Nomina Sacra*, and Textual Accuracy** | 91

55. What role did the early church creeds have in the formation of the Bible?   91

56. When do lists of the church's Scriptures begin to appear and what do they tell us about the scope of the Bible then?   94

57. What do the major ancient pandect manuscripts of Christian Scriptures, containing both Old and New Testament Scriptures, tell us about the scope of the Bible in antiquity?   98

58. What do the ancient biblical canon lists tell us about the local decisions about which books could be read in churches? What authority should be given to them?   101

59. What are the *Nomina Sacra* and how important are they for identifying ancient Christian Scripture?   102

60. What do the many variations or differences in the surviving biblical manuscripts suggest about the reliability of the church's Scriptures?   103

61. What do the most recent Greek New Testaments tell us about the *text* of the New Testament?   105

62. What ancient biblical manuscripts are involved in the preparation of the text of the New Testament for students and translators?   106

63. What books were in the church's ancient scriptural manuscripts?   108

Chapter 5: **More Christian Artifacts: Translations, Lectionaries, Hymns, and Church Councils** | 111

64. Why are the earliest translations of the Bible important? What can be learned from them about the formation of the Bible?   111

65. What are some of the earliest and most important translations of the New Testament?   113

66. What can the ancient translations tell us about the history and development of the Bible?   118

67. What are lectionaries and what can they tell us about which Scriptures were read in the ancient churches?   119

68. How important were the early Christian hymns for advancing the church's faith and reflecting which books were included in the Bible?   121

69. Were there ancient examples of hymn books in early Christianity that told the story of Jesus?   124

70. Did the ancient *local* church councils influence the formation of the Bible?   125

71. Was there an early church council that rejected the status of the Shepherd of Hermas?   126

72. What are the most important church councils that dealt with the scope of sacred texts that could be read in churches?   129

73. Did the first ecumenical council at Nicea in 325 CE settle the issue of which books would be in the Bible?   131

Chapter 6: The Challenge of Authorship and Pseudepigrapha in Early Christianity | 133

74. Was authorship a determining factor in deciding which books to include in the church's Scriptures?   133

75. What New Testament books had a disputed authorship in the early churches?   135

76. Since there was considerable debate in antiquity over the authorship of Hebrews, why was it finally included in the church's Bible?   137

77. Did the early Christians welcome and produce pseudonymous writings as Scripture?   139

78. Should churches welcome biblical books written under a false name?   140

79. Does reference to 1 Enoch in the New Testament reflect the scriptural status of nonbiblical books in early Christianity?   142

80. When was 1 Enoch finally rejected in early Christianity?   144

Chapter 7: **Early Christian Apocrypha, the Muratorian Fragment, and Scriptural Awareness in the New Testament** | 146

81. What are the *Christian* apocryphal books and how were they welcomed in antiquity? 147

82. What is the Muratorian Fragment and why do scholars cite it to establish an early dating of the New Testament? 148

83. Is the Muratorian Fragment a useful document for understanding second-century Christian thought about Christian Scripture? 151

84. Were the biblical authors aware that they were writing holy Scripture? 151

Chapter 8: **Christian Faith and the Bible** | 155

85. Can historians affirm Christian beliefs about the inspiration of the Bible? 155

86. Was God involved in the writing of Scripture and the formation of the Bible? 159

87. Is there subjectivity in biblical faith and can it ever be based on rational logic, history, and science? 161

88. Do the variants or differences in the surviving biblical manuscripts affect their inspiration or scriptural status? 165

89. Can the church survive without a Bible? 168

90. What is the value of studying the Bible in its historical and social context? 170

91. What are the most important ancient sources for investigating the origin and formation of the Bible? 171

Chapter 9: **Inspiration and the Bible** | 178

92. What is meant by "inspiration" and how is it applied to the Bible? 178

93. Does inspiration assume a perfect Bible? 180

94. What is allegory and how was it used to affirm the inspiration of Scripture? 182

95. Does inspiration involve divine "possession" of scriptural authors? Hellenistic, Jewish, and early Christian perspectives.   184

96. Was inspiration a criterion for including a book in the New Testament?   187

97. Was inspiration limited to biblical authors?   187

98. Did the early church fathers agree on what inspiration meant?   191

99. Can the church affirm the authority and inspiration of the Bible today?   192

100. What are some of the most important ancient sources that influenced Christian notions of biblical inspiration?   193

Conclusion | 209

Appendix: Photos of Ancient Religious Texts | 211
Select Bibliography | 239

Abbreviations

All abbreviations for biblical books and other ancient texts follow the conventions in the Society of Biblical Literature's *The SBL Handbook of Style*.

Introduction

THERE ARE MANY QUESTIONS related to the origin of the Bible, and that in large part is because the early churches did not leave us with a record of all that went into the formation of the collection of the church's Scriptures that we now call the Bible. While there are a lot more questions that could be addressed, I have chosen a hundred of them that deal with many of the most important issues relating to the formation of the Bible and its inspiration.

This book began with a number of questions posed to me by Michael Licona in five podcasts that I did with him a couple of years ago. While Dr. Licona and I were putting the podcasts together, we began to wonder if the material, with added reference to some resources, might also be helpful to a wider audience. The podcasts used a question-and-answer format, and this volume retains that format, with some additional questions.

In what follows I have responded to several of the questions in a short one-page response, but others required two or more pages, especially those that dealt with some of the more complex matters, such as the importance of the Dead Sea Scrolls, the books that were excluded from the church's Scriptures, and the many variants or differences in the surviving biblical manuscripts that tell the same story differently. Questions about these issues were of considerable interest in the popular media and led to the production of many books, such as Dan Brown's well-known *Da Vinci Code*, which was based largely on some ancient writings that were not included in the Bible and challenged several biblical conclusions.

Often, I will list important ancient sources and modern research texts that enable readers to pursue their own investigations. There are occasional footnotes in what follows, but mostly for clarification of some technical terms and to list some relevant current scholarly documents, the details of which can be found in the select bibliography at the end of this volume. I also include some reflections on the implications of this study for Christian faith today. Hopefully this little book will be a useful summary for students, professors, and informed laypersons in how the Bible was formed, its inspiration, and what is going on in current biblical research.

While Michael Licona was not able to continue working with me on the volume due to several pressing responsibilities, he was significantly involved in its early stages. We became friends in the process of doing the podcasts and working together on this text and I have deep appreciation for him and his faith commitments as well as his expertise in biblical inquiry.[1] While we did not always agree on how to address some of the questions, it was good for both of us to know that Christians can disagree on some matters while still agreeing on the most important issues of Christian faith that brought us together in the first place.

Scholars who examine the same ancient sources discussed in this volume often disagree on how to interpret them. Sometimes that is because all of us bring assumptions (often theological baggage) to our study of ancient sources, but also because some of our questions were seldom if ever discussed in antiquity. Because of this, we often have to draw tentative conclusions that are sometimes educated guesses on what we think was going on during the emergence of the Bible in early Christianity. Since the surviving ancient resources often do not address several modern questions, modern conclusions are often not based on what can be derived from the sources that survive antiquity. Those familiar with most of these sources often draw better solutions to those questions the ancients did not ask. Modern scholars are often more familiar with the surviving ancient resources than was possible in antiquity, though they sometimes bring theological assumptions to their work that may not have been operative in antiquity. Readers will see below that many early church fathers disagreed on how to answer many of the questions and concerns facing them in their contexts and

---

1. Michael earned his PhD in New Testament studies from the University of Pretoria and is now a professor of New Testament studies and Christian apologetics at Houston Christian University. He has also published several articles and books, most notably *The Resurrection of Jesus: A New Historiographical Approach*, *Why Are There Differences in the Gospels? What We Can Learn from Ancient Biography*, and, more recently, *Jesus, Contradicted: Why the Gospels Tell the Same Story Differently*. We are both members of the prestigious *Studiorum Novi Testamenti Societas*.

that is also true now among modern scholars in our contexts. A common assumption in some studies of ancient resources is that if one church father held to a particular position at a particular place and time, then all church fathers at that time and location held to the same position. That, of course, is almost never the case. Thoughtful biblical scholars base their conclusions on a careful study of the surviving ancient sources and those who are most familiar with them regularly form better conclusions about the formation of the Bible.

Scholars must also acknowledge that currently settled issues may one day be revisited should some unknown documents be found in an old European library collection that has yet to be catalogued or assessed or perhaps if some archaeologist discovers an unknown text or manuscript that leads to moderations of earlier settled conclusions. Some issues once thought settled long ago are given greater clarity today based on more recent research! Again, this is because many of our modern questions were not of much concern initially in the early churches—for instance, the importance of authorship and which writings were believed to be inspired by God and gave aid to churches as they formed their beliefs and practices.

Biblical scholars are very well aware that many books circulating in ancient churches, often for centuries, were not eventually included in the Bible. Some of those books have been recovered, but many of them are only known by their names and not their content. As we will see below, it has been suggested that less than 1 percent of the writings of antiquity have survived and we can only imagine what other writings of which we know nothing might have had some influence in early Christianity. And one can only wonder if the early church fathers would have formulated their beliefs differently if they had access to all of the books that we now have access to.

Readers of this work will see that I restate in a briefer and hopefully clearer format much of the research in my previous publications, some of which are listed in the Select Bibliography. I trust that this volume will lead others to pursue greater research and contribute to the growing interest in the questions below.

My own interest in the questions discussed in this book began some fifty years ago. As time allowed, I began to question what I had been taught earlier by well-intentioned but uninformed professors on such matters. At that time, in the 1960s, there were only a few (rather dated) works available that sought to clarify questions about the origin of the Bible, and many of them were unknown to professors of biblical studies.

Few Old or New Testament introductions in the early 1960s and before included more than a few pages on how the Bible was formed.

When I was in my early years as a seminary professor, I was invited to write a brief article for the seminary bulletin on how we got our Bible. That article was based largely on what I had learned earlier as a seminary student. Sometimes my earlier professors' answers were coupled with a theological agenda. That is not unusual in the history of academic inquiry. At that time I was not able to pursue this subject seriously until much later when more research became available to me in the 1970s and 1980s.

My research began more seriously when I was a pastor in Nebraska in the 1980s. While teaching a church Bible study, a student who attended a state university came home at Christmas time and attended my study. He had just finished a course on religion and the Bible, and his professor rightly told him that there were many ancient religious books that were not eventually included in the church's Bible. He asked me to tell him why some books were welcomed as Scripture, but others were not. His question was a very good one that had to do with the criteria employed by the early church fathers who selected some books that could be read in churches but decreed that others could not be read in the churches. As I was responding to young man's question, I kept thinking of exceptions to almost everything I was telling him, and I asked him if I could get back to him in a week. That began my serious study of the criteria employed to determine the scope of the church's Bible and this later became the focus of my research at Harvard Divinity School that took shape under the direction of New Testament professors Helmut Koester and George W. MacRae, who were very supportive of my research. That was over forty years ago and since then I have written over a dozen books and a hundred related articles on many of the challenging and multifaceted aspects of the formation of the Bible. Thankfully others have pursued the origin of the Bible in their investigations and now far more is known than was possible earlier.

Among the most important resources that need to be considered to understand the formation of the Bible, we must examine a limited number of citations and quotations from the early church fathers, as well as the many surviving scriptural manuscripts to see what books are in them, followed by considering what Scriptures appear in the early Christian lectionaries, which reflect the texts that were read in the ancient churches. Insight into which books were read in the churches as Scripture also requires us to study the ancient canon lists, as well as the ancient translations that have survived antiquity. Very few scholars are familiar with all of those resources, and most depend regularly on the work of other credible scholars who are familiar with them. As a result of research in all these areas, biblical scholars can now offer more plausible answers to some of the key issues than were possible earlier. Publications on the origin of the Scriptures have led almost to a cottage industry of books and articles that address many of the same questions addressed here, in this volume. While scholars often disagree on how to interpret the ancient sources, there is more agreement now than was possible earlier. In this book I would like to introduce you to the current state of research.

I am happy also to offer thanks to several individuals who have allowed me to publish this volume. I mention first George Callihan from Wipf and Stock Publishers, their Cascade publishing venue, and their editorial community who agreed to publish this book. I am also pleased to receive the help from Andrew Jacobs for clarifying to me the publishing guidelines that initially were unclear to me. He prepared the formation of this manuscript for the editor, Revd. Dr. Robin Parry who has been most helpful in editing and correcting my oversights and occasional errors. Of course, if any errors remain, they are all mine and not his. I am also grateful to Craig A. Evans for permission to make use of several of his and Ginny Evans's photos in the appendix that show examples of several ancient manuscripts of the church's Scriptures along with some examples of writings that were not finally included in the Bible. Evans has a much larger and more helpful collection of similar photos in his *Jesus and the Manuscripts: What We Can Learn from the Oldest Texts*. I was also permitted to use, with permission, several photos of biblical texts from the Dunham Bible Museum on the campus of Houston Christian University. These photos show much of what I want to say about the quality of the texts and the scope of the early Scriptures.

Finally, I am especially happy to dedicate this volume to several dear friends who served at the First Baptist Church in Alhambra, California, when I served as the senior pastor. Their dedicated service for Christ along with the fruitful exercise of their many talents and skills greatly enhanced the church's ministry, health, and growth while I was there. They include Gloria Kott, Kimlyn and Trudy Bender, Ruth Acosta, and Andy Quient. They all continue to be dear friends and have moved on to other responsibilities in their service for Christ, both in the church and in Christian teaching in other churches and academic settings.

So now let's begin!

CHAPTER 1

The Origin of the Bible

We begin here with some of the easier questions, which warrant a more detailed response than is commonly given and which also form a basis for understanding some of the more complex questions that follow. As readers will see, those more complex questions often have a significant history. Some clarifications of that history will help aid us in answering more difficult questions surrounding the development of the Bible.

1. What is the Bible and when was the term first used?

"Bible" is the collective term that refers to a collection of the church's Old and New Testament Scriptures. Christians regularly acknowledge the Bible as God's word and regularly read and cite its sacred texts in their worship services and in their classes for teaching Christian doctrine, and to identify their mission and ministry as well as for guidance for Christian living. The Bible as God's word also identifies for the church who God is, who Christ is, what the church's core beliefs are, and it speaks of God's activity in human history. The Bible enables persons of faith to root their faith in multiple divine acts that they claim are historical events, that is, they actually happened, especially God's activity in the exodus of Israel from Egypt, the wilderness wanderings, and the entrance of Israel back into the land of Canaan, and, for Christians, the resurrection of Jesus from the dead.

Along with those primary events the Bible also provides answers to the questions about the origin of life, the emergence of the nation of Israel (Genesis), and the giving of the Law to the Israelites through Moses (Exodus). Christians accept these activities that are recorded in the Hebrew Scriptures and add to them the story of Jesus of Nazareth who taught his followers the way to God. They also accept the teachings in their New Testament about Jesus' identity as the promised Christ of Jewish hopes, that he died and was raised from the dead, and that his followers pursued a mission of proclaiming him throughout the Greco-Roman world and even further.

The word "Bible" comes from the Greek word for "book" (Greek = *biblos*). The plural of *biblos* is *biblia* and simply means "books." When Christians began speaking of the collection of their Scriptures, by the ninth and tenth centuries they commonly began to call them their "holy books," the literal translation of "Holy Bible." This designation has become the very popular "Holy Bible," a text that includes all the church's Scriptures.

Some Jews have recently started to use the word "Bible" for their own sacred books, which include their Law (*Torah*), Prophets (*Neviim*), and Writings (*Ketuvim*), often using the first letters of those Hebrew words to form the name TaNaK (commonly *Tanak*) or *Miqra*. Despite continuing differences over which books belong in the Bible, the term "Bible" is widespread now and used to identify the church's Scriptures.

It appears that the term was first used by Jerome, the late-fourth and early-fifth century church father, who referred to the church's collection of its Scriptures as the "holy books," but that designation was not regularly used in churches until the ninth and tenth centuries. It became even more popular after the publication of the "Paris Bibles" in the twelfth and thirteenth centuries. With the aid of thinner paper by that time and the invention of the magnifying glass, it became possible to produce biblical manuscripts with smaller letters and thinner paper allowing the inclusion all of the church's Scriptures in one large but portable book. Those books were about the same size as a large study Bible today. Because these Bibles were first produced in Paris, they became known as the "Paris Bibles."[1]

The story told in the Bible began as an oral sacred tradition that eventually was written down over a long period of time, perhaps even a thousand years or more, but its narrative begins much earlier, in the

---

1. For a discussion of the origin and influence of the Paris Bibles, see van Liere, *Introduction to the Medieval*, 4–15; and Light, "Thirteenth Century," 380–91.

creation of the heavens and earth, and it continues to reflect the continuing revelations of God to those that honor and follow divine commands. While Jews welcome only those books that are in the Protestants's Old Testament, though in a different order as we will see below, Christians also accept those books that form their New Testament. Some Christians welcome additional books that were written largely after the books in the Hebrew Bible were written and before the writing of the books that comprise the church's New Testament. As we will see, those additional books that are not in the Hebrew Scriptures are called "apocryphal" books by Protestants, but Catholics identify those additional books in their Old Testament as "deuterocanonical books." The Orthodox churches welcome the deuterocanonical books as "readable noncanonical Old Testament scriptures"—a designation that appears contradictory, but it means that they read those books in worship for inspiration and enrichment but do not call them "canonical Scripture."

"Holy Bible" remains as the church's primary designation for its fixed collection of the sacred Scriptures. In sum, although "Bible" was not a common early designation for the church's sacred Scriptures, over time it became the most common way to identify them. As we will see below, not all Bibles in antiquity or even today are the same in terms of their contents or order, but Christians still call them their "Holy Bible."

2. What does the word "Scripture" mean and when did it emerge among Jews and Christians?

The term *scripture* comes from the Latin *script* (writing) and its plural *scriptura* (writings). This is like the Greek *graphe* (writing) and *graphai* (writings), as well as the Hebrew *ketuv* (writing) and its plural *ketuvim* (writings). These terms were first used of writing or writings in general, but in time they came to refer to the *sacred* writings of Jews and Christians. When the terms *graphe* and *graphai* are used in the New Testament, for instance, they regularly refer to the Old Testament writings present in the Hebrew Scriptures and are often translated by the Latin-derived terms "Scripture" or "Scriptures." Sometimes all three designations (i.e., *ketuv*, *graphe*, and *script*) are used of the act of writing or writings themselves without reference to sacredness, but the terms in Greek and Hebrew began to refer to sacred or holy writings, collective or individual, around 130 BCE when the first *known* use of the term for sacred religious texts

("Scripture") appears in the legendary Letter of Aristeas (#155), where it referred to the Hebrew Torah translated into Greek (*graphē*) "writing" and in translation it is spoken of as "Scripture." Whenever the terms *graphē* and its plural *graphai* are used in the New Testament, it is regularly referring to the church's first sacred Scriptures, namely its Old Testament Scriptures. There are two exceptions to this, namely 1 Tim 5:18, which cites the words of Jesus as Scripture along with the Hebrew Scriptures, and 2 Pet 3:15–17, which refers to Paul's writings along with the Hebrew Scriptures.

The term "writings" (*ketuvim*) for sacred Scriptures first appears in the sense of holy writings around 130 BCE. That designation was not used in reference to the third part of the Hebrew Scriptures until at the earliest around 180 CE to 200 CE, and it was not common among Jewish sages until the fourth to the fifth centuries CE. Although the Old Testament Scriptures are not always introduced by those scriptural designations (e.g., "as it is written") in the New Testament, all texts or citations introduced by those words are regularly citing sacred Scripture. Some scholars say that because none of the deuterocanonical or apocryphal books are introduced by those designations in the New Testament, they were not considered sacred Scripture. However, not all scriptural passages cited in the New Testament are introduced the same way. For instance, in Matt 24:15, Jesus quotes Daniel the prophet, but does not introduce the text with "as the Scripture says" or "it is written," but he is clearly referring to the sacred text of Daniel the prophet. The author of Hebrews quotes more texts from the Old Testament than any other book in the New Testament but does not use any of the usual introductory scriptural designations, except for one quote from Ps 40:6–8 and that term is in the psalm itself (see LXX translation in Heb 10:7). We should not draw hasty conclusions if the usual scriptural designations are not employed when citing an Old Testament text or assume automatically that all such uses of *graphe* ("writing") refer to sacred Scripture. Those terms are not always used in the New Testament to introduce a scriptural text, but the context clarifies that an Old Testament Scripture is being referenced.

It is unlikely that the Scriptures cited by Jesus or in the New Testament texts comprise *all* of the books that either he or the New Testament authors welcomed as Scripture, since they only cited those texts that advanced what they were teaching to specific groups or individuals. Almost a third of the Old Testament Scriptures are not cited by Jesus in the Gospels, but that does not mean that he rejected those he did not cite. We cannot say exactly which books Jesus or Paul, or other

New Testament authors accepted as Scripture since they regularly were speaking or writing to address specific situations in their respective contexts and only used or cited those sacred writings that were relevant to the issues they were addressing.

In regard to such texts as 2 Tim 3:16–17, the reference there to "all scripture" was not referring to the New Testament Scriptures, but only to the church's first Scriptures (i.e., what it came to call the Old Testament). However, it is not inappropriate to say that what was believed about the sacredness of the church's first Scriptures, its Old Testament, was also eventually held to be true of the church's New Testament Scriptures. Similarly, it is not uncommon for many today to extend the warning in Rev 22:18–19 about adding to or deleting from anything in that book and apply it more broadly to all Scriptures. However, the command not to change or delete or add to a sacred text was typical for writings believed to be sacred and from the Spirit. That notion goes back to Deut 4:2 and was also applied to the Greek translation of the Hebrew Scriptures, according to the Letter of Aristeas noted above.

Aside from the two references mentioned above (1 Tim 5:18 and 2 Pet 3:15–17)—which indicate that a written gospel and Paul's letters were starting to be cited as Christian Scripture by the time that 2 Peter was written, likely in the second century—all other New Testament references to "Scripture" refer to the Hebrew sacred texts, most of which were eventually included in the Hebrew Bible and the church's Old Testament Scriptures.

The words "as it is written" or "as the Scripture says" often appear in the Apostolic Fathers writings (ca. 90–150 CE) and, as in the New Testament, almost always in reference to the Old Testament Scriptures,[2] but there are exceptions. For instance, the reference in 1 Clem. 46.2 is to an unknown source. In Barn. 16.6, the source is also unknown, but it may be a free paraphrase of Dan 9:24. In Barn. 11.1 and 14.6, "it is written" refers to the broader teachings of Scripture. In the Shepherd of Hermas 7.4, "it is written" refers to the lost Book of Eldad and Modat. What are we to make of the fact that "it is written" or "as the Scripture says" are used of some writings unknown to us now?

---

2. See the following texts where the introductory words using the term "scripture" are referring to a text in the Old Testament: 1 Clem. 4.1; 14.4; 17.7; 29.2; 36.3; 39.3; 48.2; 50.4; Ign. *Mag.* 12.1; Barn. 4.14; 15.1.

3. What is meant by the term "canon"?

The word *canon* comes from a Greek word *kanon*, for "reed," a loan word from the Hebrew and Aramaic *kaneh* that was used in antiquity in reference to a measuring rod or stick. The reed, like a ruler, was used for measuring lengths, but it came to be used for the various rules or regulations and measurements, whether in building construction, art, philosophy guides, grammar rules, and other disciplines. In this extended sense, it came to be used of the most important texts, especially those often viewed among the Greeks as sacred texts, such as Homer's *Iliad* and *Odyssey*. In time, multiple canons were viewed as rules or guidelines and regulations to follow in antiquity long before the term came to be used for a well-defined collection of sacred books that served as guides and rules for people of faith to follow.

In the New Testament the term "canon" is used by the apostle Paul to describe the limits of acceptable beliefs in the churches (Gal 6:16)[3] and that understanding was quite common in the second century when the church spoke of its "canon [or rule] of faith" or in Latin its *regula fidei*. Yet while *canon* was regularly used in this period to designate the acceptable beliefs in churches, it was not used to refer a fixed collection of the church's sacred Scriptures. However, from the second century on some of the New Testament writings were beginning to be called "Scripture." By the late middle of the fourth century the word "canon" *began* to be employed to describe the collection of books that formed the church's sacred Scriptures and could be read in churches, and that collection of sacred texts became known as the church's "biblical canon." The Scriptures in that collection varied for centuries, but those writings accepted as sacred Scripture were regularly read in churches during their worship or liturgical meetings and used in their teaching as they were interpreted in relation to the church's core beliefs.

4. What is a biblical canon?

A biblical canon is the collection of books that comprise the church's Bible and that functions as a "rule of faith" for churches that welcome and embrace those books as sacred Scripture. The biblical canon *now* regularly refers to *fixed* collections of sacred books that form the Bibles,

---

3. Paul also uses "canon" in reference to the "limits" or scope of his ministry (2 Cor 10:13–16).

despite the variations in the Christian Old Testament books among the three main bodies of the church, namely the Orthodox, Catholic, and Protestant churches. There is a shared affirmation of all of the books in the Hebrew Bible, the Scriptures of the Jewish community, but not yet on the scope of the whole Old Testament writings. Catholic Christians accept ten additional books that they call deuterocanonical writings, and the same books are designated "apocryphal" books by Protestant churches, which do not accept them as sacred Scriptures. Orthodox Christians welcome the same additional books that Catholics welcome plus three others, but they do not call them sacred Scripture, but rather "noncanonical Old Testament Scriptures" or sometimes simply "readable" (Greek = *anagignoskomena*) texts (i.e., texts that they read in their church services). Again, there is now almost complete agreement on all of the books in the New Testament, but that took centuries to attain. Full agreement on the scope of the New Testament was eventually settled for *most* churches by the seventh to eighth centuries. As we will see, however, some minor groups of Christians, such as the Ethiopian Orthodox Christians, also welcome other books in their New Testament. And as late as the 1800s Armenian Christians also welcomed as Scripture the pseudonymous text attributed to Paul that is called 3 Corinthians.

So, "canon" originally referred to a collection of beliefs that gave direction to the churches—the "canon of faith"—but the collection of books that comprise the church's sacred Scriptures is now called a "biblical canon." The word began to be used for a fixed collection of Christian writings that could be read in churches by Athanasius, in his thirty-ninth annual *Festal Letter* in 367 CE, which was sent to churches to inform them when to celebrate Easter (more on this famous text below). Such letters regularly dealt with more than just the date to celebrate Easter and often included other admonitions as well. In this letter Athanasius listed the scriptural books that could be read in churches, but he also included some books that could be read in private for inspiration or to advance piety. Those books that could be read publicly in churches he called "canonical" books and those that could be read in private were called by him "readable" (Greek = *anagignoskomena*) books. He also spoke of "apocryphal" writings that were completely rejected because they were texts written in a false name and often heretical. Essentially books written in a false name were often also called heretical books or "apocrypha."

The "readable" books in Athanasius's list, as we will see below, along with several others are those later called "deuterocanonical" books by

Catholics, "apocryphal" books by Protestants, and "non-canonical Old Testament Scriptures" by the Orthodox. More recently some Orthodox Christians have begun to use the Catholic designation calling them "deuterocanonical" writings. Centuries later the term "biblical canon" came to be used to refer to the collection of Scriptures that can be read in the church's worship liturgies. The various churches have yet to agree on the value and use of the apocryphal/deuterocanonical/readable books, but most biblical scholars today agree that there is considerable value in them. These books will be discussed below in chapters 2 and 5.

5. When did the formation of the Hebrew Scriptures begin?

The Old Testament began as a process, and no one was thinking of a fixed biblical canon of selected Scriptures when that process began. Essentially, the ancient prophets focused on the story of the Israelites's exodus from Egypt, their wilderness wanderings, and their entering Canaan, the "promised land." There are more than eighty references to the exodus, wilderness wanderings, and entrance into the promised land mentioned in the Old Testament writings. Sanders produced a small monograph listing and discussing the importance of those references.[4] Later, that story was expanded to include the giving of the Law (Torah) at Sinai, and the beginnings of all things (Genesis). The stories of those primary events were foundational in subsequent prophetic messages. Amos, for example, speaking about the exodus from Egypt showed how much God cared for the people (2:10; 3:1–2) and as a result his people should honor and obey God and not honor or worship false gods. Amos also pointed to the Israelites rejection of the "Law of God" for they "have not kept his statues" (2:4).

Those notions became much more prominent in the messages in Amos and Isaiah and Hosea, but also other classical prophets. Eventually their messages became a collection of writings, but not for quite some time. Even the Law of Moses itself appears to have been lost for quite some time before being rediscovered by Josiah's high priest, Hilkiah, who found a copy of the Law, probably the book of Deuteronomy, in the temple when his workers were cleaning and getting things squared away in the temple. King Josiah's reading of that sacred text, the Law, led to a significant renewal among the Israelites for a brief time and there was a

---

4. For a discussion of these references, see Sanders, *Monotheizing Process*.

marvelous renewal of obedience to God in the land (2 Kgs 22:8—23:8). Soon after Josiah's death the people turned away from the Law of God and their nation was destroyed along with the temple and many of their leaders were deported to Babylon. Finally, Jerusalem was destroyed (586 BCE). When Ezra and Nehemiah and other exiles were allowed by Cyrus of Persia to return to their homeland (2 Chr 36:22–23; Ezra 1:1–4; cf. 7:1–28) they began regularly reading the same book, most likely Deuteronomy (Neh 8:1–8) and others (e.g., Ezra 1:1; 5:1–2). As a result, there was a renewal of faith among those who returned to their land, and they rebuilt their nation and temple. This was accomplished with the recognition of the sacredness of their Scriptures and commitment to observe them (Neh 8:1–12).

When the nation and its kingdom had been destroyed with its capital city, Jerusalem, and its kings and national leaders taken into captivity, what did the people have left when they had no capitol, no law, and no king, or national leader? They had nothing to give them stability, guidance, or leadership except their sacred Scriptures. From that time, we find the beginnings of Judaism, starting with Ezra and Nehemiah during the Persian occupation of the land of Israel. At that time, the Jews returning from Babylon focused mostly on the Torah, or Old Testament Pentateuch as Christians call it, which included Genesis to Deuteronomy, as we see in Ezra and Nehemiah, along with some of the prophets (see 2 Kgs 17:13).[5] John J. Collins has written extensively on this subject.[6]

6. What is the "Old Testament" and how is it different from the Hebrew Scriptures?

Those designations need some unpacking. The term "testament" is another word for "covenant," which was usually an agreement between two parties. In Jeremiah we see a reference to an agreement or covenant between God and Abraham and subsequently with the Israelites who were called on to keep the Law of God. Because that Law was broken many times with tragic consequences for the people, Jeremiah, acknowledging the nation had broken the covenant, declared that God would make a new covenant or testament with them in which he would write his covenant on their hearts, and he would forgive their sins (Jer 31:31–34).

---

5. See Sanders, *Monotheizing Process*.
6. See Collins, *Invention of Judaism*.

In the New Testament we see that Jesus in his Last Supper with his disciples took bread and a cup of wine and, after blessing it, said that the bread represented his body and the cup his blood, which was the blood of the covenant that was poured out for many (Mark 14:22–24). Matthew and Luke indicate that the bread represented Christ's body "that is given for you" and his blood was the "new covenant" poured out for many "for the forgiveness of sins" (Matt 26:26–28; see also Luke 22:14–20). The author of Hebrews in 8:7 indicates that there was fault with the first covenant (first testament) and so there was need for a second one and the new covenant made the first one obsolete (8:13), and he cites Jer 31:31–34 (see Heb 8:8–12, the longest Old Testament citation in the New Testament, which quotes this text in Jeremiah).

The first known use of the designation "Old Testament" (= Old Covenant) for the church's *first* Scripture is found in the last quarter of the second century in the teachings of Melito of Sardis (ca. 170) (also "New Testament" [= New Covenant] for the church's *Christian* Scriptures [Eusebius, *Hist. eccl.* 4.26.14, citing Melito and Irenaeus]). At roughly the same time the church father Irenaeus also made use of these terms (*Haer.* 4.28.1–2) and it is unlikely that they were invented by either church father. We see similar references in Clement of Alexandria (ca. 170–180, *Strom.* 15.5.85) and later in Tertullian, who was also familiar with "Old Testament" (*Prax.* 15). Those terms were *not commonly* used for the two collections of the church's Scriptures until well into the fourth century and by then they had a wider use in churches. In the third century Origen spoke of the "so-called Old Testament and the so-called New [Testament]" (*Commentary on John* 5.4) and Eusebius similarly in the fourth century (*Hist. eccl.* 3.9.5) It is not precisely known when those designations began to be used nor which books were included in either of them of them until the fourth century and following. Melito made a trip to Palestine to find out which Scriptures were accepted by the churches and subsequently he was able to prepare a list of the Old Testament books that is close to but not exactly like the later Old Testament canons in the churches (Eusebius, *Hist. eccl.* 4.26.14). The books that comprised the church's New Testament Scriptures were debated for centuries, but eventually by the late fourth century *most* churches welcomed most of the books of the New Testament. Again, when these designations began to be used there was no clear statement on what books were included in them except that they represented the church's "first" Scriptures (Old Testament) and their "second" Scriptures (New Testament). I will focus more on the formation of the New Testament collection in chapter 3 and following.

It has been common in recent years when communicating with Jewish colleagues to speak of the church's "First" and "Second Testaments," though Old and New Testament are still quite popular in churches and even used by some Jewish scholars.

The Hebrew Bible is a term coined by scholars to refer to the Scriptures of the Jews that are identified by them as Tanak—a name that is, as explained previously, derived from the first letters of *Torah* (Law), *Nevi'im* (Prophets), and *Ketuvim* (Writings). This collection of Scriptures is also sometimes referred to as *miqra* (Hebrew = that which is read [aloud]), which emphasizes that the Jewish sacred Scriptures were intended to be read in the synagogues and study houses (Yeshivahs). The broad order of the books in the Hebrew Bible are Law, Prophets, and Writings, but Christian Old Testaments usually are ordered broadly into Law, History, Poetry and Wisdom, and Prophets. Catholic, Orthodox, and Protestant Christians recognize as Scripture all the books in the Hebrew Bible or Tanak, but Catholics and Orthodox welcome some additional books. I will discuss this below.

7. Were the Jewish Scriptures complete and fixed in the time of Jesus?

There was no complete and fixed collection of the Jewish Scriptures in the time of Jesus' ministry (ca. 26–30 CE). Much of the answer to this question can be seen in previous one, but we can see in the time of Jesus that there were several collections of sacred writings called and treated like Scripture, though their precise contents are not always clear: namely, which books comprised the Prophets (*Nevi'im*) at that time and whether all of the books now in the Writings (*Ketuvim*), and only those, were included in the Jewish Scriptures at that time. Those clearly established collections that are easy to identify included the Torah or Pentateuch, the Twelve Minor Prophets, several prophetic books noted above, and Psalms. Other books also eventually formed the Hebrew Bible and later the church's Old Testament, but the Old Testament was not a done deal in the time of Jesus and that is reflected in the three different Old Testaments in Orthodox, Catholic, and Protestant Bibles today. We can also say that several books that later formed the Hebrew

Bible and the Christian Old Testaments were questioned or debated by Jews and Christians for centuries.

8. Was the Hebrew Bible settled for the Jews at a council at Jamnia near the end of the first century CE?

There was a popular view advocated by many well-known scholars for years claiming that the Jewish Scriptures were settled in a threefold timeframe beginning with the closing of the Torah or Law around 400 BCE, the Prophets around 200 BCE, and the Writings at a synod or council at Jamnia (or Javneh), a small town a few miles south of Joppa, around 90 to 100 CE. It was argued that those who met there were Pharisaic leaders who discussed whether Song of Songs (or Canticles) and Ecclesiastes (or Qoheleth) "defiled the hands"—a designation focusing on the cleanliness or holiness of a text. Those writings that defiled the hands were believed to form the biblical canon of the Jews. They met at Jamnia with permission following the destruction of Jerusalem and its temple and sacrificial system to focus on the future of Judaism. While there is evidence that the Song of Songs and Ecclesiastes were debated there (m. Yadayim 3.5), there is no evidence that any final decisions were made by Jews at Jamnia about the scope of the Hebrew Scriptures. The Jewish sages were still debating the sacredness of some of the biblical books for several centuries more, including the sanctity of Song of Songs and Ecclesiastes and other books (see Tosefta, Yadayim 2.13–14).

The earlier Jamnia view—that the Hebrew canon was closed at the end of the first century—was very popular well into the twentieth century, but it began to crumble when it was better appreciated that Jewish literature from that period and later reflected continuing doubts about Song of Songs and Ecclesiastes and several other books, especially Esther and Ezekiel. From the 1970s and beyond, largely due to Jack P. Lewis's detailed assessment of the relevant literature, the earlier arguments have fallen to the wayside and more reasonable arguments for the closing of the Hebrew Bible have been set forth in recent years.[7] Lewis carefully showed that no such council speaking on behalf of all Jews existed at the end of the first century CE and that no scope or canon of the Jewish Scriptures was settled there. The process of the closing of the Jewish Scriptures took much longer

---

7. Lewis, "What Do We Mean," 125–32 and his "Jamnia Revisited," 146–62. See Lewis's articles in the select bibliography.

and it was not done by a council but rather through long interactions of rabbinic Jews well into the fourth and fifth centuries CE (so there was nothing in Judaism resembling the later church councils that made such decisions on the books that could be read in churches).

9. What is the Septuagint (LXX) and why is it important for understanding the origin of the Bible?

The Septuagint is the Greek translation of the Hebrew Scriptures that was begun on an island beside Alexandria, Egypt, around 283–280 BCE. Originally it translated the Hebrew Pentateuch or Torah into Greek. It is often abbreviated by the early Christians as the LXX. The legend is that the Pentateuch or Law was translated in Alexandria by seventy-two Jewish translators from Jerusalem and the number was rounded off to the "seventy" or "LXX." Most if not all of the Hebrew Scriptures were eventually translated into Greek by around 130 BCE. The LXX designation likely came from the Christians and not from the Jews, who produced several other Greek translations after the Christians made considerable use of the old Greek, the LXX. The beginning history of the Septuagint is told in the legendary Letter of Aristeas (ca. 130 BCE) who claims that the scribes who translated the Pentateuch were separated from each other, and yet they all came to exactly the same translation! It was thus a divine translation that could not be changed.

In reality, the LXX was likely produced for the Jews living in and around Alexandria who no longer spoke Hebrew but only Greek. That collection of translated Hebrew Scriptures became very popular among the Jews of the diaspora (i.e., those living outside the "promised land") who also did not speak Hebrew or Aramaic, and was also adopted early on by most Christians for their first Scriptures, which they later called the "Old Testament." Most of the scriptural books cited in New Testament are from the Septuagint (LXX).

Sirach, a Jewish wisdom writer likely living in Alexandria, produced in Hebrew an important writing called the Wisdom of Jesus ben Sirach (ca. 180 BCE). Later, around 130 BCE, his grandson translated that text into Greek and also wrote an important prologue to it. In the prologue he mentions "the Law, Prophets, and others" for collections that were evidently highly recognized and prized at that time, but as we will see below, he did not indicate in the prologue or his grandfather's writing which specific books belonged in each grouping. Consequently, we cannot be specific on which books were included in the Prophets or what the "others" included. The Law was obviously the Pentateuch, which had gained widespread reception by the time of Sirach. That will be discussed in the next question.

The writings that Protestants regularly call the Old Testament Apocrypha are the additional books in the Septuagint that are not in the Hebrew Bible. The oldest surviving manuscripts of the LXX were copied by Christians and circulated in churches, but it is not always clear which books were included among those additional books in the LXX. The later various lists of deuterocanonical or apocryphal books included in early Christian Scripture collections are not the same in all of the surviving manuscripts or even in the canon lists that date from the latter half of the fourth century. The best examples that we have of the additional books included in the LXX are from the major fourth-century codices (volumes) commonly known as Codex Vaticanus and Codex Sinaiticus, and from the fifth century in Codex Alexandrinus and those listed in the fourth century and later lists of canonical books. The additional books in Codex Alexandrinus are mostly the ones included in current lists of the deuterocanonicals. Those included in Catholic and Orthodox Bibles are mostly from that manuscript.

The Septuagint continued as the Scriptures of most of the diaspora Jews in the Greco-Roman world well into the eighth and ninth centuries, except in Palestine, Syria, and in the East, especially Babylon. This translation was also, as mentioned above, the first Scriptures of the early Christians and that suited well the advance of the Christian mission where the majority of people in the Greco-Roman world spoke Greek. The Jews in the West, like the early Christians, also welcomed the additional books in their Greek translations and were largely unaffected by the rabbinic tradition in Palestine or Babylon.[8]

10. Why is the book of Sirach important for understanding the formation of the Old Testament?

Around 180 BCE, Jesus ben Sira (Sirach, see his name in Sirach 50:27) produced a highly-prized writing circulating among the Jews. Subsequently,

---

8. For a careful discussion of the diaspora Jews and their Scriptures, see Edrei and Mendels, "Split Jewish Diaspora"; and their "Why Did Paul Succeed?"

his grandson translated that work from Hebrew into Greek (ca. 132–117 BCE) in Alexandria, Egypt, and wrote an important prologue to it that has since been appended to Sirach. In the opening of his prologue to his translation of Sirach, the grandson speaks of "the Law and the Prophets and the other books of our ancestors" and he subsequently speaks not only of the "Law itself, but the prophecies, and the rest of the books." It is not clear what was included either in the Prophets at this time nor what "the others" refers to, since no list of the books he had in mind were listed. In 49:8–10 Sirach mentions Ezekiel, Job, and "the twelve prophets" (the "minor" prophets), but the rest of the Jewish Scriptures are not mentioned, though many heroes of faith are identified.

It is interesting that Sirach speaks of the one who devotes himself to the study of "the *law* of the Most High" and goes on to say that such a person "seeks out the *wisdom* of all the ancients, and is concerned with *prophecies*" and goes on to preserve the sayings of the famous and "penetrates the subtleties of the parables and seeks out hidden meanings of *proverbs*" (Sir 38:34b—39:3; emphasis added). While some scholars contend that the three categories mentioned in the prologue are equivalent to the Law, the Prophets, and the Writings that comprise the Hebrew Bible, there is nothing in the prologue or in Sirach itself that clarifies what may have been intended by those designations. So we cannot be sure of all of the books that were recognized as Scripture by Jews in Alexandria at that time.

Nonetheless, Sirach does appear to indicate a threefold division of Jewish Scriptures. We have other hints from the time of Jews grouping their Scriptures into categories. The Dead Sea Scrolls, the New Testament authors, and the early rabbinic sages of the second to the fourth centuries employed the most common designation for the Jewish Scriptures, namely the twofold "Law and the Prophets." Some biblical scholars have suggested there was a three-part Old Testament or Hebrew Bible mentioned by Jesus Luke 24:44 when the risen Christ comes to his disciples and reminds them of everything written about him "in the *law of Moses* and the *prophets* and the *psalms*" (emphasis added). However, in the same chapter, as he comes to the disciples on the road to Emmaus we see that "beginning with *Moses and the prophets* he interpreted to them the things about himself *in all the scriptures*" (24:27; emphasis added). Here Luke only speaks of two categories of Scripture, not three. Also, aside from Luke 24:44, no other New Testament writings speaks of three parts, and in Luke 24:44 it is *only the psalms* that are mentioned and not the whole collection that later became identified as the Writings (*Ketuvim*). If Jesus included psalms in "*all* the scriptures" in 24:27 and does not separate them from the "prophets," it is likely that they were intended or included in 24:27. Those scholars who make "psalms" a reference to the third part of the Hebrew Scriptures do so with no clear arguments from Luke or elsewhere for that conclusion. We should note that elsewhere in the New Testament Psalms (Acts 2:29–31) and Daniel (Matt 24:15) were included *among the Prophets*. All books later included in the Hebrew Bible in the later third category of Writings (*Ketuvim*) were still being called the "Law and the Prophets" in the New Testament and by the rabbinic sages well into the fourth century CE. We also see similar designations among the Dead Sea Scrolls, the closest writings in time and location to the early Christians.

This early twofold division of Scriptures can be traced back further. The author of 2 Kings (ca. 562–550 BCE; see 25:27–30) reminded the nation of their failures and mentions that they had failed the commandments of the Lord that were "in accordance with all the law that I commanded your ancestors and that I sent to you *by my servants the prophets*" (17:13). Subsequently the author praises King Hezekiah because he "kept the commandments that the LORD commanded Moses" (18:6). Clearly the Law of Moses was paramount, and the prophets conveyed what the Lord commanded to the people. Here the Law and the prophets are brought together as important sources for the people of Israel and Judah.

Returning to the Wisdom of Jesus Ben Sira (also known as Ecclesiasticus), this text itself was often called Scripture in later rabbinic writings (e.g., b. Baba Qamma 92b, citing Sirach 13:15 as Scripture) and in early Christianity and it remains in a majority of Christian Bibles. Its popularity even in later rabbinic writings reflects that it may well have been a candidate for inclusion among the Jewish Scriptures.[9] Had Sirach been included in the Hebrew Bible, one can only wonder how it would have been combined with other wisdom books to make sure the twenty-two or twenty-four numbers of books (on which see later) would have been preserved.

The issue of the orders of the Hebrew Bible and Christian Old Testament raises an important final observation here that is sometimes ignored, namely that neither order was of much interest to either Jews or Christians before their separation in antiquity (mostly between ca.

---

9. For example, see its positive mentions in b. Aboth 4:4; b. Pesahim or Pesachim 113b; b. Baba Metzi'a 112a; Tanhuma, Mikketz 10; Exodus Rabbah 21:7; Tanhuma, Va-Yishlah 8; Genesis Rabbah 73:12; b. Baba Bathra 98b; and Tanhuma, Hukkath 1.

64–65 and 135 CE). Some scholars have argued that the order in the Hebrew Bible is the only appropriate order for the Old Testament writings—and several seminaries divide their examination of Old Testament studies in the Hebrew tripartite order, but their arguments for that order, and that one alone, are not convincing and appear anachronistic. There are multiple orders from antiquity among the twelve minor prophets, which vary in their sequence, and it is surprising now that some scholars contend for the current Hebrew Bible order as the only appropriate order. If that order was important in antiquity, it is a wonder why no one, whether Jewish or Christian, made any arguments for it. The final decisions about the scope of our Bible and its order took place after a long process taking many centuries.

11. What books were in the LXX that were not included in the Hebrew Scriptures?

As we saw above, the Letter of Aristeas (ca. 130 BCE) indicated that the first Greek translation of the Hebrew Scriptures was only of the Torah (Law) or Pentateuch. Its final shape was determined later in the Christian surviving Old Testament Greek manuscripts and especially those from the fourth and fifth centuries. The Jews stopped producing copies of it in the late second or early third century, but Christians continued making copies of that translation. The contents of the complete LXX in antiquity is unclear and there were no clear and consistent lists of the additional books in the LXX before the Catholic Council of Trent in 1546. The Orthodox churches added three more books than the Catholics, but the surviving Christian manuscripts and the known canon catalogues seldom list all of the books that are now listed in the Protestant Bibles that include the Apocrypha (NRSV). Athanasius' list of the "readable" writings in the LXX but not in the Hebrew Bible (Tanak) only includes a handful of those additional writings. Melito, bishop of Sardis (ca. 170–180), listed the books in the church's Old Testament that he obtained most likely from Jews, or possibly only Jewish Christians, in Palestine and his list is much like the books in the Hebrew Bible, but not exactly. Esther is omitted and it also omits, probably by accident, the Twelve Minor Prophets, but it likely also includes Wisdom of Solomon along with Proverbs, though some scholars dispute that.

Origen in the early third century produced a list of the Jewish Scriptures but did not accept the limits of that list for himself and he welcomed and cited several of the apocryphal or deuterocanonical books despite criticism against him for doing so. The Christians before Melito of Sardis (ca. 170–180 CE) and Origen (early third century) were especially focused on which books could be read in the churches. Neither produced a list that obtained prominence among later Christians, but there was considerable overlap with the later fixed collections in terms of the books they did list. Such lists began to be more common by the middle-to-end of the fourth century and thereafter. Even the more common term "Old Testament" does not appear in reference to any collection of the church's first Scriptures until near the end of the second century, with Melito and Irenaeus (170–180). Reflecting the newness of that designation, it was identified as the *"so-called 'Old Testament'"* by Origen (*Comm. Jo.* 5.4) in the third century and also by Eusebius in the fourth century (*Hist. eccl.* 3.9.5). "Old Testament," as mentioned previously, was not a commonly used term for the church's first Scriptures until after the middle of the fourth century CE.

As noted, Origen and Athanasius welcomed several of the additional books found in the LXX and the canon lists often include some of them. The Catholic and the Orthodox (Eastern, Russian, and Oriental Orthodox) churches include the deuterocanonical or apocryphal books among their Scriptures, but not all the same books. Interestingly, Protestants did not stop including the so-called Apocrypha in their Bibles for quite some time. The first King James Version of the Bible, published in 1611, includes the apocryphal books under that title and, following Martin Luther's practice, they were placed between the Old and New Testaments. The same practice was in the Matthew's Bible of 1537 and the Geneva Bible of 1560.

Those additional books have a long tradition of use in Catholic, Orthodox, and Protestant Bibles. Catholic churches welcomed the following "additional" books in their sacred Scriptures alongside the books in the Hebrew Scriptures: Tobit, Judith, Esther with the later additions, Daniel with the later additions, 1 and 2 Maccabees, Wisdom of Solomon, Sirach (= Ecclesiasticus), Baruch, and Epistle of Jeremiah. The Orthodox churches welcome those same additional books, but add the Prayer of Manasseh, 3 Maccabees, and Ps 151, including them as inspirational noncanonical "Scriptures" to be *read* in their churches, not completely unlike the practice in many Anglican churches. The surviving lists of readable Scriptures in churches as well as the manuscripts that contain them seldom have the exact same additional writings. Only later in the medieval churches are such writings spelled out. Some of the early Christians in both the eastern and western churches often read some of that literature, but not infrequently with a different understanding of their scriptural value.

Several New Testament authors show some familiarity with several of the disputed writings. For example, Rom 1:23 (cf. Wis 11:15; 12:24; 13:10–19) and in Heb 1:2–3 (cf. Wis 7:25), and elsewhere. These evidence a considerable welcoming of many of these texts in early Christianity.

Most early church fathers did not make use of all of the deuterocanonical texts. And Epiphanius and Jerome in the fourth and early fifth centuries were the most prominent church fathers who rejected them from their Old Testaments, though both made use of them, as in the case of Epiphanius's use of Jubilees, even if it was not accepted as Scripture. And prior to them, you will find several disputed books in collections, canon lists, citations of several church fathers, and occasionally in various scriptural manuscripts.

Most of the Hebrew Scriptures cited in the New Testament are from the Septuagint Greek translation and most of them eventually formed the Scriptures for the Jews and the Old or First Testament of the early Christians. The scope or parameters of those Scriptures for both Jews and Christians took much longer to form into a fixed collection. Some of the Hebrew writings welcomed as Scripture by some first-century Jews continued to be debated both by the later rabbinic Jews in the second and later centuries but also among Christian leaders for several centuries. The early churches never fully agreed on the scope of their Old Testament and that is true even to this very day. Today Catholic, Orthodox, and Protestant churches all agree on and accept in their Old Testaments all of the books that comprise the Hebrew Bible, but, as we have detailed, they still differ on the disputed books.

In 1566 Sixtus of Siena called the first collection of Old Testament books, those in the Hebrew Bible, the "Protocanonical" (*Protocanonicos*)" books and the second often disputed collection the "Deuterocanonical" (*Deuterocanonici*) writings. The deuterocanonical writings in early Christianity varied in their reception and in the manuscripts containing them as well as the canon lists that identify them. The primary question was whether those disputed books could be read as Scripture or only privately as pious texts (sometimes called "ecclesiastical" writings by the late-fourth or early-fifth century church fathers) that were helpful in spiritual formation, or whether they should be rejected altogether, as some church fathers suggested. Initially most early church fathers appear to have welcomed several of these disputed writings as Scripture. There was not a finalized biblical canon of Hebrew Scriptures before the time of Jesus or for centuries thereafter and the early shape or scope of the Hebrew Bible and the church's Old Testament was fluid for centuries. The writings that were welcomed as Scripture by the early Christians, like some of their Jewish siblings, varied for centuries in what was in them. *Most* decisions about the scope of the Old Testament for the early churches was largely settled by the middle to end of the fourth century CE in a majority of churches, but ongoing disagreements remained. We will examine that issue more in the next chapter.

12. What are the Dead Sea Scrolls and how do they aid in our understanding of the Jewish Scriptures in the time of Jesus?

From 1948 to 1952 around a thousand ancient Jewish religious manuscripts were discovered in eleven caves at Qumran on the northwest side of the Dead Sea. A little over two hundred of them are of the biblical books that later formed the Hebrew Bible and the church's Old Testament, except that Esther is missing, but there were around seven hundred others placed side-by-side with the biblical scrolls.

The manuscripts date from around 300 BCE to roughly 40 BCE. Also, no text was found among the Dead Sea Scrolls that indicated which writings housed there were considered sacred, and which were not. Most of the Dead Sea Scrolls were also *translocal* texts, that is, they were mostly "non-sectarian" texts that were also circulating throughout Palestine at that time and were only copied at Qumran, rather than being produced there. Many of those texts were not later included in the rabbinic collection of sacred Scriptures, for example 1 Enoch and many others, but many of those texts were circulating in Palestine in the time of Jesus and before and copies of them were brought to Qumran. If the number of copies of a text is an indicator of its importance, 1 Enoch had a favored status at Qumran since multiple copies of it (somewhere between twelve to twenty) were discovered among the Dead Sea Scrolls, which is even more than several Hebrew Bible or Old Testament books.

The community at Qumran that preserved and/or wrote some of the documents found there stored them in caves, as the Romans were approaching their community, and placed them in large clay jars without any obvious distinctions between them. The books discovered there are all fragmented and include some of the books later called apocrypha and pseudepigrapha (see discussion of these terms in chapter 2). The scope or canon of the Jewish Scriptures is not identified, either in late Second Temple Judaism (i.e., before 70 CE) or in the New Testament, until for the first time in the late second century CE, for some rabbinic Jews, in the rabbinic text b. Baba Bathra 14b and in Melito of Sardis around the same time. The Dead Sea Scrolls do not reflect a closed biblical canon in the time of Jesus but the contents of that collection does clarify which books had obtained widespread reception as Scripture by some Jews in the time of Jesus. However, the presence of multiple copies of those texts that are cited most frequently can suggest which books among the Dead Sea Scrolls were more favored and possibly recognized as sacred Scripture. The multiple citations and references in the books found at Qumran, as well as in the New Testament, and in the writings of the Jewish historian Josephus in the latter part of the first century CE, may offer hints about which books were recognized as sacred Scripture in that period. Among the books most commonly cited were Deuteronomy, Isaiah, and the Psalms. These were certainly the most cited books in the New Testament and the early church fathers and were later included in the Hebrew Bible.

The scrolls let us know that some of the books later included in the Hebrew Scriptures were more cited and copied than others. They also reveal that there were other religious texts circulating among the Jews of Palestine that were often copied more than some biblical books. Most of the books there were what we call non-sectarian, that is, they were brought to Qumran and not produced there but only copied there. Those books informed the faith of those Jews, probably the Essenes, and others in Palestine from approximately 150 BCE to 68 CE, though the books that were brought to the site often date from much earlier.

As mentioned above, the most cited and copied biblical books included there were Psalms, Deuteronomy, and Isaiah, but fragments of *all* of the books that now belong in the Hebrew Bible were found there, except for the book of Esther, which seems not to have been considered Scripture by some Jews and some early Christians of the period. The important point here is that the biblical books and non-biblical books were placed side by side, mostly without distinction, and often there were more copies of the non-biblical books found at Qumran than many of the biblical books. This speaks of the value attributed to some of the books that were not later included in the Hebrew Bible.

The criteria employed to establish the canon of the Hebrew Scriptures are not easily discerned in the Dead Sea Scrolls, but they clearly reflect fluidity in the thinking of Jews and Jewish Christians at that time.

Eugene Ulrich has suggested several possible but nondeterminative criteria to discern scriptural books at Qumran. Several of them are most helpful, including whether multiple copies were made of a book, whether a commentary was written on a book, and whether a book was translated into vernacular languages. He shows that multiple copies of several biblical and nonbiblical books were present among the scrolls at Qumran, including Psalms (thirty-six copies), Deuteronomy (thirty copies), Isaiah (twenty-one copies), Genesis (twenty copies), Exodus (seventeen copies), Jubilees (fourteen copies), Leviticus (thirteen copies), 1 Enoch (twelve or twenty copies?), Minor Prophets (eight copies), Daniel (eight copies), Numbers (seven copies), Jeremiah and Ezekiel (six copies each), Tobit (five copies). The Former Prophets (Joshua to Ezra-Nehemiah) and the Writings only have four or fewer copies, which is fewer than the number copies of the Community Rule documents, the Damascus Document, the Hodayot, and the War Scroll. Ulrich also notes that only the Torah and the Prophets (specifically, Isaiah, the Minor Prophets, and Psalms) had commentaries written on them. Finally, he observes that only Torah and possibly 1 Enoch were translated into Greek, and only Leviticus and Job were translated into Aramaic (Targumim).[10] A Greek translation of the Minor Prophets was discovered at Nahal Hever. From this it is clear that Torah and the Prophets, including Psalms and Daniel, were clearly recognized as Scripture and possibly Job and Proverbs also. He adds that Job and Proverbs might also qualify, but the rest of the books were "known" to the Qumran covenanters and may or may not have been acknowledged as Scripture. As others have recognized, in some cases there appears to be no qualitative difference between some books that made it into the Jewish biblical canon and some that did not. The Dead Sea Scrolls are very valuable in showing the state of interest in the Hebrew Scriptures in the first centuries BCE and CE and they suggest

---

10. Ulrich, "Jewish Scriptures."

considerable fluidity in Jewish thinking at that time, which is also what we find in early Christianity.[11]

13. Why did the ancient Jews number their sacred Scriptures either as twenty-two or twenty-four books?

Josephus, the late-first-century Jewish historian, indicates that there were twenty-two books in the Jews' Scriptures and no more (see his *C. Ap.* 1.37–43). The books in that collection were combined to arrive at the number twenty-two, which was the number of the letters in the Hebrew alphabet. This notion precedes Josephus. Earlier portions of the Old Testament Scriptures were built around the letters of the Hebrew alphabet, as we see in Ps 119, which is divided into twenty-two sections of eight verses each and each introduced with a letter of the Hebrew alphabet with its twenty-two letters (this is clear in the NIV translation, and sometimes in other translations as well). Also, Pss 25, 32, 33, and 103 have twenty-two verses reflecting the letters of the Hebrew alphabet and their divine origin. Several church fathers also listed or referred to the Jews's Scriptures as having twenty-two books, especially Origen in the third century. In all cases some of the scriptural books had to be combined to arrive at the sacred number of twenty-two.

The first known reference to a limited collection of the Jewish Scriptures comes from Josephus, a Jewish historian, at the end of the first century CE (*C. Ap.* 1.37–43), but scholars are uncertain about the specific identity of the books in his collection. He indicated that those books numbered twenty-two, the number of letters in the Hebrew alphabet, but he only provided the genres of those writings he included, not the specific books in his collection.

The later rabbinic Jews chose instead the well-known number twenty-four, the number of the letters in the Greek alphabet that was widely known throughout the Greco-Roman world, for this would immediately reflect to readers that the Hebrew Scriptures were divinely inspired.[12] The twenty-four count was much more common and well known than the Hebrew twenty-two. This involved a different combination of the Hebrew Scriptures to make sure that the final number was

11. For a discussion and evidence of this fluidity, see McDonald, "Fluidity."

12. The widespread awareness of the esteemed Greek alphabet can be seen in the reference to God and to Christ in the book of Revelation as the "Alpha and Omega," the "beginning and the end" (Rev 1:8; 22:13).

twenty-four. This is a result of the believed divinely inspired writings of Homer, the *Iliad* and the *Odyssey*, which were the foundation of all education at that time, and those books, unlike any other, each had twenty-four chapters or books, and each began with a successive letter of the Greek alphabet. That signified their divine inspiration and all Jews, including the later rabbinic Jews, knew this (see Josephus's awareness of the Greek *Iliad* and *Odyssey* in his *C. Ap.* 1.37–43 and those writings were well attested in the rabbinic tradition, e.g., m. Yadayim 4.6; t. Yadayim 2.19; b. Sanhedrin 100a; and y. Sanh. 10.1.28a).

Alexander the Great began a cult in the name of Homer in Alexandria and Homer's work was at the heart of all Greco-Roman foundational education in the first century and after that as well. Eventually the Jews settled on the twenty-four books that no doubt were the same as the twenty-two books, but arranged and combined differently, e.g., Judges and Ruth were combined, the Samuels, Kings, Chronicles, and Ezra-Nehemiah were one book each, and the Minor Prophets are only called the Twelve but were in one scroll constituting one book. Those same books in the Christian Old Testament are thirty-nine books.

14. When did lists of the Hebrew Bible books begin to circulate among some Jews and lists of the Old Testament books among the early Christians?

There is no specific Jewish listing of the Jewish Scriptures or the Christian Old Testament until near the end of the second century CE. While Josephus, as noted above, identified the genres of writings in the Jewish Scriptures and their number (twenty-two), he did not identify the specific books in them. An uncertain though possibly Jewish text we will discuss in more detail below may have been produced around 140–150 CE, but the more certain list, found among the later Talmudic writings and commonly known as the Babylonian Talmudic book, the Bavli (designated as b.), is b. Baba Bathra 14b, dating from between 170–200 CE. It is commonly called a *baraita*,[13] that is, a text written earlier when the

---

13. A *baraita* (or *baraiyta*) is a teaching or rule formulated during the Tannaitic period, *mostly* after the deaths of Hillel and Shammai (ca. 20–30 CE), the leading first-century interpreters of Jewish Scripture and their oral traditions, and up to Rabbi Judah Ha Nasi ("the Prince") ca. 220 CE. But it was not included in the Mishnah itself, the collection of Tannaitic oral Jewish traditions and interpretations of the Law from the time of Jesus to the end of the second century. They were included later in the two Talmuds

Jewish Mishnah (or "Oral Torah") was being prepared (ca. 80–200 CE) but was not included in it likely because it was not yet a well-known tradition in the second century CE among the rabbinic sages. The two-fold description of the Jewish Scriptures as "law and the prophets" was still a common designation in the fourth and fifth centuries among some rabbis. That too will be discussed below. The text b. Baba Bathra 14b includes all of the books in the current Hebrew Bible and their three parts without the additional books seen in the LXX.

The ancient canon lists are very helpful for knowing what writings were viewed as Scripture by local church councils or individual church fathers, such as Athanasius, Augustine, or Jerome. These lists indicate which books could be read in the local churches, having been approved by local bishops or local church councils. None of the many surviving canon lists were ecumenical, that is, a universal collection of recognized Christian Scriptures. While these local collections have several differences from other collections, they also show the considerable agreement in most churches on which texts were viewed as Scripture and could be read in churches.[14]

As noted earlier, the first known Christian list of Old Testament Scriptures was prepared by Melito, the bishop of Sardis (ca. 170–180). He made a trip to Palestine to find out what writings formed the church's Old Testament. His list is similar to, but not exactly like, what was eventually the church's Old Testament. Eusebius, the fourth-century church father and author of a history of the church, relates that Melito, bishop of the important second-century church at Sardis (ca. 170–180), was unable to answer a request to identify the church's Old Testament Scriptures. So, he made a long trip to Palestine to find out and he likely received his list from Jews or Jewish Christians there (*Hist. eccl.* 4.26.13–14). His list of Old Testament books resembles the current Hebrew Bible, but not completely nor in the same order. He omitted Esther but likely also included Wisdom of Solomon and Esdras, possibly the same as Ezra and Nehemiah, but that is not clear. Remarkably, both the Jews and Christians begin to show interest in the specific books that could be read in their

---

(*Yerushalmi* and *Bavli*). The *baraita* teachings were not well-known or welcomed until later during the Talmudic period (after the second century until the fifth century CE roughly). Only later were these "external" teachings accorded equal authority to teachings in the Mishnah.

14. An excellent resource for studying these lists is Gallagher and Meade, *Biblical Canon Lists*.

communities of faith at roughly the same time, though the specific fixing of the specific books took longer for both communities of faith.

By way of another example, consider a Greek list that comes from either a *Jewish* author or a *Jewish-Christian* author and was discovered in 1873 by Philotheos Bryennios and is known by his name. It likely dates around 140–150 CE but possibly later. It is like the books listed by the church father Epiphanius (ca. late fourth century CE), but its origin is not clear. The Bryennios list does have several parallels with the first *known* Jewish list of scriptural books in a late second-century text that was not included in the Jewish authoritative oral traditions, the Mishnah, and is called a *baraita*. It was included in the later Jewish Babylonian Talmud (Bavli) and identified as b. Baba Bathra 14b. I will discuss that text more below, but here it is enough to know that it is the first known Jewish rabbinic listing of the books that now comprise the Jewish Scriptures, but it was not commonly cited until the fourth century CE.

Most of the lists of the church's *first* Scriptures, its Old Testament, *begin* to appear in the middle to late fourth century and we also see listed in some of them books that were rejected as not to be read in churches. While there is considerable overlap in the books included in those later lists, there was seldom *complete* agreement on the scope of those books. The Catholic, Orthodox, and Protestant churches have never fully agreed on the scope of their Old Testament, but all now agree on including the books that make up the Hebrew Bible. Protestants now have only the books in the Hebrew Bible in their Old Testament, though in a different order to the Hebrew Bible. A discussion of the order can be found in Q.16 and Q.17 below.

15. Were all the books in Hebrew Bible accepted as Scripture by the early Christians? Did they accept more or fewer sacred books than their Jewish siblings?

The short answer to the first of these questions is: not initially. But eventually Christians welcomed all of the books that came to be included in the Hebrew Bible. There were questions about Esther, which was rejected by several church fathers but eventually was welcomed, along with Song of Songs and Ecclesiastes. It took some centuries before complete acceptance of them was managed, but some church fathers welcomed several of the deuterocanonical or apocryphal books. The books on Old Testament canon lists were not universally welcomed as Scripture by all Christians and debates continued for centuries in early Christianity. Those lists reflect the views of those who created them and no doubt *some* of the churches, and they were produced to identify the books or writings that could be read in churches. Often, however, the lists varied on their edges and the books that could be read privately in church liturgies varied for centuries.

Likewise, the books that some church fathers said should be avoided altogether also varied in churches, as in the cases of Wisdom of Solomon, Sirach, Tobit, Judith, and 1 Enoch among others, yet these texts functioned as Scripture for some early Christians and Jews, as we see in the books found among the Dead Sea Scrolls (see discussion in Q.7 above). While there was broad agreement on most of the Old Testament books in the lists, there were still variations in many of them for centuries after they began to appear in antiquity, mostly in the fourth century and thereafter.

16. What Old Testament Scriptures do all churches now accept?

All three major church bodies *now* welcome all the books in the Hebrew Bible, but it took several centuries for all churches to agree on that. Some church fathers, as we have seen, continued to question the sacredness of Esther, Song of Songs, and Ecclesiastes. The churches still do not agree on the status of the so-called apocryphal or deuterocanonical texts (see discussion of these in chapter 2). Catholics welcome as Scripture the deuterocanonical books and place them *among* their other Old Testament Scriptures, according to their genre. The Orthodox churches include the books that Catholics welcome but have three others. The Orthodox, like Anglican and Episcopal churches, often read these additional texts in their liturgical services but not for the purpose of establishing Christian doctrine. The early Protestant Bibles included the additional books but eventually rejected them as Scripture. All churches welcome as Scripture the books in the Hebrew Bible.

17. Why are the same books in the Hebrew Bible and the Christian Old Testament ordered differently?

All churches eventually welcomed all of the books in the Jewish Scriptures or Hebrew Bible, but they ordered them differently. The rabbinic order is arranged in three parts, namely:

- Law (*Torah*) = Genesis to Deuteronomy
- Prophets (*Nevi'im*) = Former Prophets (Joshua to 2 Kings) and the Latter Prophets (Isaiah, Jeremiah, Ezekiel, and the Twelve minor prophets)
- Writings (*Ketuvim*) = the rest of the Old Testament books, that is 1–2 Chronicles, Ezra-Nehemiah, Esther, Job, Psalms, Proverbs, Lamentations, Ecclesiastes, Song of Songs.

The order of the books varied in Christian manuscripts for centuries, especially in the Writings and the Twelve.

Christians eventually welcomed all of the books in the Hebrew Bible (Tanak), but not the three-part order in the Hebrew Bible. They instead followed the order of:

- Pentateuch = Genesis to Deuteronomy (same as the Jewish Bible)
- Historical books = Joshua to Ezra and Nehemiah
- Poetry and Wisdom writings = Job, Psalms, Proverbs, Ecclesiastes, Song of Songs
- The Prophets = Major Prophets (Isaiah, Jeremiah [and Lamentations], Ezekiel, Daniel) + Minor Prophets (the Twelve).

There is nothing wrong with the three-part order that the Jews adopted or the four-part order in the Christian Old Testament, but why, if the Christians accepted the same books as the Jews, did they not follow the Jewish order of those books? Similarly, why not follow the multiple Jewish combinations of books to arrive at twenty-two or twenty-four books, combinations not found in Christian Old Testaments?

The most likely reason for these differences is because those combinations and the three-part order were not present or widely known when the Jews and Christians separated (largely between 64–135 CE). The early Jewish Christians welcomed the same books as their Jewish siblings, but neither their order nor their divine number were well-established when

Jews and Jewish Christians separated. Again, there is nothing wrong with either order nor with the combinations used to arrive at the sacred numbers of twenty-two or twenty-four, but there are no ancient arguments for either order or the combinations by Jews or Christians in first or second centuries when their separation occurred. A few later church fathers tried to follow the order in the Jewish Scriptures (especially Jerome in the late fourth century CE), but never exactly.

So the tripartite order of the Hebrew Scriptures was most likely not known at the time of the Jewish and Christian separation. After all, it would be surprising if the Christians accepted the same books, but not the same order of those books and their combinations if they had already been established before the Jewish and Christian separation.

I suggest that since most ancient Christians accepted the LXX or Septuagint translation of the Hebrew Scriptures as their Old Testament they likely followed the order in the LXX. That is not easily established since the only surviving manuscripts of the LXX were produced by the Christians, but since no early church father made an argument for the four-part order or spoke in opposition to the three-part Hebrew Bible, this suggestion may be true. It appears that the four-part order may have come from the LXX collections that early Christians received but did not invent. Perhaps the only part of the Christian order that was likely invented by them was the placing of Malachi at the end of their Old Testament Scriptures. This may have been because Malachi ends with proclaiming that Elijah would come before the "day of the LORD" (Mal 4:5) and in the first book in the New Testament (Matthew) Jesus said that John the Baptist was Elijah who proclaimed that the day of the Lord was near (Matt 11:7–15). The placement of Malachi in last place in the Christian Old Testament was likely a Christian invention, but not necessarily the four-part order of the Old Testament itself (Pentateuch, History, Poetry and Wisdom, and Prophets).

Both three-part and four-part orderings of the Scriptures postdate the first century. During the time of Jesus, all of the Jewish Scriptures were regularly called the "Law and the prophets" or "Moses and the prophets." The Writings or third part of the Hebrew Bible did not exist as a separate collection in the first century, but were included among the "prophets." By the end of the second century CE in the Babylonian Talmud (b. Baba Bathra 14b) the third part of the Hebrew Scriptures emerged but was not yet familiar to all Jews until the fourth and fifth centuries CE. In the New Testament writings only one text, namely Luke 24:44, mentions a third category (psalms). Some scholars have argued that "psalms" was representative of all of the Writings, but the evidence for that is not compelling and earlier in that chapter Jesus uses the phrase "Moses and all the prophets" to include *"all* the scriptures" (Luke 24:27), suggesting that "the prophets" included the books later placed in other sections of the Bible.

When the church was born, there was no agreement on the scope or order of the Old Testament writings except that Torah or Moses was always first. The contents of the sacred collections were not the focus of any known conversations or deliberations, but there was wide recognition of the scriptural status of most, if not all, of the books in the Hebrew Bible. The order in most of the Christian Old Testament manuscripts and canonical lists are quadripartite and there is no argument made for that order, suggesting it was inherited. It likely was what was present in the Greek Scriptures the Christians had received earlier. Thus, it could well be that the Christian order *preceded* the tripartite order that the Jews subsequently adopted for their Scriptures.

It would be surprising if the early Jewish Christians welcomed the Scriptures circulating in Palestine in the first century but did not adopt the order later established for the Hebrew Bible if it had been known. The most likely reason, to emphasize the point made above, is that order did not exist before the Jews and Christians separated in the first and second centuries—we first see the tripartite order among the Jews near the end of the second century (b. Baba Bathra 14b).

18. Why is Josephus important for knowing which books were recognized as Scripture in the late first century CE?

By the end of the first century CE, Josephus, the Jewish historian, appears to have advocated a four-part collection of the Jewish Scriptures. After indicating that "our books [Jewish Scriptures] are but two and twenty," in comparison to the multitude of Greek writings, he goes on to identify them *by categories* as follows: "five are the books of Moses, . . . the prophets subsequent to Moses wrote the history of the events of their own times in thirteen books" and he adds that the "remaining four books contain hymns to God and precepts for the conduct of human life" (see all of C. Ap. 1.37–43). These categories are not the same as the later three-part collection that made up Tanak, namely Law (*Torah*), Prophets (*Nebi'im*), and Writings (*Ketuvim*) (see his C. Ap. 1.37–43 for the complete text). By the end of the second century CE, some Jews among the rabbinic tradition produced the first clearly known three-part collection of the Jewish Scriptures in a *baraita* (b. Baba Bathra 14b noted above) in twenty-four books that listed the books that eventually comprised the Hebrew Bible, but that tradition took centuries for all Jews to affirm. Although emerging in the late second century CE, it was not a popular view at that time nor was it well-known among the Jews throughout the Roman Empire, so it was not included in the Mishnah, which reflected Jewish thinking and the "oral law" (from roughly 20 BCE to 200 CE). Jews in the fourth and fifth century were still calling their Scriptures, *the Law and the Prophets*, and not *the Law, the Prophets, and the Writings* (that is, *Torah, Nevi'im, and Ketuvim*). They were still having debates over the holiness of several Hebrew Bible books such as Esther, Song of Songs, Ecclesiastes, Ezekiel, and Sirach.

Neither Sirach nor the prologue to Sirach nor Josephus nor the New Testament make clear exactly which Hebrew Scriptures were recognized at that time. No lists of all of the sacred books existed then until the end of the second century when such lists began to be formed. It took centuries before there was a common designation among Jews and Christians on the scope of their sacred Scriptures. This is true whether we are speaking about the *Hagiographa* ("holy writings") or later when the Hebrew Bible was formed. While the early Christians eventually welcomed all of the books in the Hebrew Bible as Scriptures, they placed them in a different order (and possibly an earlier order that they likely inherited from their Septuagint Greek Scriptures, as we saw above).

19. Did some Jews believe that the Spirit of prophecy and the writing of Scripture had departed from Israel following Ezra and Nehemiah?

Yes, but not all Jews. That belief appears to have come from the religious leaders during the Hasmonean Dynasty (roughly ca. 165 BCE to the time of Herod the Great). The notion of the cessation of prophecy is first found (ca. 135–130 BCE) in 1 Macc in 4:45, 9:27, and 14:41, but it was not a uniform view held by all Jews until centuries later. The Hasmonean religious leaders, especially the Pharisees, rejected the sacred status of all religious writings produced after the time of Ezra and Nehemiah (ca. 500–450 BCE). Many other Jews did not accept that view and some believed that the Spirit of prophecy was *still* present among them, especially some among the residents of Qumran, where the Dead Sea Scrolls were found, who from around 150 BCE produced copies of Scriptures (originally written ca. 300–40 BCE, or even 40 CE) circulating among them and wrote others themselves (see discussion of these scrolls in Q.7 above). They continued to produce what some believed were divinely inspired texts, and the early Christians did the same and also believed that some of their texts were written under the power of the Holy Spirit (2 Pet 1:20–21). The early Christians also believed that in Jesus, the Christ and Lord of the church, the Spirit was present and active among them (e.g., Mark 1:9–12; Luke 3:21–2; Matt 3:13–17; 4:1; John 14:15–17; Acts 1:8; 2:1–4, 14–18).

20. Which Jewish and Christian writings were welcomed as authoritative Scripture in the time of Jesus?

The short answer is that *we do not know specifically* which Hebrew writings were acknowledged as Scripture in the first century of the common era, but from the New Testament authors who cited multiple texts as Scripture, we can know many of them. If what has survived among the ancient manuscripts that we now possess is any indication, we can say that there was considerable agreement over most of the books in the Hebrew Bible and in the church's Old Testament. Since no one at that time produced a list or collection the specific books that informed the faith of either Jews or Christians, we are left with collections of citations from the first-century New Testament writings, the Dead Sea Scrolls, Philo of Alexandria, and Josephus. Those are the closest writings to the time and location of Jesus and the early Christians. Those writings, however, do not address the limits of sacred Scripture and the citations in all of them only address the current issues or concerns facing the communities where those writings were produced or read. The New Testament authors likewise addressed specific issues or concerns important to churches and cited many of their first (Old Testament) Scriptures to support their mission and proclamation, but the New Testament authors never make that claim about their own writings as Scripture. The most disputed book in the New Testament, Revelation, claims to be a revelation from God (Rev 1:1–3; 22:18–19), but does not use the term "Scripture" for itself (though it comes close).

The sacred status of the religious or scriptural texts cited by the early Christians depends on *how* they were cited, namely whether as authoritative texts or just as illustrations. While some ancient religious texts are seldom cited in the Dead Sea Scrolls or in the New Testament, that does not mean that they were *not* consider sacred Scripture. Because so little is known about how the (likely Essene) community at Qumran viewed all of their religious texts, it is seldom easy to determine what was sacred and what was not. Because the sacred books were placed side by side with books that were later not included among the Hebrew Scriptures, it is difficult to say with assurance how all of that literature was viewed. Since other historical books (Joshua, Judges, 1–2 Samuels, Ezra-Nehemiah, and Esther) were eventually welcomed as Scripture in the Hebrew Bible, without comment on any distinctions, it should not be surprising if the Qumran residents accepted the Books of Kings and Chronicles as Scripture as well despite few if any citations of those books. The only book in the later Hebrew Bible that was clearly rejected at Qumran was Esther, but it was later welcomed by the rabbinic sages. Similarly, not all of the books in the Hebrew Bible are cited in the New Testament, but that does not mean that they were not viewed as Scripture. Most of the citations of sacred texts in the New Testament were employed to advance particular arguments or notions that were relevant to the persons for whom they were written. Since no one at that time and for another century made a list of the church's first (Old Testament) Scriptures, it is not possible to say what books were included in the church's Scriptures in the time of Jesus.

As suggested above, care is needed before imposing our modern notions of "Bible" or "biblical canon" on first-century Jews or Christians. Nothing in the New Testament or the second-century church fathers indicates that anyone at that time decided which sacred books were the church's Scriptures and which were not. By the end of that century those questions were asked by a few (Melito and Irenaeus), but their answers were not uniform until much later. Again, the multiple copies of some books found among the Dead Sea Scrolls that were not later included in the Hebrew Bible or the church's Old Testament suggest the texts were viewed with considerable favor, but it says nothing specific about their scriptural status. We cannot easily impose modern notions of "Scripture" or "Bible" on ancient religious texts unless they are cited or treated like Scripture. In some cases, they were.

It could well be that because the historical books did not focus on the theology prominent among the Jews of that community that they were not copied as much or cited as much as others like the Psalms, Isaiah, or Deuteronomy. Emanuel Tov, the past international director of the Dead Sea Scrolls, has indicated that some of the books that were later included in the Hebrew Bible were written in the old Hebrew with the more-square fonts, but that was not the case for all the biblical books found there.

The New Testament authors and early church fathers seldom cite texts from the Kings or Chronicles or the other historical biblical books, but there is no evidence that they rejected them. The New Testament authors' interests were more focused on other subjects and the issues confronting them as communities of faith. Had they or others in the first century been asked to list all the books they believed were divinely inspired texts, they probably would have listed the historical books because of their long-standing history among their Jewish siblings. No one then was asking our questions about whether those texts were inspired Scripture. That is true for both the residents at Qumran and the early Christians who believed that the Spirit was present and active among them. There was no indication among the early Christians that prophetic writings could no longer be produced. We see in the surviving manuscripts at Qumran and in the later writings of church fathers uncertainty pertaining to the scope of the Scriptures of both the Jews and the early Christians. Again, few authors in the first century in Palestine were talking about lists of sacred books that could be read as *Scripture* in Jewish or Christian gatherings. While Josephus comes close to that, we cannot tell specifically what his list was. No Christians were asking such questions at the end of the first century CE and such discussions were largely held in the fourth and fifth centuries.

21. Did the Diaspora Jews and early Christians read the Greek translation of their Scriptures or their Hebrew Scriptures?

Jews living outside of the land of Israel (diaspora Jews)—whether in the north, south, or west of Israel—could not speak or read Hebrew or Aramaic and so the Scriptures that were used were those in Greek translation. Some early Jewish Christians (Paul and Matthew) were familiar with the Hebrew language and occasionally cited scriptural passages from the Hebrew Scriptures, but diaspora Jews and gentile Christians generally did not speak Hebrew and could only understand their Scriptures in Greek and later in Latin. Thus, the Greek Old Testament Scriptures (LXX) were the first Scriptures for the majority of the early Christians, both Jews and gentiles. Although the Old Testament Scriptures were all written in Hebrew, most citations of them in the New Testament are from the Greek translation of them and not from the Hebrew. Greek was a universal language in the Greco-Roman world in the first century and as the Christian message was proclaimed to both Jews and Greeks in the first century, Greek was the primary language to proclaim the message and that was true of the Scriptures they cited in their proclamation as well. It made sense for them to speak and write in Greek. Greek was well-known in the land of Israel in the time of Jesus, though many Jews there could communicate in Hebrew and Aramaic as well as Greek. Outside of the land of Israel, however, speaking or writing in Hebrew was not a viable option in which to proclaim the church's message—a prime example, of course, is the ministry of the apostle Paul.

In the first century CE, Greek was a common language even in Palestine among gentiles and many Jews and many Jews in Palestine even had Greek names. Consider the complaint about favoring the Hebrew-speaking Jewish widows against the Greek-speaking Jewish widows in Acts 6:1–7. The solution was the selection of leaders to take care of the problem, and those selected had Greek names. Archaeologists have found many Greek inscriptions with Greek names of Jews on many of the burial ossuaries (bone boxes) dating roughly from the late first century BCE to 100 CE. There is a Greek inscription at Caesarea Maritima that says in Greek, "Do you fear authorities? Then do right and you do [will] not have to fear." Greek inscriptions were all over the Middle East despite local languages such as Hebrew, Aramaic, Latin, and others. Many Jews in the first centuries BCE and CE had Greek names, including some prominent Jews in the Hasmonean Dynasty, e.g., Alexander Jannaeus, Salome Alexandra, and others. When the early Jewish Christians began their mission work, they generally went to places where Greek was spoken and generally not where Hebrew or Aramaic were widely spoken. As we saw earlier, Edrei and Mendels have shown that the diaspora Jews followed the LXX writings in Greek and content well into the eighth and ninth centuries (see footnote 8 above).

When the New Testament literature was written, its authors chose to write in Greek, the language of most of their readers and hearers, and the New Testament authors translated the sayings of Jesus into Greek, except for a few sayings that are transliterated (e.g., Matt 27:46; Mark 15:34;

see also 1 Cor 16:21). Eusebius noted that Papias, the church father of Hierapolis (ca. 120–130 CE), indicated that Matthew wrote sayings of Jesus in Hebrew (Aramaic) that were later translated into Greek (*Hist. eccl.* 3.39.14–16). The present Gospel of Matthew, however, was written in Greek and not Hebrew, though perhaps some of the sayings in it were written originally in Hebrew, as Papias said. Greek was the universal and dominant language throughout most of the Greco-Roman world in the time of Jesus, even in the West, despite many Latin works by leading Roman authors such as Cicero, Livy, Tacitus, the Elder and Younger Pliny, Suetonius, and others. By the end of the fourth century, Latin had became the official language of the Western church fathers. Tertullian (ca. 200) was the first Latin church father who wrote in both Greek and Latin. Latin began to be more prominent after him. The Orthodox Christians in the East and West regularly read their Scriptures in Greek, but some Latin translations began to appear around the end of the second century and later, especially Jerome's Latin translation of the Hebrew Old Testament books, the Vulgate, that soon had several editions in the fifth century and later for Christians in the West.

It is important to note that even now several scholars contend that the Hebrew manuscripts used to translate the Scriptures into Greek (the Pentateuch ca. 283–280 BCE and the rest of those Scriptures by around 130–100 BCE) were earlier and perhaps more reliable than the later Hebrew manuscripts used by the Masoretic Jews (ca. seventh to tenth centuries CE) who produced the text of the Hebrew Scriptures used in most Old Testament translations today. The copies of the LXX that were produced ca. 283–280 BCE were earlier and often more reliable than the later ones produced by the Masoretic scribes. Also, the Hebrew manuscripts among the Dead Sea Scrolls are often more reliable than the later Masoretic Texts.[15] In several instances it is likely that the Greek text reflects an earlier Hebrew text than the Masoretic text of the Hebrew Bible. Because the Greek Old Testament (LXX) Scriptures are cited more frequently in the New Testament and in the early churches, they should not be ignored.

15. The Masorah, a Hebrew term meaning "handed down," often refers to the accepted text of the Hebrew Scriptures that "Masoretes" or scribes worked on from largely 500 CE to 1000 CE and produced the accepted text of the Hebrew Scriptures finally determined by Aharon ben Mosheh ben Asher of the Hebrew school of Tiberias. That text has antecedents in some of the Dead Sea Scrolls and generally functions as the Hebrew text that scholars use to produce their translations of the Hebrew Bible and the church's Old Testament Scriptures.

22. Do the Old Testaments in early Christian Scripture collections include all the books in the Hebrew Scriptures?

Yes, eventually, but translations of them are sometimes derived from the Septuagint for Eastern Christians rather than from the Hebrew text. The well-known differences in the Hebrew Scriptures and those in Greek translation reflect the fact that some of the Old Testament texts cited in the New Testament are from the *Hebrew* Scriptures and translated into *Greek* by the writer but most of them are straight from the Greek Old Testament, the LXX (or Septuagint). The question of which text and translation from the Jewish Scriptures is used is very important and just as difficult to answer. Most of the citations of the Old Testament Scriptures in early Christianity are from the LXX up until the time of Jerome in the early fifth century, who made a new translation of the Old Testament Scriptures into Latin, but instead of using the Greek LXX, he made use of the Hebrew text of those Scriptures. Sometimes the Greek and Hebrew texts differ significantly. Since both Hebrew and Greek texts of the Old Testament Scriptures are cited in the New Testament writings, there may be implications regarding which text or texts Christians should view as Scripture. Occasionally the differences between the Greek and the Hebrew texts of the Bible are significant, yet both are considered Scripture in the New Testament. Orthodox Christians still generally rely on the Greek LXX text as their Old Testament Scriptures, and we cannot ignore the fact that, as already mentioned, their LXX text was based on an earlier Hebrew antecedent than the Masoretic Hebrew text used in most Bible translations today.

As noted earlier, Emmanuel Tov, the past director of the Dead Sea Scrolls, contends that the Septuagint is often more reliable and earlier than the Hebrew Masoretic manuscripts we now have. He observes that the Septuagint version of Jeremiah is almost 15 percent shorter than the Hebrew text and claims that the Greek text is often the earlier and more reliable text. There are several passages in the Old Testament/Hebrew Bible where the Septuagint probably preserves the better and earlier text. Moreover, the Septuagint and Samaritan Pentateuch are often closer to each other than they are to the Masoretic Hebrew text, and in such cases Tov often favors the Greek text over the Hebrew.

While biblical scholars acknowledge that the New Testament's citations and quotes from the LXX often differ from the Hebrew, they generally prefer the earliest available Hebrew text, which until the discovery of the Dead Sea Scrolls was the Masoretic text of the Hebrew Bible, dating from the tenth and eleventh century CE. That view is beginning to change, and many seminaries now encourage students to read both the Hebrew and Greek texts of the Old Testament Scriptures. That is an important change.

This, of course, does not answer the question satisfactorily for the average reader of the Old Testament who does not have access to either the Hebrew or Greek and is unaware of how to do a careful analysis and comparison of texts. Serious students of the Scriptures will be better informed by reading also the modern translations of the Septuagint.

Since the LXX and the Hebrew text differ significantly at some points, it is likely best to read both and determine which best fits the context of the passage *in the New Testament* and prefer the text that best fits the New Testament context.

I often encourage students and all readers to prefer the New Testament's preference of texts when our Hebrew and Greek texts diverge, depending on the importance of the passage in question. The New Testament authors often depend on an earlier text of their Scriptures, possibly as early as the biblical texts in the Dead Sea Scrolls and certainly earlier than the later Masoretic text (ca. 975–1000 CE) on which current Jewish Scriptures and most of the church's Old Testament translations are based.

23. What are the "unknown" or "lost" books cited in the Old Testament and what influence did they have in ancient Israel?

Besides the books now in the Hebrew Bible and the Christian Bibles, several other religious texts also informed the faith and life and history of early Israelites, but they do not appear to have had much influence after the fifth century BCE. These other religious texts were written and were circulating in Israel before, during, and after the time of Josiah's reforms in 621 BCE, and they apparently had some effect on the Jewish people until around the fifth to fourth centuries BCE. We do not have the contents of the books, but because some of them were written by those considered to be prophets, they were not negligible texts, if the many references to them are anything to go by. They include:

A. In the Law or Torah:

   Book of the Wars of the LORD (Num 21:14)

B. In Joshua, Judges, and 1–2 Samuel, 1–2 Kings:

   1. Book of Jashar (Josh 10:12–13; 2 Sam 1:18–27; 1 Kgs 8:12–13 in LXX)
   2. Book of the Annals of the Kings of Judah (1 Kgs 14:29; 15:7, 23; 22:45; 2 Kgs 8:23; 12:18; 14:18; 15:6, 36; 16:19; 20:20; 21:17, 25; 23:28; 24:5)
   3. Book of the Annals of the Kings of Israel (1 Kgs 14:19; 5:31; 16:5, 14, 20, 27; 22:39; 2 Kgs 1:18; 10:34; 13:8, 12; 14:15, 28; 15:11, 15, 21, 26, 31)
   4. Book of Acts of Solomon (1 Kgs 11:41)

C. In Chronicles, Ezra, and Nehemiah:

   1. Book of the Kings of Israel (1 Chr 9:21; 2 Chr 20:34)
   2. Book of the Kings of Judah and Israel (2 Chr 16:11)
   3. Book of Kings of Israel and Judah (2 Chr 27:7)
   4. Annals of the Kings of Israel (2 Chr 33:18)
   5. Records of the seer Samuel (1 Chr 29:29)
   6. Records of the seer Gad (1 Chr 29:29)
   7. Records of the seer Nathan (1 Chr 29:29)
   8. History of the Prophet Nathan (2 Chr 9:29)
   9. Prophecy of Ahijah the Shilonite (2 Chr 9:29)
   10. Visions of the seer Iddo (2 Chr 9:29)
   11. Records of the Prophet Shemaiah and the seer Iddo (2 Chr 12:15)
   12. Annals of Jehu the son of Hanani ("which are recorded in the Book of the Kings of Israel"; 2 Chr 20:34)
   13. Records of the seers (2 Chr 33:19)
   14. Story of the prophet Iddo (2 Chr 13:22)
   15. Commentary on the Book of the Kings (2 Chr 24:27)

16. A book written by the prophet Isaiah son of Amoz containing the history of Uzziah (2 Chr 26:22)

17. A vision of the prophet Isaiah son of Amoz in the Book of Kings of Judah and Israel (2 Chr 32:32; cf. Isa 1:1)

18. Annals of King David (1 Chr 27:24)

19. Annals of your ancestors (Ezra 4:15)

20. Book of the Annals (Neh 12:23)

21. Laments. This additional book mentioned in 2 Chr 35:25 is not a reference to Lamentations but rather to a book evidently produced by or for Josiah that is now lost.[16]

Most of these references are made after Josiah's reforms (ca. 610 BCE) and the exile, but some were written earlier and show that various unknown religious and historical texts played an influential role in the life of ancient Israel before, during, and after Josiah. None of those listed are in the Hebrew Bible, with a possible exception of Isaiah (C16 and C17 above). However, notice in the list the presence of several books by a "prophet" or a "seer," as in the case of "Records of the seer Samuel" (1 Chr 29:29; cf. 1 Sam 9:9, 11, 11,18, 19; 1 Chr 17:1; 26:28). Similarly, a second source for the account of the activities of David is the "Records of the prophet Nathan" (1 Chr 29:29; 2 Chr 9:29; 29:25); we also see a book by the prophet Iddo who saw the end of Solomon's reign (2 Chr 13:22), the prophet Shemaiah and the seer Iddo (2 Chr 12:15), and Iddo is also mentioned again when we are told that the acts of Abijah are written in the "story of the prophet Iddo" (2 Chr 13:22), and the acts of Manasseh, along with the "words of the seers" are recorded in the "Annals of the Kings of Israel" (2 Chr 33:19), and "Records of the seer Gad" (1 Chr 29:29, cf. 1 Chr 21:9 and 2 Sam 24:11).

All of these books are now lost, but they appear to have had an authoritative role for a time in ancient Israel. It is difficult to draw any conclusions about these lost books and we do not know what was in them, though we have some idea from the citations of the book of Jashur, but

---

16. The references to the "Book of the Acts of Solomon" (B4 above) and the "Book of the Annals of the Kings of Israel" (B2 above) as well as the "Annals of the Kings of Judah" likely existed in the courts of Samaria and Jerusalem. The authors and editors of the Kings doubtless used independent sources that circulated during the Deuteronomistic period of Israel's history. For a discussion of these lost books, see McDonald, "Lost Books"; Davila, "Questions from Lost Books."

more importantly the references to prophets and seers concern those who were perceived to receive and communicate the will and word of God. Likewise, while it is possible that the records or annals may only refer to histories, we must remember that such writings eventually were welcomed as sacred Scripture and called "prophets" in the Hebrew Bible (e.g., Joshua, Judges, 1–2 Samuel, 1–2 Kings). What one makes of these unknown writings is difficult to say since we do not know for the most part what they contained, but the context in which they are listed or referred to suggests that some of them at least *functioned* in an authoritative manner in Israelite and later Jewish contexts. That function lies at the heart of the notion of Scripture.

The lost books that did not make it into the Hebrew Bible canon then likely functioned scripturally, for a time at least, in the Jewish community. Though it is difficult to tell the *extent* to which the ancient Israelite community accepted them as scriptural writings.

Besides those writings that appear to have been lost, many others have survived antiquity and likely functioned either as Scripture or as trusted sources for the faith and life of various Jewish sects before the second century CE. These texts are what we anachronistically call Jewish apocrypha and pseudepigrapha.

The references in biblical and nonbiblical texts to writings that did not survive the canonization processes suggest at least some level of importance for such texts in the nation of Israel, or at least in some segments or sects of Judaism in Second Temple Judaism. Some of these lost books were important enough to require written commentary, as seen in the reference to "the Commentary on the Book of the Kings" (2 Chr 24:27). That a commentary was written on a now-lost book suggests the book's sacredness, or at least its high significance and influence, since, like today, commentaries were made only on the most significant writings. The "Laments" mentioned in 2 Chr 35:25 is not a reference to the biblical book of Lamentations, but rather to a book produced by or for Josiah. Undoubtedly other ancient texts that we know nothing about have been lost, and it is impossible to determine how much authority the ancient communities attributed to them. Since at one time the "book of the law" itself (Deuteronomy) was lost (2 Kgs 22–23), it is also likely that other sacred books either mentioned or not mentioned in the Bible were also lost. When they no longer functioned authoritatively in a religious community, their "decanonization" or marginalization was set in motion.

24. When did the lists of Scriptures appear in ancient Judaism and early Christianity?

The lists of sacred books that were produced to make clear which books could be read *in the churches* largely emerged in the fourth century. A couple of lists come from the second century—namely the Bryennios list (middle to late second century) and the one prepared by Melito of Sardis (170–180 CE). In the third century, Origen produced a list of the Jews' Scriptures (not his own list), but most of the lists were produced in the mid-fourth century and for centuries thereafter. As we will see in chapter 2, below and in the discussion of Christian canon lists in chapter 4, the ancient "canon lists" overlapped considerably, but seldom completely. Several of those lists included *some* of the additional books from the LXX and the order in the lists often varied as well. Some disputed or later rejected books are cited as "Scripture" by some church fathers, even though they were not specifically called "Scripture" in the first century when the church was formed.

The lateness of such lists in early Christianity suggests that the earliest Christians did not yet accept Christian writings from the first century as Christian Scripture nor were they considering producing Christian Scripture. That move only begins to emerge in the second century, and mostly toward the end of that century, and even then not for all of the Christian texts that eventually were recognized as Christian Scripture. The earliest followers of Jesus were not intent on producing a collection of Christian Scriptures, but they did find several of those writings helpful in their mission to proclaim the Christian message. By the middle of the second century a number of church fathers were *citing* the earliest surviving Christian writings *like Scripture* before they began *calling* them Scripture. That is likely the period of considerable changes in the Christian writings that were reflected in subsequent Christian manuscripts. After *using* early Christian writings in the same way as Scripture—that is, authoritatively—soon they began *calling* several of those texts Scripture, especially the Gospels and several letters of Paul and later other texts that were included in the New Testament.

25. What criteria were employed to determine which books to include in the churches' Old Testament?

While the bottom line is that we do not know for sure in all cases, there are several helpful hints that allow us to know with some assurance why some books were selected, and others that were not. A part of our problem in discerning a factual answer to this question is that no one in antiquity wrote a book or article telling us why some books were accepted, and others were not. Some books were quite popular and were obvious candidates for acceptance (Genesis, Deuteronomy, Psalms, Isaiah), but others (Chronicles, Ecclesiastes, Song of Songs) were not and yet were still included. Eugene Ulrich from Notre Dame has put together a list of possible criteria that might be used to see the most popular and welcomed books (a canon?) among the Dead Sea Scrolls. His suggestions might well also be criteria for the selection of the books in the Hebrew Bible or the recognition of selected books and Hebrew Scriptures.

These include: (1) if a document is listed or identified *in a collection* of Scriptures; (2) if a book was accepted as a part of the Law or Prophets; (3) if a book is cited or introduced with the usual scriptural designations (e.g., "it is written"); (4) if multiple copies of a book were made; (5) if a commentary was written on a book; and (6) if a book was translated. He concludes that, if any of these or a combination of them was true of a book it was likely accepted as Scripture.[17] Some books were likely rejected because they were written after the time when some Jews (mostly Hasmonean) believed that the Spirit had departed from Israel and prophetic voices ceased in the land after the deaths of Ezra, Nehemiah, and Malachi. The belief in the absence of the Spirit in the Jewish nation is first mentioned in 1 Macc 4:45–46, 9:27, and 14:41. After that time, the cessation of prophecy among the Jews became a common belief, though not a universal one.

Again, no one known in antiquity listed the criteria for including books in the Hebrew Scriptures or subsequently in the church's Old Testament. The later rabbinic sages were especially mindful of the date of a writing and generally rejected anything written after Ezra, Nehemiah, and Malachi. Some books were rejected if they were not originally written in Hebrew, as in the case of 2 Maccabees, Wisdom of Solomon, and others. Sirach was a very popular book among the Jews and even cited as Scripture by some rabbinic Jews using the designation "as it is written"

---

17. See Ulrich, "Jewish Scriptures," 116.

in reference to it. Although it was later rejected by the majority of Jews, there are over two hundred references to it in rabbinic literature. Like the residents at Qumran, the early Christians also welcomed Sirach, and several other books not later included in the Hebrew Scriptures.

Among the Dead Sea Scrolls at Qumran, there are some twelve to twenty copies of Enoch (depending on whether some fragments are from the same manuscript). Several early church fathers until the time of Origen cited Enoch as Scripture e.g., Irenaeus, Tertullian, and initially Origen. Again, Ulrich contends that if you find a book circulating within a body of texts that are already recognized as Scripture, that book was probably also viewed as Scripture. If there were translations made of it, it was likely recognized as Scripture. There are multiple copies of the Temple Scroll in the Dead Sea Scrolls at Qumran, far more than many of the biblical books. As noted above, that is also true of several books that were not later included in the Hebrew Bible. The point here is that several noncanonical or nonbiblical books were quite popular in late Second Temple Judaism and during the birth of the early church.

26. Scholars have long acknowledged the many variants or differences in the surviving biblical manuscripts. What do those differences show about the formation of the Bible?

This question is a special concern to a growing number of biblical scholars and students who are well aware that until the invention of the printing press no two manuscripts are exactly alike even when telling the same stories. There are more than nine thousand Hebrew manuscripts that have survived antiquity and occasionally others come to light as portions of ancient biblical manuscripts are discovered, sold, and catalogued. The best-known ancient manuscripts were discovered in the Judean Desert at Qumran (Dead Sea Scrolls), but others have been found at Masada, the Nahal Hever cave, and Murabba'at, along with the Nash Papyrus, the Cairo Genizah fragments. Others include the Ben Asher manuscripts, the Leningradensis (Codex Leningrad codex, ca. 1008 CE), the Petersburg Codex of the prophets, the Erfurt Codices, and the "Lost Codices" (= Codex Severi, Codex Hillel, Codex Muga, Codex Jericho, and Codex Yerushalmi). Within the Christian

Septuagint manuscripts, the most important include especially Codices Vaticanus, Sinaiticus, and Alexandrinus, plus others.[18]

Among the surviving Hebrew scriptural manuscripts, there are, according to Emanuel Tov, over nine hundred thousand variants in them. He shared this with me after I gave a paper on the variants in the New Testament manuscripts in which I noted that of the roughly 5,750 surviving New Testament manuscripts some text-critical scholars say that there were minimally around two hundred thousand variants in them and some go as high as four hundred thousand, but three hundred thousand is not an unusual estimate. I indicated to Professor Tov that I was going to quote him, and he said: "Be my guest. They are all there!"

Most of the variants are easily corrected by comparing them with other manuscripts from the same era and most are simple oversight errors, but some variants are not easily reconciled, and questions still remain over the less-common intentional changes made by copiers and scribes. However, the vast number of variants in the manuscripts make clear that while the specific books that comprised the Old and New Testament canons were largely settled, the precise words in them varied for centuries and no two manuscripts are exactly alike until the invention of moveable type fonts and the Johannes Gutenberg printing press in Mainz, Germany that produced the first printed Bible in the 1450s. It has taken hundreds of years of comparing the multiple biblical texts by textual critics to determine the most likely original text of the Jewish and Christian Scriptures, but determining the precise original text is still a work in progress for both Testaments.

In our next chapter, we will focus on the writings that are now called "apocrypha" or "pseudepigrapha" and how they were welcomed in ancient churches.

---

18. For a discussion of this, see McDonald, *Old Testament*, 1:419–47.

CHAPTER 2

The Old Testament Apocrypha and Pseudepigrapha

IN ALL CHRISTIAN BIBLES there are both an Old Testament and a New Testament. The Old Testaments regularly contain the same books as are found in the Hebrew Bible, but as we saw earlier, Catholic and Orthodox Bibles include several other books besides. We will focus here on how to understand those books and an ever-growing collection of ancient religious texts now known as "pseudepigrapha." Those books have had a history of use in Jewish and Christian religious texts and provide a broader understanding of the context of both religions in the history of their emergence and growth.

27. What was meant by the term "apocrypha" in antiquity and currently?

In antiquity the term *apocrypha* had a variety of meanings, and they were not initially negative in earlier Jewish writings, but that changed over several centuries. Initially the designation simply referred to *what was secret or hidden*. It came to be used of more esoteric writings, much like apocalyptic literature and sometimes introduced by saying something like: "I will not say what I want to say now, but I will save it for a later and more appropriate time." See, for example, Dan 12:4–9, which speaks of keeping the words of a book (prophecy) secret and hidden "until the time of the end." Also 4 Ezra 14:5–6, 45–46 (= 2 Esd, ca. 90 CE) speaks of Ezra along with five scribes restoring the sacred Scriptures for the nation. According to 4 Ezra, it took forty days to recover the twenty-four books lost in the destruction of Jerusalem and they were to be made public, but Ezra was told to keep seventy additional books private, kept for the wise.

The reported seventy additional books along with others that were said to be recovered after the destruction of Jerusalem are now likely called "apocrypha" and "pseudepigrapha." The passage in 4 Ezra does not say anything bad about the "hidden" or "secret" seventy books. As we shall see, the term "apocrypha" eventually came to refer to "rejected" or "heretical" writings or those that were deemed "pseudonymous" writings, but initially it was used of special texts reserved for a more appropriate occasion or for those with wisdom that was not present in the average readers or hearers.

By the fourth century CE, "apocrypha" began to refer to rejected books that could not be read in churches and that were either heretical or pseudonymously written under a false name, such as 1 En. So the meaning of "apocrypha" varied in antiquity from its earlier use to documents that were eventually rejected by churches in the fourth century. For examples of "apocrypha" referring to that which was "hidden" or "secret," and kept secret or hidden until a later more appropriate time to reveal their contents, see Dan 8:26 and 12:4, 9–10; 4 Ezra 12:37–39; 14:5–6, and 44–47; 2 Bar. 20:3–4 and 87:1; cf. Jub. 1:5. An example of this can be found in Sib. Or. 11.163–11, which tells the story of a divine oracle given to one who conceals it. It reads in part: "For he ['an elderly wise man'] will write the chief points with power . . . for he will be the first to unfold my [divine] books. Afterward he will also conceal them and will no longer show them to men until the goal of wretched death, the end of life."[1] Unsealing the hidden divine documents was the motivation for the author of Revelation to speak of scrolls that were unsealed now because it was time (see Rev 5:2, 10; 6:1–8:1; 10:4; 22:10). Perhaps Jesus' parables could be understood in this way, namely they were intended to hide truth from unbelievers (Mark 4:10–29).

This notion of "apocrypha" for Jews and some ancient Christians may have its roots in Deut 29:29 in which the "secret things belong to the Lord our God" and only the "revealed things" belong "to us and our children." Apocrypha is similar to the Greek *aporreton* (= "not to be spoken"). Again, initially neither designation had negative connotations

---

1. For a discussion of this text, see J. J. Collins's translation in *OTP* 1:438.

(Dan 12:4; 4 Ezra 12–14; cf. Rev 5:1–5; 10:4–11, and elsewhere), but by the end of the second century CE it began to have pejorative connotations among some church fathers.

Since the council of Trent (1546 CE), Catholics have included in their "deuterocanonical" books Tobit, Judith, Esther with the several additions to it, 1–2 Maccabees, Wisdom of Solomon, Sirach, Baruch with the Letter of Jeremiah, Daniel with the additions (song/prayer of the three young men, Susanna, and Bel and the Dragon). The Greek Orthodox welcome all those plus three other texts (the Prayer of Manasseh, 3 Maccabees, and Ps 151) as "readable" texts, which can be read for enriching personal piety. Officially they are not called canonical Scripture. The Russian Orthodox churches are similar, but their books are in a slightly different order. Protestants now generally reject the apocryphal or deuterocanonical books, but many did accept them as sacred Scripture well into the 1800s despite placing them between their Old and New Testaments like Martin Luther did in his translation. Protestant lists of the apocryphal books are often larger and more inclusive than those in the Catholic and Orthodox lists.

Orthodox Christians welcome the deuterocanonical writings as valued texts that advance piety, following the decision of Athanasius, in his *Thirty-Ninth Festal Letter* in 367, who did not call them canonical Scripture, but encouraged the private reading of some of them for personal devotion. There is no question that some of the deuterocanonical books were *cited as Scripture* by some church fathers and some of them were *included in multiple canon lists* produced in the fourth, fifth, and sixth centuries as well as included in some *local* church council decisions and are also included in several surviving ancient biblical manuscripts.

No ecumenical church council representing all of the ancient churches produced a list of Old or New Testament writings that were to be read in churches. Many churches in antiquity recognized the value of many of the apocryphal/deuterocanonical writings. The initial King James Version of the Bible in 1611, for example, included these writings, but some of those debated Christian books that were later rejected were included in some churches well into the nineteenth century, such as 3 Corinthians in the Armenian Bible, but by then the majority of Orthodox, Catholic, and Protestant churches had long excluded such books from their Scriptures. Some Protestant Bibles began to include the apocrypha/deuterocanonical books again, well into the twentieth century (NRSV), and many Protestants now have found special interest in them.

Whenever Protestant Bibles include these books, they are always placed between the Old and New Testaments while Catholic Bibles include them alongside other biblical books sorted according to their genre. These writings had considerable use in many ancient churches and several of them are variously found in some ancient biblical manuscripts.

There is potential for some terminological confusion in that Catholic and Orthodox Christians do not use the term "apocrypha," as Protestants do, for deuterocanonical books but rather in reference to heretical or rejected writings. Protestants use the term "pseudepigrapha" for the collection of rejected writings.

28. Are there examples in the New Testament that show familiarity with the apocryphal books in the Septuagint (LXX)?

The earliest examples of Christian familiarity and use of the apocryphal or deuterocanonical books included in the LXX are in several New Testament texts and subsequently in the early church fathers where there are multiple word parallels. In the New Testament there are several examples of use, even if not direct citations, in Romans and Hebrews as well as elsewhere in the New Testament. Many scholars have also shown the use of the additional LXX writings by both the New Testament authors and early church fathers. Paul shows considerable familiarity with both the Hebrew Scriptures and some writings in the LXX. We have multiple examples of this, but no list of them was made until much later when arguments in favor of the LXX translation were made by several early church fathers, including in the writings of Origen and Augustine's *On Christian Doctrine* (2.7.24–2.16.56). The most cited deuterocanonical/apocryphal books included in lists or manuscripts are Tobit, Judith, Wisdom, Sirach, and 1–2 Maccabees. While none are introduced with the familiar scriptural designations such as "it is written" or "as the scripture says" in the New Testament, the multiple word parallels (see below) suggest familiarity. Several of these texts include but are not limited to the following examples:

1. Receiving God's forgiveness depends upon forgiving one's fellow human beings, extending to others the forbearance and mercy one seeks for oneself (Sir 28:2–5; Matt 6:12 // Luke 11:4; Mark 11:25 // Matt 6:14

2. Charitable giving toward those in need *now* is the best means by which to lay up one's treasure for the future (whether for this life of the next) rather than hoarding resources to rust and rot doing no one any good (Sir 29:9–12; Tob 4:6b-11; 12:8–9; Matt 6:19–20 // Luke 12:33; Mark 10:22 // Matt 19:21 // Luke 18:22)

3. Hypocrisy and presumption upon God's favor and forgiveness, for example on the basis of performance of acts of personal piety, have no place in the life of the covenant people (Sir 7:5, 8, 9; Pss. Sol. 4:2–3; Luke 18:10–14; Matt 7:3–5)

4. Humility and other-centered service is the path to honor in God's sight, not the practices and orientations modeled by the competitive, precedence-seeking culture (Sir 1:30; 3:18; Luke 14:11; 18:14; MTT 23:12; Mark 10:42–44 // Matt 20:26–28; Mark 9:35 //Luke 9:46–48).[2]

The various canon lists that include some deuterocanonical writings that can be read in churches overlapped considerably but varied often. This can also be seen in the surviving New Testament manuscripts, as we will see below. No one even in the fourth and fifth centuries lists all of those books that are now included in Christian Bibles.

29. What is "pseudepigrapha" and how common was it in antiquity?

We will see examples of this use and practice later in our discussion of production and use of pseudepigrapha in early Christianity, but for my purpose here pseudepigrapha is essentially writing a document in a false name. As we will see later, this practice appeared for multiple reasons, but most often to deceive readers into thinking that such texts were written by well-known prophetic or apostolic figures. Sometimes this was done in order to sell such pseudonymous writings to a library under the name of a famous author or to promote ideas that were not well-known seeking the name of a famous author to ensure such ideas got into current thinking. It is difficult to neatly distinguish writings in "the apocrypha" (or deuterocanonical writings) from "the pseudepigrapha" since pseudepigraphical texts appears in both collections. For instance, no one believes now that the Wisdom of Solomon was written by Solomon

---

2. For more examples, see McDonald, *Old Testament*, 1:302–14.

but it is included in many Scriptures. The authorship of several of the apocryphal/deuterocanonical texts are likely pseudonymous, including the additions to Daniel and Esther (indeed, the Book of Daniel itself is pseudonymous). Such texts were known throughout the ancient world, and they became well-known also in Judaism of late antiquity and, as we will see below, also in early Christianity.

30. How common was the production and use of pseudepigraphal texts in antiquity?

As we saw earlier, the pseudepigrapha (singular = *pseudepigraphon*) are essentially writings produced in a false name. A pseudonymous text is a text written in an assumed or fictitious name normally by authors for multiple reasons, such as choosing to hide one's identity, or to advance a perspective under the name of better-known person to ensure its reception, or perhaps to advance a view that could affect the actual author's personal security by authorities. The current use of a pen name, such as Mark Twain (whose actual name was Samuel Langhorne Clemens), is not unlike a pseudonym. There appear to be multiple reasons for producing and using such writings in antiquity. Most of those who produced those texts *now* regularly called "pseudepigrapha" likely intended to deceive readers (or hearers) with the false names.

The widespread use of pseudepigrapha in Judaism and early Christianity, often in the name of well-known prophets or apostles, is well known and our current categories of apocrypha and pseudepigrapha were not considered issues initially for the early churches. As we will see below, authorship did not appear to be a significant matter to the early churches unless a document was written to advance heretical teachings. The categories we now use were not precisely defined in antiquity and there were no well-known or standard or limited boundaries for either group, especially when authorship was not a factor in the early Christian writings. For example, more than half of the New Testament writings were produced anonymously, as in the cases of the four Gospels, Acts, Hebrews, and 1–3 John. Eventually both terms, apocrypha and pseudepigrapha, were used of heretical and or pseudonymous writings. That is similar in the Christian apocrypha (the so-called New Testament Apocrypha) that also had no chronological boundaries, with some of its writings dating well into the seventh century CE for some Christians even then were penning pseudonymous writings.

By the fourth and fifth centuries "apocrypha" overlapped with "pseudepigrapha" in that both designations often contained falsely attributed texts some of which were considered heretical. While Jerome believed that some of those disputed texts were worthwhile reading for edification (see his *Prologus Galeatus* prologue to 1–2 Kings), he also said in his letter to a woman named Laeta to have her daughter avoid them altogether because he argued that they contain questionable doctrine and were not written by the authors to whom they were ascribed (*Let.* 107.12). Later church fathers regularly identified heretical texts as "apocrypha" or as texts falsely written in prophetic or apostolic names. Some of the pseudonymously written texts were theologically orthodox, but in such cases not much attention was given to their authorship.

As noted above, pseudonymous writings are well-known in ancient Judaism, mostly from the late-fourth or early-third century BCE, though the practice existed even earlier in Babylon and certainly among some Greeks who often wrote in names of earlier well-known authors. Jewish authors who produced such writings generally wrote in well-known names of prophets, leaders of ancient Israel such kings or prophets (e.g., Moses, David, Solomon, Jeremiah, Ezra, and others), and also in similar genres that we find in the Old Testament (history, poetry, wisdom, prophecy). The early Christians also produced and used pseudonymous writings in Christian communities from the second century CE and for centuries thereafter. That will be a focus below but for now we should simply note that they wrote in the names of well-known apostles (e.g., Peter, Paul, John, James) and in similar genres to those found in the New Testament (histories, gospels, acts, epistles, apocalypses).

As already noted, some of the "apocryphal" or "deuterocanonical" texts are also pseudonymous (e.g., Wisdom of Solomon, 2 Esdras, and others). Scholars generally acknowledge that several Old Testament writings were pseudonymously written in another's name, such as Deuteronomy (in Moses' name), some of the psalms (attributed to David), or Proverbs and wisdom literature (attributed to Solomon). Some prophetic texts were attributed to well known prophets, such as 40–54, 55–66, and perhaps 24–27 of Isaiah, all of which were attributed to Isaiah, but were not written by Isaiah. This also includes the later textual insertions in Daniel in the LXX (the Prayer of Azariah and The Song of the Three Jews inserted between Dan 3:23 and 24; Susanna in the expanded Dan 13, and Bel and the Dragon as in the expanded Dan 14 in the LXX). This includes the multiple insertions in the LXX version of Esther and the six later textual insertions in the book of Esther comprising 105 additional verses along with several textual changes in the Hebrew text by its translators.

The distinction between apocrypha and pseudepigrapha was for a long time that the former is the additional books in the LXX while the latter is ancient religious texts that are not in the so-called "apocrypha." These two designations often overlap in scope, genre, and content. Modern distinctions between these two collections are often confusing to students in part due to the fact that a pseudepigraphic text is now considered a literary forgery that was created or modified with the intention of deceiving readers. This was also true in some Old Testament apocrypha (e.g., Wisdom of Solomon and 4 Ezra) and in early Christian apocrypha (e.g., Apocalypse of Peter, Acts of Paul). Scholars debate over whether all such writings were intended to deceive, but clearly some were, e.g., 1 Enoch. Again, the current designations do not always fit easily with the ancient texts and how they were viewed at the time of their production. I will say more below about the production and use of pseudonymous texts when dealing with the New Testament and early Christianity. There were many more ancient Jewish and Christian pseudonymous writings now dubbed pseudepigrapha or apocrypha than the number of books included in the Old and New Testaments.

It is interesting that these ancient pseudepigraphal texts were preserved by Christians but not by their Jewish siblings who welcomed some of them before the separation of Jewish Christians from other Jews beginning in first century BCE and completed by the end of the second century CE. That is likely because some Jewish Christians were reading such texts when the church began and the separation between Jews and Christians had not yet begun. After that separation started (ca. 62–135 CE), some pseudepigraphal texts continued to be welcomed among Jewish Christians. Some of these texts were translocal texts circulating in Palestine and some were present among the Dead Sea Scrolls, including later in a large collection of sacred texts discovered in the famed Cairo Genizah.[3] Centuries after this most Jews adopted as their Scriptures the

---

3. The term is Hebrew (*genizah* = "storage") and a *geniza* is a storage room often attached to a synagogue in its basement or attic or even a cemetery to store old worn-out religious texts, especially those with divine names in them in Hebrew. The Cairo Geniza was discovered in 1896, but some visited it earlier in 1752 and 1753. This genizah

books in the Hebrew Bible. While many of the fragments discovered in the Cairo Genizah have been catalogued, many have not. Many Jews in the diaspora continued using some non-biblical books for centuries and the early Christians also continued using several of them as sacred texts.[4]

31. Did some early Christians welcome Jewish pseudepigraphal books as Scripture?

As we saw above, the *pseudepigraphal* books are those writings that were widely acknowledged to be produced under a false name and they were eventually rejected by Jewish and Christian teachers,[5] but some of them were welcomed as, or like, Scripture in Jewish and Christian communities for centuries. By the fourth century those books now called "pseudepigrapha" were widely rejected as Christian Scripture. For example, the writings attributed to the biblical Enoch (Gen 5:18–23) were widely acknowledged as texts falsely written in Enoch's name and widely rejected by the mid-third century, though not universally, and some Ethiopian Christians still consider 1 Enoch to be Scripture. In the New Testament, the most commonly cited evidence of early Christianity welcoming a pseudepigraphal text is the citation of 1 Enoch 1:9 as *prophetic* Scripture in Jude 14. Jesus' reference in Matthew 19:28 to "when the Son of Man is seated on his throne of glory" (see a similar phrase in Matt 25:31) uses a phrase only found in 1 Enoch (see 67:27–29 and others). Jesus may have read 1 Enoch, which was circulating in Galilee region in the first century and was a trans-local text taken to Qumran and found among the Dead Sea Scrolls, or Jesus may only have known the oral tradition about it circulating at that time. We will see below that several early church fathers

---

contained a collection of some four hundred thousand mostly fragments of Jewish religious and non-religious texts including Sirach and the Damascus Document. This *genizah*, was obtained in 882 CE when a Cairo church was taken over and for financial reasons it was given to Jews who changed the building into a synagogue. Many of the texts in it were brought by Jews to the synagogue and likely date from the sixth century CE, but some date well into the nineteenth century CE. See a discussion of this important *genizah* in McDonald, *Old Testament*, 1:406–8.

4. See Edrei and Mendels, "Split Jewish Diaspora."

5. Note that some texts now universally considered to be pseudonymous are contained in the apocrypha/deuterocanonical collection of texts and were not rejected in some scriptural collections (2 Peter, the Pastorals, and possibly 2 Thessalonians and others).

cited 1 Enoch as Scripture. The last and best known was Origen in the third century, though he did eventually reject it.

32. What are some of the popular pseudepigraphal texts welcomed among some Jews and some early Christians?

In recent years many pseudepigraphical texts have been published in new formats and those texts significantly outnumber the ones that were eventually included in the Hebrew Bible and in the Christian Bibles. As noted earlier, the Old Testament pseudepigrapha (i.e., those written in the names of Old Testament characters) is now a growing collection that includes more than a hundred texts and extends well into the sixth century CE. Many of the pseudepigrapha often classified as Old Testament Pseudepigrapha were written by Christians and those include some of the Sibylline Oracles (books 6–8), 5 Ezra, 6 Ezra, Questions of Ezra, Greek Apocalypse of Ezra, Vision of Ezra, Apocalypse of Elijah, Apocalypse of Zephaniah, Apocalypse of Sedrach, Apocalypse of Daniel, Testament of Adam, Testament of Isaac, Testament of Jacob, Testament of Solomon, Ascension of Isaiah, and Odes of Solomon. The books identified as "apocrypha" are *not* all focused on hidden teachings nor are all of them ascribed in false names. The terms, therefore, can be confusing because they are understood differently in Christian tradition.[6]

The widely rejected ancient religious writings circulating in some ancient churches were initially welcomed in several churches as Scripture but were later rejected by the majority of churches and eventually fell out of use in most churches. However, they have considerable value for today because they often reflect the social and historical contexts of late Second Temple Judaism and Judaism of late antiquity (roughly 300 BCE–300 CE) and also of early Christianity. They also clarify the meaning of many important terms and issues later included in the New Testament and early Christianity, including "Son of Man," developing messianic views, notions of life after death, the emerging understandings of Scripture. Some of these texts continue to be regarded by some churches today as Scripture, as in the case of 1 Enoch in the Ethiopian churches, and it is important to see how they influenced subsequent doctrinal and practical

---

6. The best resources for these and the other Jewish texts that are continuing to be published are Charlesworth, *Old Testament Pseudepigrapha* (2 vols.) and the more recent additions in Bauckham et al., *Old Testament Pseudepigrapha*, vol. 1 (vol. 2 is on the way).

matters of faith and conduct in some ancient churches. We, of course, see this influence in the citation of 1 En. 1:9 in Jude 14, which will be discussed in more detail in chapter 7. Many churches, though not all, did initially welcome some of the disputed writings as Scripture and several of those writings are found in the canon lists that began to appear in the second century and especially in the fourth century and later and also among several of the surviving biblical manuscripts, as we see in the major pandect codices of Christian Scriptures in the fourth and fifth centuries (Codex Sinaiticus, Vaticanus, and Alexandrinus).

Some of the pseudonymous texts that the early Christians welcomed were also found among the Dead Sea Scrolls. They were taken to Qumran, not created there, and their presence at Qumran reflects the popularity of several trans-local texts in the land of Israel in the first century BCE. So we can see that these were nonsectarian texts that were circulating in the land both before and during the time of Jesus and up until there was a separation of Jewish Christians from Judaism (roughly 62–65 CE to ca. 190 CE). This reflects both the fluidity in the notion of Scripture at that time and the origin of such writings in some early Christian churches.

All of the pseudonymous writings have a story to tell that frequently enables scholars to construct more complete histories of the Jews and Christians in their social settings and not infrequently they allow for greater clarity on the meaning of some New Testament issues, such as the meaning of Son of Man. Some of these writings are simply interesting and occasionally inspirational reading and reflect the religious piety of the ancient Jews, and sometimes the early Christians, who continued to make copies of these writings. Although such texts were popular among some Jews before the Jews and Christians separated, it was the Christians who preserved them. This was because some of the books continued to be recognized as sacred texts in some early Jewish Christian and later even gentile Christian communities, but fell out of use among the mainstream of the Jewish community.

33. Who was Athanasius and what did he say about which Scriptures could be read in churches?

Athanasius (296–373 CE) was bishop of Alexandria and since the date of Easter changed every year, he was eventually asked to inform churches annually of the date to celebrate Easter. In his celebrated *Thirty-Ninth*

Letter (367 CE) informing churches on the appropriate date, he also included other directives related to which Scriptures could be read in churches and which could not. He had an important impact on many churches in the East and on some western churches in the fourth century and later. This *Letter* was not equally received by all churches but did have significant influence well past the fourth century. Athanasius' *Festal Letter*, noted above in question 4 above, was taken to many places not only in Africa, but also as far as Syria and even to some western churches. In it, he listed the "canonical" Scriptures that could be read in churches, but also some books that were not "canonical" but could be read privately to advance piety. He then listed some books that were considered heretical that could not be read at all. His list of scriptural texts included all the Old Testament books in the Tanak and Protestant Old Testament except Esther, but it also included Baruch and the Epistle of Jeremiah (both in the apocrypha). His New Testament included for the first time all of the books of the current New Testament (2 Peter was included for the first time). These books *could be read in churches as canonical Scripture*. While he did not include Esther in his "canonical" Old Testament Scriptures, he included it in his private "readable" list. Besides Esther, his "readable" list included Wisdom of Solomon, Wisdom of ben Sirach, Judith, Tobit, and the Christian Didache and Shepherd of Hermas, which, when read privately and not as canonical Scripture, could advance piety, especially among new converts.

The full extent of the influence of Athanasius's *Festal Letter* at that time is unclear. Obviously, it did not carry much weight in those Syrian churches that received his *Festal Letter* but also welcomed as Scripture the *Diatessaron* and 3 Corinthians for centuries and rejected for centuries 2 Peter, 2 and 3 John, Jude, and Revelation. In Egypt at the same time there were other churches—gnostic and others such as early Coptic Christians—that welcomed books besides the canonical ones listed by Athanasius. So, his influence was clearly notable, but not final for all churches. It appears that Athanasius's *Thirty-Ninth Festal Letter* had mixed responses.

34. Do Catholic and Orthodox churches welcome the apocryphal or deuterocanonical books the same way?

While Catholics welcome the deuterocanonical writings as sacred Scripture they are welcomed differently by Orthodox Christians, who take them seriously as "readable" (Greek = *anagignoskomena*), that is "non-canonical" readable texts, but not as canonical Scripture. The Orthodox Christians only accept as sacred canonical Old Testament Scripture the books in the Hebrew Bible that all Christians also welcome in their Old Testament Scriptures. While that appears like a contradiction in terms, it seems to work for the Orthodox churches. They consciously welcomed all the same canonical books that Athanasius affirmed in his *Thirty-Ninth Festal Letter* (plus Esther) but included more of the deuterocanonical writings among their "readable" texts than he listed. They never had an ecumenical council meeting that listed all of the approved texts for reading in churches, and freedom was allowed in eastern churches for individual churches to decide the matter. But the basic approach was set by Athanasius, who rejected all of the deuterocanonical books, except for Baruch and Epistle of Jeremiah, *as Scripture* but accepted some of them as "readable" in private. He also emphasized that the "apocryphal" writings—here meaning heretical writings, not the writings Protestants call apocrypha—have no place in Christian gatherings because "they are an invention of heretics, who write them when they choose, bestowing upon them their approbation, and assigning to them a date, that so, using them as ancient writings, they may find occasion to lead astray the simple" (Athanasius, *Thirty-Ninth Festal Letter* 4–7, *NPNF*).

35. What books did the ecumenical church councils affirm for reading in churches?

The seven ecumenical or universal church councils that represented all churches in both East and West never discussed or determined the scope of the church's Scriptures and there is no clear ecumenical statement on the contents or scope of the apocryphal or deuterocanonical writings. Although eventually all churches welcomed as Scripture all of the books in the Hebrew Bible, they varied on which "additional" books could be read publicly or just privately. Those decisions were made by local church councils, as we will see below, but they did not reflect the thinking of *all* churches, both East and West. Few ancient lists that include these "additional" writings include more than a handful of them. The more recent listing of these books in current Bibles regularly includes a larger list than what we find in the ancient canonical lists or even in ancient manuscripts. The standard and most frequently cited LXX texts in the recent LXX editions of the Rahlfs and Rahlfs-Hanhart *Septuaginta*—which is largely based on the pandect uncial codices of Vaticanus, Sinaiticus, and Alexandrinus—regularly list more apocryphal/deutero-canonical books than those in the surviving ancient biblical manuscripts or in the canon lists. Only a few uncial and minuscule manuscripts from the fifth to tenth centuries include more than a handful of the deuterocanonical or apocryphal texts. Longer lists of these texts are included in recent Protestant editions of the Old Testament, especially *The New Oxford Annotated Bible: New Revised Standard Version with the Apocrypha*.

There is little that is controversial in this literature, though, as noted above, Luther was especially concerned over the prayers for the dead in 2 Macc 12:39–45 and the notion of offerings seeking divine favor in Tobias. Most of these writings, however, are both interesting and informative and many are often inspirational and educational, as in the cases of Judith and 1 and 2 Maccabees. They also help "fill in" several gaps in our understanding of the time between the two Testaments and often clarify several topics in the New Testament. Again, several of those disputed books are useful for understanding the context of early Christianity and the issues churches were facing at that time, but none were affirmed by any ecumenical council representing all churches. They sometimes aid in the interpretation of several New Testament teachings that we would not fully understand without knowing some of that literature.

36. Why do most Protestants reject the Old Testament apocrypha as Scripture?

Protestants eventually decided to adopt as their Old Testament only the books in the Hebrew Bible, though not their order. That stance was not prevalent at their beginning, but by the late 1800s Protestants stopped including apocryphal books in their Bibles. Like the Jews, they accepted no books written after the time of Ezra and Nehemiah, concluding that prophecy ceased among the Jewish nation after Ezra, Zechariah, and Malachi. That was not initially a Christian view and, like the residents of Qumran, early Christians initially believed that the Spirit and prophetic activity continued in the time of Jesus (Luke 1:41, 67; 2:36–38; 3:17, 22 and //s; John 20:22–23; Acts 1:8; 2:1–4; *passim*). There came a time during the Reformation, and especially with Martin Luther, when Protestants *began* to take exception to accepting some of the deuterocanonical (apocryphal) books that had regularly been appealed to as Scripture in most western churches at that time. Some Protestant Bibles continued to include a collection of the apocryphal/deuterocanonical writings well into the early nineteenth century. For example, the well-known Matthew's Bible in 1537 had sixteen of them. The Geneva Bible in 1560 had fourteen. Even the first edition of the King James Bible in 1611 contained ten of them, but following Martin Luther's example, placed them between the Old and New Testaments and identified them as "apocrypha."

At the Catholic Council of Trent in 1546, the Catholic Church made its final decision on which books it accepted as Scripture, including the deuterocanonical texts. It was recognizing and formalizing the use of sacred texts in the church that began centuries earlier, before those books were called "deuterocanonical" books. They continue as biblical books in Catholic Bibles to this day. Variations in the specific apocryphal/deuterocanonical books in Protestant Bibles continued well into the 1800s. Luther, interestingly, made use of some of the deuterocanonical writings but he rejected their scriptural status, much like the Orthodox. He especially opposed 2 Maccabees because it supported the Catholic doctrine of purgatory (see 2 Macc 12:39–45) though he did include those books in his Bible due largely to popular support for them in the Protestant churches.

We will now begin our focus on the Christian writings that eventually formed the New Testament canon.

CHAPTER 3

The Formation of the New Testament Canon

37. What key factors were involved in the formation of the New Testament?

THE ANSWER TO THIS question is, of course, the identity of Jesus and the church's core traditions about him. That is the first factor. Jesus' early followers believed that he was the anticipated Messiah who soon was acknowledged as the Lord of the church and this affirmation was rooted in his resurrection from the dead (Rom 1:3-4). This was central in all of the earliest affirmations about him. The second factor included the core beliefs about Jesus and the church's central traditions about the Christian faith. Without the eventual affirmation of this teaching Christian faith would not have survived, and without broad agreement on these central features of Christian faith the New Testament would not have emerged. These core beliefs—focused mostly on the identity, mission, and teachings of Jesus—are the presupposition for all Christian faith and for all the writings that make up the church's New Testament. His teachings, practices, beliefs, and death and resurrection are central beliefs in the emergence of early Christianity and in the writings that eventually formed the New Testament.

The earliest Christian writings presented something new about Jesus that was not a part of their early Jewish traditions and their first Scriptures, which they welcomed from their Jewish siblings. They interpreted the Hebrew Scriptures, often in Greek (they most often used the LXX), generally in *Christological* fashion, namely citing those Scriptures that found their fulfillment in Jesus, and eschatologically, that is, those Scriptures that supported the church's views about the coming kingdom of God.

38. What are the most important ancient resources for the study of the formation of the New Testament?

There are essentially seven major resources that enable scholars to make the best-informed decisions about the formation of the New Testament as Christian Scripture. None of them are in themselves without dispute, but a reasonable examination of all of them is the best way to find an adequate explanation of this question. These include: (1) the biblical literature itself and what we can glean from its texts that sometimes have similar words to the apocrypha and pseudepigrapha and sometimes contain later inserted texts; (2) the canon lists that have survived antiquity, which show considerable overlap, but not infrequently some (now) non-biblical books are included and some biblical books are not included; (3) the surviving scriptural manuscripts—most of which are from dry arid regions, such as Egypt or the Sinai Peninsula and the deserts in Israel and Jordan—which can let us know the most important books circulating in early Christianity and which texts were not so well received; (4) the books included in the translations of the biblical writings; (5) the insertions of specific texts in the surviving manuscripts, some of which are insertions put into them by often well-intentioned scribes or copiers; (6) the citations of ancient sacred literature in the church fathers and how books were received by the fathers, whether as Scripture or "ecclesiastical" writings (or "readables" noted earlier); and (7) local church councils.

Few scholars are proficient in all these fields of inquiry, and so they regularly depend on the research of other scholars to arrive at a coherent understanding of how the Bible came to be. Along with the texts cited above and below in the questions, I have added in the subsequent chapters several other important resources for understanding the formation of the New Testament, including the creeds, councils, and also hymns of early Christianity.

39. Did the ancient churches accept only the four Gospels or did some also accept other gospels?

Although the canonical Gospels in the New Testament received the majority of citations and use in early Christianity, some churches also welcomed other gospels that were not later included in the New Testament. There were many gospels that were not included in the New Testament, but the canonical Gospels were by far the most favored and most cited by the church fathers. In the latter part of the second century, Irenaeus insisted on only the four Gospels as canonical (see his arguments in *Haer* 1.31.1; 3.1.1; 3.11.8–9). His insistence was likely in part because of some second-century Christians from Asia Minor, sometimes called the "Alogists," who rejected the Gospel of John and Revelation. Their name was given to them by their opponents based on their opposition to the Logos (Greek = word/reason) in John's Gospel, hence "Alogists," a name that also served to indicate they were considered "unreasonable" (i.e., without *logos*/reason).

About the same time (ca. 180–200 CE) Tertullian chided Marcion because he cited the Gospel of Luke and not an *apostolic* author, such as Matthew or John. Tertullian thus appears to have a lower view of Luke than of Matthew and John (*Marc.* 4.2.2). This is presumably why Luke and Mark were the least cited of the four canonical Gospels in antiquity and Matthew and John were the most cited. The earliest manuscript that contains all four Gospels and Acts is P45 (= papyrus manuscript 45) penned from around the early third century. Many of the earliest manuscripts that include the Gospels only have one of them (mostly Matthew) and only a few have two Gospels in them. But that may not be because they rejected the others as much as that in some cases they only possessed one Gospel, and indeed that Gospel may have been the only one that was known to those churches.

In the second century and following, the most cited New Testament book was the Gospel of Matthew, whose contents, especially the words of Jesus, were cited far more times than the other Gospels. It may be going too far to say that the canonical status of our four Gospels was never disputed or that no other gospels were known from that time, but from the third century onward the manuscripts that contained canonical Gospels regularly included *only* the four canonical Gospels, e.g., Codex Vaticanus, Codex Sinaiticus, and Codex Alexandrinus. Following the second century, whenever the Gospels are listed in canonical lists, they appear together without any others beside them.

40. What other gospels were read in some ancient churches?

After the second century, no one in the proto-orthodox churches (a majority of early orthodox churches before the fourth century) accepted any gospels other than the four canonical Gospels that are now in Christian Bibles, but for a time several other gospels were circulating in some second- and third-century churches, as in the cases of the Gospel of the Hebrews, and the Gospel of Peter, noted by Eusebius in the fourth century (*Hist. eccl.* 3.25.5 and 6.12.3–6). As we have seen, Tertullian did not think that Mark and Luke had as much authority as Matthew and John, because the former books were not written by apostles. Tertullian did accept them, but not on the same level as Matthew and John. From the third century on, those four canonical Gospels, and no more, appear to circulate together or just individually in the surviving manuscripts or they are listed together in the various catalogues of the church's Scriptures. The earliest manuscript containing all four canonical Gospels and Acts is, as noted above, in the early-third-century papyrus manuscript P45. But at that time, several single Gospel manuscripts were still circulating in some churches. From the early fourth century when Eusebius speaks of the four canonical Gospels as the "holy tetrad" (*Hist. eccl.* 3.25.1), the most popular gospels were the canonical Gospels alone. See also his description of the New Testament writings that were widely accepted, those that were disputed, and those rejected (3.25.1–7). From that point on, perhaps 320–330 CE, it is almost only the four canonical Gospels that were widely read in churches.

By the end of the second century, it appears that only a few churches were still open to reading other gospels. For instance, according to Eusebius, some Jewish Christians preferred the Gospel According to the Hebrews. By the early third century the four canonical Gospels *began* to be circulated together (P45), though not everywhere and there were other gospels circulating in churches that were eventually rejected or even condemned (as in Irenaeus, *Haer* 1.31.1; and 3.1.1; 3.11.8–9). While Irenaeus argued strongly for only the four canonical Gospels, not everyone in his generation or shortly thereafter agreed with him. For example, we see some thirty years later that the church at Rhossus (ca. 200 CE) read the Gospel of Peter in its services, which led to disputes in that church. Initially, Bishop Serapion of Antioch encouraged them to go ahead and allow its reading if that was the only problem among them, but he himself had not yet read it until he returned to Antioch and found a copy and read it. He then found what he believed was heresy in it and reversed his ruling, telling the church not to read it any longer (Eusebius, *Hist. eccl.* 6.12.3–6). Aside from Irenaeus, no one in the second or early third century was talking about a fixed biblical canon for the Gospels or other writings for all churches. Even Irenaeus, who accepted only the four canonical Gospels, did not suggest that *only* the Gospels and no other texts were Scripture. He simply did not set forth a list of the other books that formed his New Testament. Serapion, a leading bishop of a major church, evidently was unaware of a limited collection of Gospels for all churches and initially allowed that church to read a different gospel that was later rejected by all churches. Soon after that, however, whenever the Gospels are listed, it is almost exclusively only the four New Testament Gospels.

Biblical scholars are well aware that there were many gospels initially welcomed in some churches and written and in the names of well-known New Testament figures, such as the Gospel of Thomas, the Gospel of Peter, the Infancy Gospel of Thomas, the Gospel of Philip, the Gospel of Mary, the Gospel of the Egyptians, the Gospel of the Hebrews, and others. Some churches possessed and read these texts, as we saw at Rhossus above, and they likely read them like Scripture because at that time there was no notion of a fixed biblical canon circulating in churches or in most church fathers. When these other gospels were written, mostly in the second and third centuries, there were no decisions made about the formation of a biblical canon. Those decisions were largely made in the late fourth century and thereafter. However, the other gospels eventually were rejected when canon formation began to become a significant part of the church fathers' focus in the middle to late fourth century following the Council of Nicea (325 CE) when the identity of Jesus was established for most of the churches. After that, several biblical canons (lists of writings that could be read in churches) began to appear among several local church councils at Laodicea (360), Rome (382), Hippo (393), and Carthage (397 and 419).

41. What was the status of the Book of Acts when churches began forming their New Testament?

Acts was included alongside all four Gospels at the end of the second or beginning of the early third century in P45. Acts is often cited by several church fathers beginning with Clement of Rome (e.g., 1 Clem. 2.1–2; 18.1 [See 1 Sam 13:14 and Acts 13:22]; 59.2; cf. also 2 Clem. 4.4 and 20.5; Pol. *Phil.* 1.2; 2.3; 6.3; 12.2; Did. 1.5; 4.8; Barn. 7.2 and 19.8), and in several texts after that, including in Justin's *Dialogue* and his *1 Apology* as well as later by Tertullian in his arguments against Marcion (*Marc.* 5.1–2 and *Praescr.* 22). Acts was cited often, sometimes like Scripture but sometimes not. Its importance for understanding several of the New Testament writings and consequent use in the early church fathers' writings suggests that its reception in early Christianity was never much in doubt despite the rejection of many other non-canonical books of acts in the names of apostolic figures circulating in the second- and third-century churches. There are no known ancient objections to its inclusion among the church's Christian Scriptures.

Several events in Acts are cited in the collection known as the Apostolic Fathers and in later church fathers. Irenaeus makes frequent authoritative use of Acts on multiple occasions without calling it "Scripture" (*Haer.* 1.26.3; 3.12.1; 4.23.2). However, it is unclear if there are any clear references to Acts as "Scripture" until the fourth century, despite its being employed to tell the church's proclamation multiple times throughout the second and third centuries. At some point, either in the first or second century, it was separated from the Gospel of Luke, though written by the same author, and later it circulated in connection with the Catholic Epistles. In the early fourth century (c. 315–323), Eusebius clearly places Acts in the category of "recognized" Scriptures among most of the churches (*Hist. eccl.* 3.4.6 and 3.25.1). While Acts was not always a bridge between the Gospels and the Catholic epistles or Paul's epistles, it generally functioned that way following the example of Athanasius. Only later did it become a bridge between the Gospels and the Epistles of Paul.

42. When were Paul's letters recognized as sacred Scripture?

In a second-century text, Polycarp (150–155) recognized the scriptural status of one of Paul's letters. His letter to the *Philippians* 12.1 is as follows: "I am confident that you are well trained in the sacred scriptures and that nothing is hidden from you"; and subsequently he adds, "Only, as it is written in these scriptures, 'Be angry and do not sin, and do not let the sun go down on your anger.'"[1]

This, of course, fits in well with how the early churches recognized the value of some of Paul's letters and cited them *like* sacred Scripture before actually *calling* them *Scripture*. They were often treated *like* Scripture, that is authoritatively, and then later, in the second century, some of Paul's letters began being *called* Scripture. The above text in Polycarp does not come to us in Greek, the original language of that text, but is preserved in a late fifteenth-century Latin text (*ut his scripturis dictum est*). Although some scholars question its authenticity because chapters 10–12 are only preserved in late Latin (dating ca. 1498), it nevertheless fits in well with what we find happening in the beginning in the second half of the second century when some of Paul's letters and the Gospels were beginning to be called "Scripture." The earliest references to the Gospels and some of Paul's writings as "Scripture," according to Hippolytus of Rome (ca. 200 CE), appears to come from Basilides around 123–140 CE, who cites three of the Gospels (not Mark) and four of Paul's letters using the scriptural introduction "as it is written" to refer to them (see Hippolytus, *Refutation of All Heresies* 7.22.4).[2]

It is important to repeat that texts regularly *functioned like Scripture* before they were *called* Scripture in antiquity. In other words, they were first treated like authoritative writings—which church leaders were called to read in the churches (Col 4:16) and which were used to give directions for Christian teachings and Christian living (1–2 Corinthians and others)—before they are called Scripture. And they are *called Scripture* before they are *placed* in a biblical canon or called canonical Scripture and put into a fixed collection of sacred books. There were several writings that were *called* Scripture long before they were listed with other sacred texts that make up the Bible, and some of those books initially called Scripture were not later included in the New Testament. For example, Shepherd of Hermas and Enoch were regularly called Scripture in early Christianity for more than a century but were not eventually included in the church's biblical canon.

We should note that Paul's letters were not called Scripture in the first century and, as we will see, their use and the value seen in them

---

1. Polycarp is citing here both Eph 4:26 and Ps 4:5 (Bart Ehrman, LCL trans.).

2. For other examples of parallels in wording in various Gospels and some of the letters of Paul, see McDonald, *New Testament*, 2:45–59.

preceded their recognition as Scripture in many second-century churches. This raises questions of the authorship of 2 Peter 3:15–16, which says of Paul's writings: "The ignorant and unstable twist [them] to their own destruction, *as they do the other scriptures.*" Those who use this argument for an early acceptance of Paul's writings as sacred Scripture in the first century ignore the more recent scholarly arguments regarding the date of 2 Peter. It was thought that since 2 Peter has parallels with the apocryphal Apocalypse of Peter (c. 110–140), that it was written shortly before then, but more recently it has become clear that 2 Peter *depends on* the Apocalypse of Peter and was likely written c. 120–140. Since 2 Peter is not cited before the end of the second century nor listed in any New Testament canon list before Athanasius in 367 CE, it was obviously a disputed text. It was ignored by Lucian of Antioch (d. 312), and the prominent Bishop John Chrysostom of Constantinople (347–407) and Theodore of Mopsuestia (350–428) never mentioned it. The Syrian churches never accepted 2 Peter until the sixth century, and it was still disputed much later by Martin Luther, who said that the Christian message did not shine well in it. It is quite possible that the references to the use of Paul's letters by heretics in 2 Pet 3:16 could be a reference to Marcion or gnostic Christians and it is without parallel in the first century. Finally, the significant differences between 1 and 2 Peter and the broader acceptance of 1 Peter suggests 2 Peter was written later and not by the author of 1 Peter. Thus, 2 Peter attests to Paul's writings being considered Scripture by some Christians in the second century, but it is not evidence that they were so considered in the first century.

43. Did Paul write the book of Hebrews and when was its scriptural status affirmed?

Paul did not write Hebrews. By the late fourth century several local canon councils list *thirteen* letters attributed to Paul and began to speak of *fourteen* letters of Paul, meaning that Hebrews was attributed to Paul at the council of Rome in 382 and clearly at the Council of Carthage in 419. That view was not accepted by all church fathers, but the book's long-standing use in the churches from the first century had gained it a wide reception and it was not going to be rejected. By the fourth century, when authorship of Christian writings became more important—unlike in the first century when more than half of the New Testament writings were written anonymously—Hebrews was attributed to Paul. Although Pauline language and the major theological issues in Paul's undisputed letters (justification by faith, reconciliation, the role of the Holy Spirit, and others) are not in Hebrews, it was likely attributed to Paul to keep it in the church's sacred collection of Christian Scriptures when authorship became an important criterion for acceptance.

The thirteen letters widely attributed to Paul before then included the Pastoral Epistles but did not include Hebrews, though P46 (c. 200) includes Hebrews after Romans and before 1 Corinthians, clearly welcoming it among Paul's letters, while the Pastoral Epistles attributed to Paul were omitted in that manuscript. The thirteen letters *without* Hebrews are attributed to Paul at the council at Hippo (393) and Hebrews is distinguished from Paul's letters even later at the Council at Carthage (397), but it was finally connected to Paul's letters at the Council of Carthage in 419 CE. Marcion omitted both the Pastoral Epistles and Hebrews, but he may not have known of the Pastoral Epistles, or, if he did, he rejected them.

Like Hebrews, the Pastorals are unlike the widely accepted letters of Paul due largely to the absence of the major themes found in Paul's writings, such as justification by faith, reconciliation, the role and ministry of the Holy Spirit, and the mission of the church. Also, the style of the writing and vocabulary is considerably different in those writings from Paul's widely accepted letters (Romans, 1–2 Corinthians, Galatians, Philippians, 1 Thessalonians, and Philemon).

Interestingly, the late second- or early third-century manuscript P46, the earliest manuscript that we have of Paul's letters, does *not* include 2 Thessalonians, the Pastoral Epistles, or Philemon, but it does include Hebrews. Because the manuscript is fragmented, it might have included others, including 2 Thessalonians and Philemon, but it seems there is not sufficient space in it to have also included the Pastoral Epistles. Now, the exact number of pages of P46 is now known and that has been the source of considerable debate among scholars, some of whom have suggested that the Pastorals could have been included if the copier wanted, even if he was running out of space, because he could have used smaller letters. However, even with decreasing the size of letters P46 still would not have been able to include the Pastorals. Some of those arguments are, of course, guess work, and it could have been possible that additional pages were added to that manuscript, but the evidence for that is lacking. Consequently, that suggestion is not widely accepted, and the issue prompts us to ask afresh whether the Pastoral letters (1–2 Timothy and Titus) adequately reflect the Paul that we see in his undisputed letters. Since most of the surviving manuscripts before the fifth century are fragmented, it is difficult to say precisely what was included among the letters attributed to Paul before the fourth century. The Pastoral Epistles are also missing in the later manuscript Codex Vaticanus (ca. 350–375 CE), but again, because it ends in the middle of Heb 9:24, it is possible that those books could have been included in the manuscript. Centuries later, other books, including the Pastorals, were added to Codex Vaticanus to make it more complete, and the Pastorals are in Codices Sinaiticus and Alexandrinus and follow the book of Hebrews.

The usual order of Paul's writings seems to be based on length, and it concludes with Philemon, the smallest writing of Paul, *followed by* Hebrews, a much longer writing. This is suggestive of the doubts about the authorship of Hebrews. The later fourth- and fifth-century church councils and manuscripts regularly attribute the Pastorals to Paul and by the early fifth century Hebrews is regularly attributed to Paul. The authorship of Hebrews was debated by several church fathers, the most famous contribution coming from Origen, who concluded that only God knows who wrote Hebrews. But he was not willing to dismiss the book, for by his time Hebrews had gained the "irresistible momentum" noted above.

There are, of course, ongoing questions about the authorship of Hebrews, as we will see below. The Councils (or Synod) of Laodicea (360) and Rome (382) attributed fourteen letters to Paul, including Hebrews, but the Council of Hippo (393) and Carthage (397) had some question about Paul's authorship of Hebrews. By the subsequent council at Carthage (419), all fourteen epistles are attributed to Paul, which means that the Pastorals and Hebrews were also attributed to Paul. When the church fathers began to cite the Pastoral Epistles, they generally attributed them to Paul.

44. If any of Paul's lost letters (1 Cor 5:9; Col 4:16) were found, should they be included in the New Testament?

Paul wrote letters that we no longer have. For instance, he mentioned that he wrote an earlier letter to the Corinthian church (1 Cor 5:9) before writing the letter that we now call 1 Corinthians. What if it, or one of his other lost letters, was found? This question has long been debated among scholars and church leaders, but there is little agreement among them on what should be done if one of Paul's lost letters were to be found.

Publishers would certainly be pleased because it would lead to many new publications and many media reports around the world. It is unclear what the churches would do with it, but likely it would at the least be cited and quoted in a lot in churches and in academic research.

It would, of course, be amazing if an actual lost text written by Paul or any other well-known follower of Jesus in the New Testament writings were found. It would surely have to be taken seriously, but it is hard to believe that it would change any of the church's core teachings, which are well supported in the Scriptures that we now possess. There could hardly be any lost book by a genuine apostolic figure that would go contrary to the core teachings of the early churches. And I doubt that many people would toss away their current Bibles and look for a new one that includes the newly discovered writing, but this does not give a definitive answer to the question posed. Some Christians would likely say yes, the newly discovered text should be in the Bible, and others would say no.

It could be argued that if an authentic letter written by Paul was discovered, the New Testament would not be affected since the church in its wisdom only included what we now have and so it would not be included in the church's Bible. The church preserved only those books that were most beneficial for its life and no writings not included by any of the major local church councils—like those at Rome, Laodicea, Hippo, Carthage, and later Trent—should now be included in the Bible. Since such a discovered work was never included in any ancient canon lists or council decisions, it should not be included in the Bible now.

Not all agree on this matter, however, and we see in Hal Taussig's *A New New Testament* that he and scholars working with him added several ancient Christian writings in their New Testament. However, despite the sensational response that emerged after its publication, there is currently not much support among most biblical scholars or the church to change the scope of the current Bible. It is likely that the same would be true of any new findings, unless they made very significant contributions to our understanding of early Christianity and its core beliefs.

Some early Christian collections of sacred texts initially included some Christian writings that were not later included and were even lost for centuries (e.g., Didache, Shepherd of Hermas, Epistle of Barnabas). Perhaps those and other writings were purposefully not included in the church's New Testament for unknown reasons or perhaps they were lost or destroyed during the Decian and Diocletian persecutions of churches in the third or fourth centuries. Some of the lost early writings have now been found and important commentaries have been written on some of them (e.g., Didache, Shepherd of Hermas, and others), yet they have not been added to the New Testament.

Again, what would churches do if some archeologist or biblical scholar discovered that collection of some twenty-two to twenty-six lost books mentioned in the Old Testament, which we listed above, some of which were cited as prophecy. It is doubtful that many churches would be willing to change their Bibles after so many centuries of having the matter settled, but no doubt such a find would generate a lot of excitement, research, and new publications.

For all intents and purposes, the Bible is *closed* for Orthodox, Catholic, and Protestant churches despite the many differences between them. While the current processes of canonization are often imprecise and complex, it is not likely that any widespread changes will be forthcoming on the scope of Christian Bibles.

Expanding the Bible now would more likely bring more havoc in churches than any perceived value that a new book or books might bring to the church, or the problems any dismissal of disputed biblical books would cause churches. Again, the biblical canon for all intents and purposes is finished and the current scholarship is largely focused on how the ancient churches arrived at the scope of the Scriptures that we have today and have been largely settled for centuries. The core theology and message of each of the included books advance the church's core teachings about Jesus and the Christian faith.

It is also worth bearing in mind that a tight connection between authorship and scriptural status was not made by the church to start with. Various New Testament texts, including all four Gospels, are anonymous and the authorship of the sacred writings circulating anonymously in churches was not posted in more than half of the New Testament books, and their names were not widely known or cited for more than a hundred years. This suggests that the matter of authorship was not so important then. We should note that most people even today do not know the authorship of several Old Testament books but would not consider rejecting them, e.g., the Samuels, Kings, Chronicles, some psalms and Proverbs (Prov 25:1). They are a permanent part of the Old Testament irrespective of their authorship. When the Gospels were read in churches or cited by the early church fathers, the authors of the Gospels were not generally mentioned by name until the later second century. That, too, suggests that authorship was not as important initially as it was later. When the Gospels began to be cited, the citations were not anchored in the names of the authors, but rather in the word and deeds of Jesus, the Lord of the church. That began to change around 170–180 CE and probably earlier, but it was not the case much earlier. So although authorship became an important factor in the canonization process by the fourth century, it was not so to start with.

Future research on this question will best be served, I suggest, by focusing on the multiple authorities in the churches *before there was a Bible*. These include some of the artifacts included below, but they especially include Jesus himself, the church's first Scriptures (i.e., its Old Testament), apostolic authority, early church tradition, church creeds, the increased role of church leaders (bishops), baptismal and eucharistic affirmations, hymns, lections, canon lists, the books that were included in the ancient manuscripts, and translations of the church's Scriptures. Since neither Jesus nor the authors of the New Testament ever spoke about open or closed biblical canons or the emergence of a New Testament canon of Scriptures, it is probably best not to be dogmatic about what would happen if . . . ![3]

45. Which New Testament writings were most disputed in the early churches?

In the fourth century Eusebius indicated that several New Testament writings were disputed in some churches, especially James, Jude, 2 Peter, 2–3 John, and Revelation (*Hist. eccl.* 3.25; ca. 320–330 CE). The widely accepted books at that time, according to Eusebius, included the four canonical Gospels, the letters of Paul (of which he includes Hebrews), the book of Acts, 1 Peter, and 1 John. Eusebius includes Revelation in the disputed category but with some question later, after listing the "not genuine" (*nothois*) books he adds, "And in addition, as I said, the Revelation of John, *if this view prevail*. For, as I said, some reject it, but others count it among the Recognized Books" (Greek = *tois homologoumenois*) (3.25.4, LCL). He was aware that Constantine liked the book of Revelation and so was careful not to offend him, but later he gave considerable space to Dionysius

---

3. For a study of the earliest authorities in early Christianity, see McDonald *Before There Was*.

of Alexandria to express his doubts about the authorship of Revelation (*Hist. eccl.* 7.25.1–9). For centuries Revelation was rejected in the Eastern churches, and it is still not read in the Orthodox liturgies despite its acceptance as Scripture in the seventh and eighth centuries.

Eusebius also acknowledged that "some" church fathers (generally the Jewish Christians) "counted" or recognized the Gospel of the Hebrews. Along with making clear which writings were disputed in churches, he listed the "not genuine" books (Greek = *en tois nothois*) and included among them the Acts of Paul, Shepherd of Hermas, Apocalypse of Peter, Epistle of Barnabas, and the Didache (i.e., Teaching of the Twelve). In a final word, Eusebius referred also to the "not encovenanted" (Greek = *ouk endiathekous*) books—that is, the "counterfeit" and "not canonical" books—and he included among them the pseudonymous gospels attributed to Peter, Thomas, and Matthias (not Matthew), as well as the pseudonymous Acts attributed to Andrew, John, and the other apostles (*Haer. eccl.* 3.25.6).

Unlike today, the early churches had few if any who questioned whether Paul wrote the letters now called Ephesians, Colossians or 2 Thessalonians. There are several letters mentioned among Paul's writings that are apparently lost, such as a first letter to the Corinthians mentioned in 1 Cor 5:9 and later his letter to the Laodiceans mentioned in Col 4:16. Scholars are mindful that despite universal recognition of Paul's authorship of 2 Corinthians it may be a letter combining two or even three of Paul's letters that were written over an extended time when circumstances changed. Similarly, the break in Phil 3:1b appears to suggest that Paul's Letter to the Philippians combined another of Paul's letters, with the first letter closing in 3:1a and the second beginning in 3:1b. The loss of Paul's letter to the Laodiceans led others later to construct a pseudonymous letter in Paul's name, likely written by someone in the fourth century, and it is likely mentioned—and rejected—in the late-fourth-century Muratorian Fragment. Marcion referred to a letter from Paul to the Laodiceans, but Tertullian claimed that Marcion thought that the letter to the Laodiceans was Paul's Letter to the Ephesians.

There is no evidence in antiquity that anyone ever denied Paul's authorship of the Letter to Ephesians. However, the address to the church "in Ephesus" (Greek= *en epheso*) in Eph 1:1 does not have good textual support, and this suggests that the name "Ephesus" was likely added later to that letter, and it may well have been written to the Laodiceans, or it could have been an encyclical letter that Paul wrote to a broader number of churches than just the Ephesians. F. F. Bruce concluded that Ephesians is "the quintessence of Paulinism,"[4] but it was not likely written to only the church at Ephesus. It may be that Ephesus is where a copy of that letter was found and so "in Ephesus" was later attached to it. It may also be that Marcion confused this letter with Paul's letter to the Laodiceans (Col 4:16) or even another of his letters that is lost, but this is speculation and uncertain.

The Letter of James was sometimes omitted from early canon lists and was disputed because of its differences with Paul on the role of works in Christian faith. Some biblical scholars argue that James, the brother of Jesus and leader of the church in Jerusalem (Acts 15 and 21), did not write this letter, partially because it is suggested that Jesus' brother would not have been adequately literate or have the ability to write with such high-quality Greek in what is among the best literary writings in the New Testament. That, of course, is not necessarily the case, since like Paul he could have used an amanuensis or secretary (see Rom 16:22, and also 1 Pet 5:12, where Silvanus was used to write the letter). Some of the highly educated writings were produced by a more literate amanuensis. Cicero was one of the most highly educated persons in all of Rome, yet he also made extensive use of a secretary named Tiro. According to Cicero himself, Tiro was responsible for a whole lot more than merely taking dictation. Paul likewise was well educated and still made use of secretaries. In three of his letters, Paul speaks of writing a concluding greeting with his own hand (Col 4:18; 2 Thess 3:17; Philm 19. See also Gal 6:11). His letter to the Roman Christians was his crown jewel and the best written of all of Paul's letters, but it was written by Tertius, who identifies himself in Rom 16:22. Like Tiro for Cicero, Tertius's role in the composition of Romans almost certainly far exceeded merely taking dictation from Paul.[5] James also could have used a secretary to take notes and then compose the letter that he approved prior to sending it to churches. It was not only written in good Greek, but it is also very Jewish-Christian in its content.

This raises an important question, namely whether the scriptural status and canonicity of James was questioned because of its disputed authorship or because of its content. It was finally recognized as Christian Scripture by some early Christians, likely Jewish Christians, and

---

4. Bruce, *Paul*, 424.
5. See Richards, *Paul and First Century*.

eventually included in the New Testament, but not without doubts. The canonicity of James was questioned later by Luther and others because of its differences with Paul on justification by faith and not works. Luther marginalized Hebrews, Jude, and Revelation and put them at the back of his Bible.

If the Letter of James was written by James the brother of Jesus, who died around 62–64 CE, it would be among the earliest writings in the New Testament and likely written in Palestine. If James's secretary wrote it, the amanuensis secretary was well-educated, with considerable skills in Greek, not unlike in the writings of Philo of Alexandria. Several modern scholars thus conclude that it was not written by James the brother of the Lord, but by a well-informed Hellenistic Jew. The date and authorship of James is not easily determined, but the message of James fits well with early Jewish-Christian theology and Jewish traditions circulating in Palestine in the first century.

46. Why were some of the Catholic Epistles (James, 2 Peter, 2–3 John, Jude) and Revelation disputed well into the fourth century and even later?

Disputes about these texts emerged before there was much thinking about a fixed biblical canon and the debates became clearer in the fourth and fifth centuries and even later. The Catholic or General Epistles were not generally cited by the church fathers as much as they cited the Gospels and letters of Paul. For several centuries, the Syrian Christians did not recognize or accept the Minor New Testament Epistles (2 Peter, 2–3 John, and Jude) and Revelation. The reason is not always clear in the surviving traditions, namely whether it was a question of content or something else, such as the size of these texts. On the other hand, the Syrians welcomed as Scripture Tatian's unified or harmonized gospel, the *Diatessaron* (Greek = "through four") also called the "Gospel of the Mixed." They also welcomed 3 Corinthians in their Scriptures for several centuries and that text continued in the Armenian church Scriptures well into the early 1800s. Eventually, rejection of most of the Catholic Epistles was overcome and, by the fifth century, following the increased Greek influence in the East, these letters were finally welcomed as Scripture, but the book of Revelation was still rejected until the late sixth or seventh centuries, and even after that it continued to be marginalized in their worship services and still is not read it in their liturgies. While these disputed writings were all attributed to apostles or those connected to them and welcomed in the Syrian New Testament, they did not have a prominent place in those churches. It may be that Syrian rejection of these five Catholic Epistles was largely because of questionable authorship or perhaps due to their contents, and Revelation continued to be a problem for many centuries after that. It also took several centuries (most likely the fifth or sixth century) before the Syrian churches welcomed all canonical Gospels over Tatian's *Diatessaron* and 3 Corinthians.

The Oriental Orthodox churches generally followed the Syrian tradition in regard to Revelation but eventually they welcomed it into their New Testament books as Scripture. Even though it is now in all of their New Testaments, Revelation is never read in the Eastern, Russian, or Oriental Orthodox worship services, along with those of Eastern Catholic communities who use the Byzantine rite liturgy. (One recent Orthodox author questioned how the book of Revelation could be in their New Testament and yet not read it in their worship.)[6]

No one in the second or third centuries focused on which *Christian* Scriptures formed a fixed biblical canon, even though Irenaeus was certain about the four Gospels (and only those gospels), but he did not speak about a complete New Testament for all churches, nor did he construct a list of the other writings that churches now accept as their New Testament Scriptures. In the third century Origen was well aware of a Jewish canon of Scriptures and even a Jewish list of their sacred books (*Comm. Jo.* 5 and *Hom. Josh.* 7.1), but such lists did not yet play a prominent role in early Christianity. It appears that Origen accepted most if not all of the New Testament (he is not precise in regard to some of the letters), but he may have advocated a limited list of New Testament books for reading in the churches based on the criterion of catholicity, i.e., texts that were widely welcomed in the majority of churches. However, at that time a fixed biblical canon was not the same everywhere for all churches (see Eusebius, *Hist. eccl.* 6.25.3–14). Origen cited approvingly several deuterocanonical texts as Scripture, contrary to the Jewish collection of Scriptures, and defended this in his *Letter to Julius Africanus* (4.12–14). His New Testament collection appears mixed on the reception of James, 2 Peter, 2–3 John, and Revelation, and he never quotes 2–3 John, but

---

6. Scanlin, "Old Testament Canon," 300–312.

he did cite 2 Peter a few times, which points to his reception of it.[7] He had doubts about Revelation and 3 John (*Hom. Josh.* 7.1; *Comm. Matt.* 1; 10:17;[8] *Comm. Jo.* 5) but cites it positively elsewhere along with the Gospel of Peter in regard to the perpetual virginity of Mary.

It is clear that questions about the formation of the Bible were primarily a fourth- and fifth-century discussion when most decisions about the scope of the New Testament took place, but not for all of New Testament books. Most of the known decisions occur after the Nicene Council (325 CE), which focused primarily on the identity of Jesus and not on the scope of the biblical canon. It would hardly have been possible to have a *Christian* New Testament canon before there was broad agreement among most churches on the identity of Jesus.

47. Does Revelation 22:18–19 say that the whole Bible is a divine revelation and inspired?

That passage, of course, only refers to the revelations in the book of Revelation and not to the whole Bible, but eventually it was cited to refer to all of the church's Scriptures in both Old and New Testaments. The passage in Revelation reflects a common admonition in antiquity that no one who copied a book could add to it or take something away from it or that person would receive the wrath of God for doing so. The passage in Revelation is reflective of Deut 4:2 in which Moses commands, "You must neither add anything to what I command you nor take away anything from it but keep the commandments of the LORD your God with which I am charging you." This command is followed in Deut 12:28 with, "Be careful to obey all these words that I command you today so that it may go well with you and your children after you forever" (see also 12:32). There is an implied threat in several such passages in antiquity, including in the Letter of Aristeas (#311), not to change or add anything in the LXX Pentateuch, the Greek translation of the Hebrew Torah, or there would be serious consequences. This is much like what we see in Rev 22:18–19. Irenaeus makes a similar warning against changing the text of a sacred writing (*Haer.* 1.27.2 and 3.30). Similarly, Tertullian (*Herm.* 22).

---

7. It is also worth noting that P72 includes both Jude and 1–2 Peter as Scripture—in that order, but also several of the non-canonical writings.

8. See Gallagher's and Meade's comment on the citation of *Comm. Matt.* 10.17 in *Biblical Canon Lists*, 96–99.

Those verses have been cited by many about adding or deleting anything from the Bible, but as we saw above in the many variants in the biblical manuscripts, that warning was not always followed by the copiers of Scripture, who often made changes in the wording of the Scriptures whether to make it more clear to readers at a later time or to insert their own theological positions, as we see in 1 John 5:7–8 (the so-called Johannine Comma), John 7:53—8:11; Mark 16:9–20; and elsewhere.

Even the Greek philosopher Plato reflects such changes to texts of authors while commenting on his and Socrates's doubts and concerns about the reliability of writings altogether. He wrote,

> For this invention [writing] will produce forgetfulness in the minds of those who learn to use it, because they will not practice their memory. Their trust in writing, produced by external characters which are no part of themselves, will discourage the use of their own memory within them.
>
> He who thinks, then, that he has left behind him any art in writing, and he who receives it in the belief that anything in writing will be clear and certain, would be an utterly simple person, and in truth ignorant of the prophecy of Ammon, if he thinks written words are of any use except to remind him who knows the matter about which they are written. (Plato, *Phaedr.* 275AC, LCL)

The practice of changing written texts in antiquity took place up until there was a printing press. As another example, consider Tatian, a student of Justin Martyr (ca. 165 CE), who later produced his famous *Diatessaron*, an attempted harmony of the four canonical Gospels that was used by the Syrian Christians well into the fifth century. He obviously appreciated the four Gospels but also felt the need to change them into one harmonious gospel.

The ancient biblical manuscripts were regularly changed, whether by accident or by intention, in their transmission and no two manuscripts are exactly alike, but their scriptural status remained unchanged. Often the copier of biblical manuscripts changed words or phrases to make clear to readers what was intended in the passage and changed the text to something like "in other words" for the sake of clarity.

So, in Rev 22:18–19, the author was doing something that was typical in antiquity by making this familiar long-standing warning about adding to or deleting anything from an important text. He knew of those who had changed written texts and is the only writer in the

New Testament who explicitly says this about his work, a work that contains divine revelations. Paul hints at others changing his words (Gal 6:11 and in 2 Thess 2:2–3) and he surely did not appreciate those who would do so.

In practice, however, all ancient texts were modified in transmission, most accidentally, but some intentionally, for clarification. It is interesting in this regard to see in the Qumran Dead Sea Scrolls that some scribes who copied texts often freely made changes in them in their production of other copies and yet still they recognized their sacred status. They did the same in their making additions to Ps 145 and other scriptural texts as well.

In sum, the use of this admonition in Rev 22:18–19 was a common means of declaring the sacredness of a writing by claiming its inviolability, but the author only intended his admonition for the book of Revelation.

48. Were there other collections of Scriptures in antiquity that included books that are not in the New Testament today?

Yes. Among the best known are the Syriac Scriptures that included well into the fourth century 3 Corinthians and the *Diatessaron* (Tatian's harmony of the Gospels) and the Syrian churches omitted the minor New Testament texts (2 Peter, 2 and 3 John, Jude) and Revelation. Well into the nineteenth century the Armenian Christians welcomed as Scripture 3 Corinthians and the Repose of the Blessed Disciple (John). Codex Sinaiticus included in its New Testament the Epistle of Barnabas and Shepherd of Hermas. Codex Alexandrinus (fifth century) also included 1 and 2 Clement and strangely in their New Testament also the Psalms of Solomon. The Ethiopian Orthodox New Testament now includes Syndos, Book of the Covenant, Clement (not 1 Clement), and Didascalia. While there was broad agreement on most of the New Testament books by the fourth and fifth centuries in a majority of churches, Chrysostom (407 CE) never cited the last four of the Catholic/General Epistles or Revelation. Some churches also added other texts to their sacred Scriptures as we can see in the Stichometry of Nicephorus (ca. 850 CE), which condemns the use and reading of the noncanonical books that were still being read in churches hundreds of years after they had been rejected by church councils and prominent church fathers.

49. Because 1 Clement was a popular book and called Scripture by some Christians, why was it not included in the New Testament?

Since 1 Clement was likely written by Clement of Rome before some of the New Testament books were written and because it was popular in early Christianity and called Scripture by some (including the pseudepigraphal author of 2 Clement, who is not Clement of Rome)[9] many wonder why it was excluded from the New Testament. It was clearly an orthodox book with many carefully articulated teachings more so than many of the smaller books in the New Testament. It was also included among some church Scriptures in Codex Alexandrinus (fifth century), so why not include 1 Clement in the New Testament? We know that Clement of Rome wrote 1 Clement (ca. 75–90 CE) and that Clement was likely a bishop of the church in Rome when he wrote it and that he also had some apostolic ties, especially with the apostle Peter. So, why exclude it?

The scriptural status of 1 Clement is like the situation with the Gospel of Mark in that Mark was not an apostle and, according to Eusebius, he wrote what he had learned from the apostle Peter, and that may also be also true of Clement of Rome. 1 Clement may arguably have a greater claim to canonicity than Hebrews or some other writings that were included.

For sure, we do not know the answer to the question of why some books that do not seem as important as 1 Clement were included (e.g., 2–3 John, Jude) while Clement's text is not. As already made clear, 1 Clement is certainly orthodox in its teachings and can be dated in the later part of the first century, though some scholars date it as early as the 60s or 70s. It is likely earlier than some New Testament books—Matthew, John, Revelation, and others. It thus overlaps in time with writings that were included in the Bible, and it is clearly acceptable in its content.

Clement of Rome was a prominent teacher in Rome who wrote to the Corinthians to encourage them to be attentive and helpful to the leadership in their church and not to abuse them. 1 Clement remained a highly regarded text by the church fathers even long after they no longer accepted it as Scripture. Clement also and interestingly claimed that his own work

---

9. Most scholars agree that 2 Clement was not written by Clement of Rome but was falsely written in Clement's name considerably later. That, of course, reflects the popularity of 1 Clement in the second century, otherwise Clement's name would not have been included on a pseudonymous text.

was inspired by the Holy Spirit (47.2 and 63.2) and wrote, "For you will make us joyful and happy if you become obedient to what we have written through the Holy Spirit" (Ehrman, trans. LCL 149). Nevertheless, despite this it was still eventually rejected as Christian Scripture. Why? The specific reason is uncertain and we will likely never know.

50. What led the ancient churches to see a need for a fixed list of books (a canon) that could be read in churches?

Several biblical scholars[10] have argued that the Christian biblical canon emerged in response to many heresies circulating in churches and the production of heretical writings in the false names of apostolic figures, and there is much that is appealing about this position. Eventually, by the fourth century, the church fathers wanted to have a fixed list of the church's Scriptures that could be read in churches and eliminate the reading of any writings containing what was believed to be falsehoods and heresy circulating in several churches. The call for such fixed collections of both Old and New Testament writings begin to appear after the Council of Nicea (325 CE) when the identity of Jesus was established for the majority of churches.

51. When did a single biblical canon begin to emerge in early Christianity?

The notion of a single canon begins to emerge in the middle to late fourth century following the Council of Nicea when the identity of Jesus was broadly established. There could hardly be a collection of Christian Scriptures established before there was significant agreement on the identity of Jesus, the Lord of the church.

There never was a time when all churches agreed on the scope of the books to include in their Old Testaments, but by the end of the fourth century most churches agreed on the books that are now included in the New Testament, though that was not complete for all churches until centuries later—as we saw above, the eastern churches took longer to welcome the minor New Testament writings (2 Peter, 2 and 3 John, and Jude) as well as Revelation. Eventually all churches welcomed all

---

10. See Metzger, *Canon of the New* and von Campenhausen, *Formation of the Christian*.

of the books in the Hebrew Scriptures, but they differed on whether to welcome the deuterocanonical or apocryphal books, mostly seen in the Greek or LXX manuscripts, and on which deuterocanonical books were to be accepted. By the late seventh century it appears that all churches except the Ethiopian churches accepted all of the New Testament writings, but even after that some churches still welcomed reading other nonbiblical books in their liturgical church services.

52. What criteria were employed by the ancient churches to determine which books would be included in their New Testament?

Those examining the formation of the Bible recognize early on the complexity of this question because no one in antiquity told this story. Some uninformed inquirers have sometimes assumed that the formation of the Bible was a neat and clear-cut process with little disagreement involved, but the answer is much more complex than that. Recent canon research has made many positive advances in our understanding of how we got our Bible, but no one suggests that the processes are easy to articulate or demonstrate. Some scholars have worked on this question for years now and we are only beginning to get a clearer picture of how the early church developed and how its need of a biblical canon emerged. Forming the biblical canon was a much longer process than was earlier thought, but some aspects of it can now be seen with greater clarity than has previously been possible.

Without question some church fathers spoke of issues related to whether some books should be accepted when canon formation was being openly discussed in the fourth century and later, and by then *authorship* had become an important issue for many in the church. Who wrote a book was not *initially* of significant concern for the church. Again, since the four canonical Gospels, Acts, Hebrews, and 1–3 John were all written anonymously, it is clear that authorship only became an important matter later. By the end of the second century authorship was becoming more significant. Those who accepted a book generally, but not always, also accepted its attributed authorship, but when the *content* of a writing was questioned or considered heretical, the question of authorship was scrutinized, since how could an apostle write heretical teachings? That is also why so many falsely written documents in apostolic names appear when *apostleship* became an important criterion of authenticity, namely by the end of the second century and again in the fourth century when canonicity was in focus. So the concern for apostolic authorship was grounded in the desire to avoid heretical teachings.

The most commonly acknowledged criterion was widespread acceptance, often called "catholicity." That is, did most churches accept a book as Scripture and read it in their churches? Origen affirmed widespread use of a writing as a primary criterion that should be followed when in doubt about a particular book. About a century later, Eusebius, who had access to Origen's library at Caesarea, followed widespread use as a determinative criterion that he called it *homologoumena* or "recognized" writings that were assumed sacred by a majority of churches and acceptable for reading in churches (*Hist. eccl.* 3.25.1–7). This was his first criterion. We also find it later in Augustine who wrote,

> In the matter of canonical scriptures, he [the reader] should *follow the authority of the great majority of catholic churches*, including of course those that were found worthy to have apostolic seats and receive apostolic letters. He will apply this principle to the canonical scriptures: to prefer those accepted by all catholic churches to those which some do not accept. *As for those not universally accepted, he should prefer those accepted by a majority of churches.* (*On Christian Doctrine* 2.21, OWC trans, emphasis added)

He adds to widespread acceptance by mentioning the importance of certain churches that had a long-standing tradition that was more important than lesser or minor churches. One scholar has recently said that it was likely that the famed churches of Rome or Jerusalem or Alexandria had more influence in the selection than the smaller churches.

Orthodoxy broadly understood was also an important factor for determining the scope of the church's Scriptures. It is reflected in the primary core traditions of the churches and was regularly summarized in church creeds, hymns, and in baptismal and eucharistic affirmations. If the core teachings of the earliest churches were not found in various books, those books were not included in the biblical canon. Although the apostle Peter most likely did not write 2 Peter and it was most likely a second-century document, its core teachings were very much in keeping with the core teachings of early Christianity. Its apocalyptic teachings have many parallels in early Christianity. While 2 Peter was finally included, following considerable doubt about its authorship, its inclusion was likely because many did believe that the apostle Peter wrote it. When doubts arose about a particular document, its reflection of the orthodoxy in early Christianity no doubt helped those who made decisions about whether it should be included in the New Testament. The essential church orthodoxy was about the identity of Jesus and that was largely affirmed for most churches at the Council of Nicea (325 CE). That affirmation was necessary for the later local church councils to produce lists of writings that complied with that core teaching and could be read in churches. After Nicea, beliefs about which books could be read in churches and the authorship of those books became more important than it had been before. It was important in the formation of the New Testament canon in order for churches to have a clear understanding of Jesus' identity.

Apostolicity (later), *catholicity* (widespread use), and *orthodoxy* were the primary considerations for canonization, but also the dating or *antiquity* of the writings was also an important factor, welcoming texts that were written near the time of Jesus. The Muratorian Fragment later indicated that the Shepherd of Hermas could not be included because it was written later, in a subsequent generation. To that we must also acknowledge the continuing *adaptability* to issues facing churches. The late James Sanders claims that "adaptability" means that those writings that were able to be applied to the new situations relevant to later churches were also those that remained permanently in the church's Scriptures. Once the biblical canon was settled, then multiple ways of interpreting those books (hermeneutics) took on a more prominent role in churches, namely whether a book should be interpreted literally or allegorically or figuratively.

53. When was the Bible officially closed or was it ever closed?

This question may also ask whether it is possible to add anything new to the Bible. As noted above, some recent biblical scholars have considered adding other books to the Bible and deleting writings they do not consider relevant to Jesus and his earliest followers.

There are no Scriptures that say that the Scriptures are complete or closed and as church historians know well, there were Montanist Christians at the end of the second century who believed that their many writings were also inspired by God, and they garnered considerable support from their best-known convert, Tertullian. At a much later point the

Catholic Church believed that they needed to clarify this issue, and they affirmed a closed biblical canon at the Council of Trent (1545). It was also closed at one point for the Protestants, too, and at another for the Orthodox churches but without a church council to do it.

This raises the question of whether the biblical canon is forever closed. If so, when was it closed, by whom, and why? Was it determined by an ancient church council and if so, was that council representing *all* of Christianity? Such questions are not easy to answer and, as noted above, no *ecumenical* church council ever identified the books included in the church's Bible. While there are several Bibles functioning in the major church bodies (Orthodox, Catholic, Protestant, and Ethiopian), all include the books in the Hebrew Bible books and also (now) all the current New Testament books. Apart from that core agreement, the Bibles vary among the major church bodies today.

Since there is no verse or passage in the Bible, whether Old or New Testament, that identifies a specific number of books to include in the Bible, that is, no biblical passage says, "these books and no others," and since no ecumenical council issued any final decrees on the matter, one is pressed to say that the biblical canon is closed. However, each major body of the churches has long settled the question of which books could be read as Scripture in their churches. For all *practical* purposes the biblical canon is closed and while *in theory* it could still be open, a move to change it would not be without considerable challenges within the churches.

In the second century no one to our knowledge was thinking about a closed biblical canon until much later. Bishop Serapion, as observed earlier, did not reject the Gospel of Peter initially, but later rejected it because of the theology in it, not because it was not in an already-fixed list of Christian Scriptures. It is only with Origen in the third century, who indicated that the Jews had a fixed collection of their Scriptures, that we find such an interest in fixed lists. And even then Origen himself did not accept only those books contained in the Jewish list. He also accepted others among the deuterocanonical writings, especially Susanna, and he appears to have accepted most of the New Testament writings, but with some uncertainty over some of the smaller letters in it.

There were serious discussions about which writings could be read in churches in the fourth and fifth centuries more than a century after Origen and even after the Council of Nicea. At that time there was no universal agreement on which Old or New Testament books could be read in churches despite very considerable overlap in what was accepted by most churches. While canon interest and discussion emerge largely after the Council of Nicea (325 CE), when the identity of Jesus was largely settled for most churches, that council did not provide a list of books that could be read in churches (the essence or meaning of a biblical canon).

As noted above, a few scholars today advocate deleting some books from the Bible or including others in it. Thus, members of the Jesus Seminar, under the editorship of Hal Taussig, produced *A New New Testament*, in which several books that were not included in the New Testament are added—including the Gospel of Thomas, the Odes of Solomon, the Thunder: Perfect Mind, the Gospel of Mary, and the Gospel of Truth. Taussig and the authors in that volume obviously wanted readers to be informed by more than the current New Testament books that were selected by the early orthodox Christians.

While other scholars agree with the importance of those additional books for our understanding of the context of early Christianity, most have not chosen to add to or delete anything in the current New Testament. One can learn from such texts without declaring them Scripture. Serious students of early Christianity know that it is important to be aware of such noncanonical writings, for they informed some early Christians for a time. Indeed, several of the rejected books were still being read in some churches centuries later, as we see in the case of the Stichometry of Nicephorus (ca. 850), which condemned the reading of such books. Why condemn writings rejected centuries earlier if no one was still reading them?[11]

One does not need to accept the teachings in the rejected books as valid Christian teaching, but they often offer interesting perspectives that reflect the wider history of early Christianity and help readers understand the multiple paths and positions that we find in early Christianity and often the social contexts in which they emerged. Our understanding of the books in the New Testament is often enhanced by some of the marginalized books. Most Christians and biblical scholars understandably give preference and priority to the New Testament books because for the most part they were written in the first century and closer to the time of Jesus but such scholars also recognize that the

---

11. Some early Christians continued to read writings rejected earlier and this reflects the fluidity in canon formation for centuries. Bruce Metzger identified those books as having "temporary canonicity," or they were "temporary Scriptures." Later, they continued to be rejected and eventually were found to be less useful and valuable to churches.

rejected writings help us understand the growth and development of early Christianity and the challenges the churches faced.

In sum, the church fathers widely and eventually affirmed those writings that were closest in time to Jesus, were widely read in churches, and reflected the core traditions and beliefs of early Christianity. In all practicality the church closed the biblical canon, employing some of the criteria listed above. Because the Scriptures themselves do not speak of a limited collection of sacred texts others in antiquity felt free to produce more writings that they believed were inspired by God. That was true in the late second century when the Montanists (later called Cataphrygians) wrote many texts that they believed were inspired by God. Tertullian, as noted above, agreed that the Spirit of God had not ceased speaking in the churches. That view is not unlike the Mormon Church that has added to the Bible the *Book of Mormon*, the *Pearl of Great Price*, and the *Doctrines and Covenants*. The criteria for canonicity mentioned earlier were not listed in the Scriptures themselves and that gave to some followers of Jesus the freedom to write what they believed were inspired texts. For most Christians, however, the biblical canon is closed.

54. When were the final decisions made about the formation of the Bible, that is, when could nothing more be added?

When the processes of the formation of the New Testament began, what actually happened is seldom reflected in current popular discussions of the formation of the Bible. The first step in the canon process was the recognition of the authority of the life, teachings, and fate of Jesus, whether in writing or oral traditions.

Jesus was the first "canon" (rule or authority) of the early church, acknowledged as the Messiah or Christ and eventually the Lord of the church. The teachings and miracles of Jesus were taught in early Christian gatherings (Acts 2:42) or written down (1 Tim 5:18), some of them, according to James Dunn, were likely written *before Jesus died* and were later included in Matthew and Luke (the so-called Q material). From the church's beginning, the teachings of Jesus were viewed as authoritative, or "canonical" in its original Charistian sense of "functioning as a 'rule' of faith." Whatever Jesus said or did was authoritative in the early churches. Consequently, when stories about him—his teachings and activities—were written and shared in early churches they had an immediate positive reception and were recognized like Scripture (1 Tim 5:18), despite not initially being called Scripture. Paul's letters were not initially read as sacred Scripture and he himself never calls them Scripture. That is likely also why Paul supported his own teaching with a word "from the Lord" (1 Cor 7:10–12) and even though he thought he was led by the Spirit in the matter (1 Cor 7:40) he acknowledged that he had no word or command "from the Lord" on the issue before him but was only positing his own "opinion" (1 Cor 7:25). Paul's words to the Corinthians were written before any of the Gospels, but the oral traditions of Jesus' teachings were present in churches from the beginning and if Jesus the Lord commanded or addressed whatever issue was in view, the matter was settled, and one could not find a better authority in early Christianity.

In Matthew, Jesus said, "All authority in heaven and on earth has been given to me. Go, therefore, and make disciples of all nations, baptizing them in the name of the Father, and of the Son, and of the Holy Spirit, and teaching them to obey everything that I have commanded you" (Matt 28:18–20a NRSV). In other words, whatever Jesus said or did, including the interpretation of his death and resurrection, that was authoritative for the churches and a command "from the Lord" (see 1 Cor 14:37) was a rule for the church. *Jesus* was the canon.

Whenever the Gospels cited the words of Jesus, they did not cite them as "according to Matthew, Jesus said," but regularly as the words of Jesus, the Lord of the church and founder of their faith. Whatever Jesus said was like Scripture for the early churches. You find that attitude reflected in 1 Tim 5:18, which cites Deut 25:4 *and the words of Jesus* in Matt 10:10 (cf. Luke 10:7) *as Scripture*. This helps us understand how the Gospels were first read in the churches and treated like Scripture before they were called Scripture later in the second century.

After the death of the apostles, it seemed to the early church fathers that what the apostles and those they mentored had written was especially important in the churches. Thus, the church's collection of recognized Christian Scriptures soon also included a recognition of the value and practicality of the letters of Paul for churches, at least seven of which were circulating by the end of the first century. Like the Gospels, Paul's writings were beginning to be called Scripture in the second century, as we saw earlier.

The final decisions about the scope of the church's Scriptures were long in the making, some as late as the nineteenth century, and few decisions were officially made before the middle to end of the fourth century, and those decisions were mostly made in local church councils. No ecumenical church council representing all of the churches ever made a list of the church's Scriptures or ever indicated that the Scripture collection was complete, but by use there came a time when no new books were added to that collection and some writings that had a long history, as in the case of 3 Corinthians, were no longer included in any body of Christian Scriptures.

We will now focus on some important ancient artifacts that help us tell a more informed story about the formation of the New Testament.

CHAPTER 4
Important Christian Artifacts

Creeds, Canon Lists, Manuscripts, *Nomina Sacra*, and Textual Accuracy

AMONG SEVERAL IMPORTANT ANCIENT artifacts that contribute to our understanding of the status of Christian Scriptures in the fourth and fifth centuries, the most formative time for the origin of the Christian Bible, the following factors are important components that aid our understanding of the formation of the Bible.

55. What role did early church creeds have in the formation of the Bible?

The most important core traditions and beliefs of early Christianity, the "*regula fidei*" or "rule of faith," were summarized in the early creeds circulating in the early churches. The early creedal formulations or summaries of core teachings in the New Testament include, but are not limited to, Matt 16:16; 28:18–20; Mark 12:29–31 (likely also 10:45); John 1:1–3, 12–14, 49; 6:68–69; 20:28; Acts 2:22–36; 8:36–37; 16:31; Rom 1:3–4; 4:25; 10:9; 1 Cor 8:6; 11:2, 23–29; 12:3; Eph 1:3–14; Col 1:12–20; 2:9–15; 2 Thess 2:15; 3:6; 1 Tim 2:6; 3:16; 2 Tim 2:8; 1 Pet 3:18; 1 John 4:2. Of these, the most important is Rom 10:9, "Jesus is Lord," which is likely the earliest New Testament creed, and also 1 Cor 15:3–8, and Phil 2:6–11. Most early creeds reflect the heart of the emerging beliefs of the post-Easter followers of Jesus and are primarily focused on Jesus' identity, e.g., Son of God, Christ, Lord, and his passion and crucifixion and resurrection. Books that did not affirm these core beliefs were not later included in the New Testament. The church creeds over time expanded to address current issues facing the churches, but at the heart of them was the identity of Jesus and his acts for the salvation of humanity, namely his death and resurrection. Essentially, we can say that those core beliefs were determinative of which books would later form the church's New Testament canon.

The early New Testament and church fathers' creeds generally included summaries of core Christian beliefs about Jesus (e.g., Rom 10:9; 1 Cor 15:3–8; Phil 2:6–11; see also Ignatius, *Trall.* 9 and Polycarp, *Phil.* 2). These beliefs also focus mostly on Jesus' divine identity and special relationship to God, as well as his role in the salvation of humanity. Eventually they also focused on divine creation, the Holy Spirit, Christian mission, and responsible Christian living. Irenaeus's summary of the core Christian beliefs about Jesus are as follows:

> The church, though dispersed throughout the whole world, even to the ends of the earth, has received from the apostles and their disciples this faith: It believes in one God, the Father Almighty, Maker of heaven and earth and the sea and all things that are in them and in one Christ Jesus, the Son of God, who became incarnate for our salvation and in the Holy Spirit, who proclaimed through the prophets the dispensations of God, the advents, the birth from a virgin, the passion, the resurrection from the dead, and the ascension into heaven in the flesh of the beloved Christ Jesus, our Lord. He also proclaimed through the prophets his future manifestation from heaven in the glory of the Father "to gather all things in one," and to raise up anew all flesh of the whole human race. [This will take place] in order that to Christ Jesus, our Lord, God, Saviour, and King, according to the will of the invisible Father, "every knee should bow, of things in heaven, and things in earth, and things under the earth, and that every tongue should confess" him. And he will execute just judgment towards all sending into everlasting fire "spiritual wickednesses," and the angels who transgressed and became apostates, together with the ungodly, and unrighteous, and wicked, and profane among men. But he will, in the exercise of his grace, confer immortality on the righteous and holy, and those who have kept his commandments, and have persevered in his love, some from the beginning of their Christian course, and others from the time

of their repentance. He will surround them with everlasting glory. (*Haer.* 1.10.1, *ANF* adapted; cf. 3.4.2)

He argued subsequently that this core teaching had been passed on from the apostles to the bishops (Irenaeus, *Haer.* 3.3.3).

Tertullian, promoting the "rule of faith" (*regula fidei*) and its connection between the church's core beliefs and the church's Scriptures, said that whenever the church's rule of faith is proclaimed the true Scriptures will be present: "*For whenever it shall be manifest that the true Christian rule and faith shall be, there will likewise be the true scriptures and expositions thereof,* and all the Christian tradition" (*Praescr.* 19, *ANF*; emphasis added). In his *Against Marcion*, Tertullian speaks against those who subvert "the rule of faith" (3.1; *ANF*).

There were multiple early creeds formed and expanded in the early church fathers. Among the most familiar early church father creeds are those of Irenaeus and Hippolytus. Eventually the Nicene Creed (c. 325 and 390) and later the Apostle's Creed (c. 340) were the most popular circulated creeds in churches.

Some core Christian teachings were commonly expressed in the texts that became parts of the New Testament but not initially in creedal form: for instance, God as creator of the heavens and universe (e.g., 1 Cor 8:6; John 1:3; Col 1:15–16), the virgin birth, the humanity of Jesus ("crucified under Pontius Pilate"), the church, the Holy Spirit, and life everlasting. Such beliefs were affirmed in churches before they appeared in the later creeds. The creeds always summarized the church's core beliefs, but not what each individual church member believed. What is important here is that no book that denied those core beliefs—beliefs that were embraced by the church before the New Testament was written or formed and that eventually became formalized in creeds—was included in the New Testament. The early Christian creeds were central in churches, and Jesus is always at the heart of Christian creeds. Jesus' identity was affirmed at the Council of Nicea and only after that do we begin to see canon lists of the New Testament Scriptures.

56. When do lists of the church's Scriptures begin to appear and what do they tell us about the scope of the Bible then?

The value of the canon lists—that is, lists of books that could be read in churches—is that they let us know which texts church leaders believed were the sacred writings that could be read in the churches and were identified as Christian Scripture. Those lists are not always the same, but there is considerable overlap in the books listed that were usable in churches throughout the Greco-Roman world and considered sacred Scripture. The lists also show which books were marginal and not accepted by all churches, namely, Hebrews, James, 2 Peter, 2 and 3 John, Jude, and Revelation.

The lists generally reflect which scriptural texts were commonly read in various *local* churches, especially those located where church councils were held. While some church fathers made lists of writings that were acceptable for reading in churches, especially Athanasius, the *local* councils generally reflected what was already read in the churches in their *local* areas. While Athanasius made a list of books that could be read in churches and that could be read privately for personal piety, generally it was the councils, not individuals, that made those lists. Again, let me stress that these lists were always local and not reflective of *all* churches, despite considerable overlap in the selections. To repeat, there were no ecumenical church councils that decided the scope of the church's Bible. Below are examples of Old and New Testament lists, most of which date from the fourth century and later. The following list is a small selection of some of the surviving canon lists that include Old and New Testament books as well as others. Their value is that they show that there was considerable overlap in the recognized scriptural books, but also several differences.

A. Old Testament and New Testament Canon Lists from the East

1. Origen (ca. fl. 210–253): Old Testament = includes, alongside the books found in the Hebrew Bible, 1–2 Esdras, Epistle of Jeremiah, *possibly* 1–2 Maccabees, but also Susanna and other deuterocanonical books that he defended. The Twelve Minor Prophets are likely accidently omitted. His New Testament may exclude 2 Peter and possibly but not clearly 2–3 John and Revelation. See his *Selectae in*

Psalmos 1 where he says there are "twenty-two encovenanted books *according to the Hebrew tradition*" in his *Commentary on Matthew* 1 (preserved in Eusebius, *Hist. eccl.* 6.25.3-6), and Origen's *Commentary on John* 5; and *Homily on Joshua* 7.1. But this may not be his own view of which books are sacred.

2. Eusebius (ca. 320-339): his Old Testament apparently follows Origen's list, which he includes in his *Historia ecclesiastica* 6.25.1-14. His New Testament books = "Recognized books" = four Gospels, Acts, letters of Paul (identity not given), 1 John, 1 Peter, possibly Revelation. "Disputed books" = James Jude, 2 Peter, 2-3 John, and possibly Revelation and the Gospel according to the Hebrews. "Spurious books" = Acts of Paul, Shepherd, Apocalypse of Peter, Epistle of Barnabas, Didache. And finally, "Heretical books" = Gospels of Peter, Thomas, Matthias, and other Gospels, Acts of Andrew, Acts of John, and other Acts—all of which are to be "shunned altogether."

3. Cyril of Jerusalem (ca. fl. 350-87): in his *Catechetical Lectures*, Lecture IV.33-36 in which he lists in all of the books in his Old Testament (4.35) and New Testament (4.36). His New Testament does not include Revelation. His Jeremiah includes Baruch and the Epistle of Jeremiah, and his Daniel includes the additions, namely Susanna and Bel and the Dragon. He numbers the books of the Old Testament as "twenty-two books." His New Testament includes all of the New Testament books except Revelation.

4. Athanasius of Alexandria (ca. 367): in his *Thirty-Ninth Festal Letter*, the Old Testament, in addition to most of the books of the Hebrew Bible, includes in Jeremiah also Baruch, Lamentations, and Epistle of Jeremiah. Daniel includes Susanna and possibly Bel and the Dragon. He excludes Esther. The whole New Testament is present. "Readable" books (= some deuterocanonical books) include Wisdom of Solomon, Sirach, Esther, Judith, Tobit, plus the Christian texts, Didache and Shepherd of Hermas. Rejected books = "apocrypha" (= heretical texts that he says are "invented by the heretics") including Enoch, possibly Ascension of Isaiah, Testament of Moses, and Apocalypse of Elijah. He does include the whole New Testament canon.

5. Synod of Laodicea, Canons 59–60 (ca. 360–380): the Old Testament includes Baruch and Epistle of Jeremiah and 1–2 Esdras. The whole New Testament is included except Revelation.

6. *Apostolic Canons* 85 (ca. 375–380): the Old Testament includes 1–2 Esdras, Judith, 1–4 Maccabees, Ps 151, Wisdom and likely also Sirach. The New Testament includes 1–2 Clement, but not Revelation. The author adds eight books of the Constitutions for bishops.

7. Gregory of Nazianzus (ca. 330–391): his Old Testament likely includes in Jeremiah both Baruch and Epistle of Jeremiah, but no other disputed or deuterocanonical texts. His New Testament questions but still includes Revelation (see his *Iambi ad Seleucum*, lines 251–320).

8. Amphilocius of Iconium (ca. 380): his Old Testament raises questions about Esther and includes the Epistles of Baruch and likely Epistle of Jeremiah in the book of Jeremiah. His New Testament includes most of the New Testament books, but like Syrian churches also raises questions about 2 Peter, 2–3 John, Jude, and Revelation.

9. Epiphanius of Salamis (ca. 315–402): his three lists of Old Testament writings number them as twenty-seven instead of twenty-two or twenty-four books and in all three he includes 1–2 Esdras, and the Epistles of Jeremiah and Baruch (see *Panarion* 8.6.1–4; *De mensuris et ponderibus* 4–5 and 22–23). After listing the complete New Testament, he adds Wisdom of Solomon and Sirach (see *Panarion* 76.22.5).

B. Old Testament and New Testament Canon Lists from the West

1. *Muratorian Fragment* (ca. 375–400): the current *fragment* includes most of the New Testament books but does not include Hebrews, 1 and 2 Peter, or James. Strangely, the author includes Wisdom of Solomon at the end of the New Testament list, much like Epiphanius above. The MF rejects the public reading of Shepherd of Hermas but encourages its private reading. The author also rejects reading texts by Arsinous, Valentinus, and Miltiades, along with two pseudonymous texts in Paul's name (Laodiceans and Alexandrians). Its references to Pius as the brother of Hermas, Miltiades as heretical, the Cataphrygians (instead of the second-century designation

Montanists), and the lack of parallels of New Testament canon lists before the fourth century date it in the middle to late fourth century.

2. *Codex Claromontanus* (ca. mid-sixth century): a Greek manuscript with a Latin insertion between Philemon and Hebrews listing both Old Testament and New Testament books. The Old Testament includes Wisdom, Sirach, likely the additions to Jeremiah, 1–4 Maccabees, Judith, and Tobit. The complete New Testament is included along with Epistle of Barnabas, Shepherd of Hermas, Acts of Paul, and Revelation of Peter.

3. Mommsen or Cheltenham List (ca. 365): the Old Testament includes 1–2 Maccabees, Tobit, Judith, Ps 151, and likely Wisdom of Solomon and Sirach (based on the number of lines listed for Solomon). Ezra is not included. It includes the New Testament canon but with questions about 2 Peter, 2–3 John, and likely only affirms 1 Peter and 1 John since after noting that there were two letters of Peter, the author inserts *una sola* ("only one") and after noting three letters of John also adds *una sola*. This New Testament list does not include Hebrews, James, or Jude.

4. Hilary of Poitiers (ca. 310–367): the Old Testament includes Epistle of Jeremiah and indicates that *some* add Tobit and Judith making a twenty-four-book Old Testament. No New Testament canon is listed. See his *Instructio Psalmorum* 15.

5. Jerome of Stridon and Bethlehem (ca. 347–420): his Old Testament includes Tanak books and mostly in that order adopting the Hebrew twenty-two-book canon *at that time* with its usual combinations (Ruth with Judges, Ezra-Nehemiah, 1–2 Samuel, 1–2 Kings, 1–2 Chronicles, the Twelve [Minor Prophets]). The New Testament canon includes all the New Testament books, though Jerome expresses some doubts about Hebrews. He said some noncanonical books could be read in church, but not to settle doctrinal issues. These include Wisdom of Solomon, Sirach, Judith, Tobit, 1–2 Maccabees, and the Shepherd of Hermas. See Prologus Galeatus, *Epistle* 53, *Epistle* 107.

6. Rufinus of Aquileia (ca. 345–410, here ca. 404): the Old Testament includes all the Tanakh books and possibly Baruch and Epistle of Jeremiah. His "ecclesiastical" category encourages *reading* several non-Tanak/Hebrew Bible and non-New Testament texts, but *not* as

Scripture. These books include Wisdom, Sirach, Tobit, Judith, 1–2 Maccabees. The Christian "ecclesiastical" texts for reading include Shepherd of Hermas, Two Ways (= Didache), and Judgment of Peter. See his *Commentary on the Apostles' Creed*.

7. Hippo Council (ca. 393 report): the canonical Old Testament established by this council includes Tanakh plus also Wisdom of Solomon, Sirach, Tobit, Judith, and 1–2 Maccabees. The Hippo council's New Testament includes all and only the New Testament books but also includes as readable in the churches the Passion of the Martyrs. See the *Breviarium of Hipponense* 36.

8. Augustine of Hippo (ca. 354–430): Old Testament includes all Tanakh books but did not mention Lamentations, Baruch, or Epistle of Jeremiah. He also includes 1 and 2 Esdras, Tobit, Judith, 1–2 Maccabees, Wisdom of Solomon, and Sirach. The New Testament includes all and only the New Testament books. See his *On Christian Teaching* 2.8.12.24–13.29.

9. Pope/bishop of Rome Innocent I (ca. 402–417): Old Testament includes Tanakh books and Wisdom of Solomon, Sirach, Tobit, Judith, 1–2 Esdras, and 1–2 Maccabees. His New Testament includes all and only the New Testament books. See Innocent, Epistle 6 *ad Exsuperium Tolosanum* (ca. 405).

The above lists reflect early notions of what comprised the church's Old and New Testament Scriptures in various locations and although there was considerable overlap in their contents, there was also variation on the fringes of several of the collections. They reflect the variations in the scriptural collections well into the fifth and sixth centuries.

57. What do the major ancient pandect manuscripts of Christian Scriptures, containing both Old and New Testament Scriptures, tell us about the scope of the Bible in antiquity?

The most important pandect or complete copies of the church's Scriptures in the important uncial or capital-lettered manuscripts from the fourth and fifth centuries show that the development of the codex (book form) enabled the inclusion of all of the church's Old and New Testament Scriptures in a single volume. This was only possible because of the considerable technological advances made in the production of the codex (book format) by in the fourth century that could include between fourteen hundred and sixteen hundred pages). The most important of these New Testament manuscripts from the fourth and fifth centuries include the following:

Vaticanus (B, 4th c.)[1]	Sinaiticus (ℵ, 4th c.)[2]	Peshitta (Syr^p) (5th c.)[3]	Alexandrinus (A, 5th c.)[4]	Claromontanus (D, 4th c.)[5]
Matthew	Matthew	Matthew	Matthew	*Gospels*
Mark	Mark	Mark	Mark	Matthew
Luke	Luke	Luke	Luke	John
John	John	John	John	Mark
Acts	Romans	Acts	Acts	Luke
James	1 Corinthians	James	James	John
1 Peter	2 Corinthians	1 Peter	1 Peter	Paul:
2 Peter	Galatians	1 John	2 Peter	Romans
1 John	Ephesians	Romans	1 John	1–2 Corinthians
2 John	Philippians	1 Corinthians	2 John	Galatians
3 John	Colossians	2 Corinthians	3 John	Ephesians
Jude	1 Thessalonians	Galatians	Jude	1–2 Timothy
Rom	2 Thessalonians	Ephesians	Romans	Titus
1 Corinthians	Hebrews	Philippians	1 Corinthians	Colossians
2 Corinthians	1 Timothy	Colossians	2 Corinthians	Philemon
Galatians	2 Timothy	1 Thessalonians	Galatians	
Ephesians	Titus		Ephesians	To 1–2 Peter[6]
Philippians	Philemon		Philippians	James
Colossians	Acts		Colossians	1, 2, 3 John
1 Thessalonians	James		1 Thessalonians	Jude
2 Thessalonians	1 Peter		2 Thessalonians	Barnabas[7]
Hebrews	2 Peter		Hebrews	Revelation

   1. The manuscript breaks off in Heb 9:24 and a later minuscule hand completed the mss and added Revelation, but not the Pastorals and Philemon.

   2. This manuscript has Acts following Letters of Paul and before the Catholic Epistles. It also includes the Epistle of Barnabas and Shepherd of Hermas.

   3. Revelation is missing and the Catholic Letters follow Acts and Paul stands at the end.

   4. Note that the Catholic Letters follow Acts and Paul comes at the end before Revelation, but it includes 1–2 Clement, and Psalms of Solomon.

   5. This Catalogue is inserted in Codex Claromontanus (D; ca. 350–400, likely from Alexandria, Egypt), written in a Latin hand and inserted between the texts of Philemon and Hebrews. See its order of Gospels and additional books in it. It is likely that the omission of Philippians and 1–2 Thessalonians is accidental. The order in the catalogue differs from the order of books in the rest of the manuscript itself.

   6. It appears that the author here listed 1 and 2 Peter as having come from Paul to Peter.

   7. The reference to "Barnabas" here may be a reference to Hebrews since the line

Vaticanus (B, 4th c.)[1]	Sinaiticus (ℵ, 4th c.)[2]	Peshitta (Syr^p) (5th c.)[3]	Alexandrinus (A, 5th c.)[4]	Claromontanus (D, 4th c.)[5]
Hebrews	2 Peter		Hebrews	Revelation
	1 John		1 Timothy	Acts
Omitted:	2 John		2 Timothy	
(1 Timothy)	3 John	2 Thessalonians	Titus	Others:
(2 Timothy)	Jude	1 Timothy	Philemon	Shepherd
(Titus)	Revelation	2 Timothy	Revelation	Acts of Paul
(Philemon)	Barnabas	Titus	1 Clement	Revelation of
(Revelation)	Shepherd	Philemon	2 Clement	Peter
		Hebrews	Pss of Solomon	Missing:
				Philippians
				1–2 Thess
				Hebrews?

Sinaiticus and Vaticanus are both mid-to-late fourth-century manuscripts and Alexandrinus is a fifth-century manuscript. Some scholars think Sinaiticus was penned first, but I put it second, probably toward the last quarter of the fourth century and Vaticanus around 350–375, based on some of the texts that have been expanded in Sinaiticus that were not in Codex Vaticanus (e.g., Mark 1:1b). Sinaiticus has all the New Testament books plus the Epistle of Barnabas and the Shepherd of Hermas. Vaticanus does not have all the books of the New Testament, though that manuscript is fragmented and ends at Heb 9:24.

It is unclear if Revelation was in the manuscript or whether it was purposefully omitted or lost. Like P46 (papyrus manuscript number 46, ca. 200), Vaticanus is also missing the Pastoral Epistles and Revelation. In the 1400s, the omitted New Testament books were added to Codex Vaticanus by a different scribe along with a table of contents at the end of Vaticanus. Sinaiticus and Vaticanus are both fragmented more than the fifth century Codex Alexandrinus, which is much more complete. In its New Testament, Alexandrinus includes all of the books of the New Testament but also 1 and 2 Clement (2 Clement is only mentioned in the table of contents but not in the current manuscript) and strangely also included is the pseudonymous Psalms of Solomon.

A study of even more ancient manuscripts and the canon lists are helpful for knowing what books informed the faith of the early

count is the same as Hebrews. This may be following Tertullian (*Pud.* 20) who also lists Hebrews as "Barnabas."

churches. These reflect most likely the Scriptures that informed the faith of the earliest Christians. While only a fraction of the ancient biblical manuscripts have survived, perhaps less than 1 percent,[8] they do reflect considerable agreement on most of the books recognized as Scripture in emerging orthodox Christianity, but also with multiple differences in them as noted earlier.

58. What do the ancient biblical canon lists tell us about the local decisions about which books could be read in churches in local regions? What authority should be given to them?

The local canon lists tell us what certain church fathers and local church councils decided were texts that could be read as Scripture in the worship gatherings of their churches. Those lists reflect what those leaders decided was Scripture, but not necessarily what the churches themselves believed and read in their worship and teaching settings. The lists are very important, but the surviving manuscripts often reflect the actual texts read in the churches. As we will see, the surviving biblical manuscripts do not always reflect the decisions of early or later church councils of leaching church officials. In some cases, they contain other books not approved by church councils or their leaders.

Of the approximately 5,750 surviving New Testament manuscripts, we occasionally find other texts that likely functioned like Scripture even if they were not called Scripture. For example, in P72 in the Bodmer papyri, a third- or fourth-century manuscript and the first that contains 1 and 2 Peter and Jude (though not in that order—Jude was first). It also includes texts side by side without distinction between them. There are eight other writings in that manuscript: the Nativity of Mary, 3 Corinthians, Melito's *Homily on the Passover*, the 11th Ode of The Odes of Solomon, the Apology of Phileas, Pss 33 and 34, and a fragment of a hymn. The texts that the early churches read in their worship liturgies functioned as Scripture for the churches that had them. We will see below that the variations in the manuscripts and the canon lists show considerable overlap in what was welcomed, but also several differences in some of the books listed or in the manuscripts. These differences are also seen in the translations and lectionaries that I will mention below.

---

8. According to Hurtado, *Earliest Christian Artifacts*, 24–25.

It is important not to overstate the scope of the Scriptures in the early churches despite considerable overlap in the ancient lists. Most of the time current New Testament scholars do not examine the lectionaries that are often listed at the bottom of the page in of their Greek New Testaments. While the Greek New Testaments today have twenty-seven books in them, the ancient lectionaries do not include all of those books. Also, in terms of the manuscripts, there is no New Testament manuscript before the year 1000 CE that has all of the New Testament books and no others. Codex Sinaiticus (ca. 375) has all of the New Testament books, but it also has the Epistle of Barnabas and the Shepherd of Hermas. More about this below, but for now it is important to know that the churches that made copies of their Scriptures were not always familiar with all the church's Scriptures or were even aware of church council decisions and the multiple canon lists of scriptural books to be read in churches. It appears from comparison of the differences between the books included in the biblical manuscripts and those in the church's canon lists that if the church's local leaders were aware of council decisions and canon lists, they often ignored them.

59. What are the *Nomina Sacra* and how important are they for identifying ancient Christian Scripture?

The *nomina sacra* ("sacred names") are abbreviations of sacred or holy names common in early Christian texts. Normally the words in question included the first and last letter of a Greek word, occasionally with a middle letter included between them, and with a short line over the top of each abbreviation. They are in abundance in ancient Christian Scriptural manuscripts, but also in other Christian texts. Their presence in a manuscript identifies the text as *Christian*, but not necessarily as Christian *Scripture*, though scholars are divided on that issue. The most common of these abbreviated "holy words" are God, Lord, Jesus, Christ, and often Spirit. Eventually there were some fifteen such contracted words. The practice likely originated with the Jewish use of the abbreviated *Tetragrammaton*, that is the four-letter abbreviation of the divine name YHWH (or Yahweh).[9] When the Jewish Scriptures were translated into Greek, it appears that some contractions of God (Greek = *theos*) and Lord (Greek *kyrios*) were used to identify those sacred names.

9. Bokedal, *Formation and Significance*, 84–123.

These designations have received considerable attention in recent years, and while there are important differences among the scholars on their use,[10] they agree on several matters, including:

> (a) that the practice is well-established and consistently applied in the earliest Christian MSS we possess and its practice must go back earlier still, (b) that it was *not* a simple space-saving device, (c) that it was probably a *Christian* innovation, (d) that it represents an attempt to reflect the *sacred*, religiously "special" nature of the referents of the nouns being abbreviated in this way: hence the description "*nomina sacra*," and (e) such sacredness is probably to be related to the reverence shown in Judaism to the divine name.[11]

The early Christians identified Jesus with *kyrios* (Lord) and *christos* (Christ), but other distinct designations eventually included *man, king, mother, father, crucify, son, man, heaven, savior, mother*, and several others. It is quite possible that initially several of these so-called *nomina sacra* reflect the nonliterary or documentary hand style of communication in early Christian writings since abbreviations were seldom used in literary texts. They have been found in all kinds of *Christian* texts, including in sacred, literary, and personal correspondence.[12]

60. What do the many variations or differences in the surviving biblical manuscripts suggest about the reliability of the church's Scriptures?

Textual critics are those who labor over the surviving manuscripts of biblical and religious literature from antiquity with the goal of establishing the earliest and most reliable texts of the Scriptures, whether Old or New Testament. Historically their goal was to establish the "original text" of Scripture, but while many textual critics still aspire to find the originals, it is a highly complex task and many textual scholars have concluded that, unless archaeologists, librarians, or biblical scholars find significantly more ancient manuscripts, that goal is beyond

---

10. See Tuckett, "Nomina Sacra"; Hurtado, *Earliest Christian Artifacts*, 95–134; Hurtado, "Origins of the Nomina"; Bokedal, *Formation and Significance*, 83–123.

11. Tuckett, "Nomina Sacra," 432.

12. For a summary of these, see also McDonald, *Before There Was*, 148–52 and McDonald, *New Testament*, 2:230–34.

anyone's reach and they are as close as they will likely get, with the possible massaging a biblical text here or there. If we could arrive at the elusive "originals," would we also find in them the humanness and variants in the manuscripts we now have?

Establishing the *precise words* of the Bible, from studying the surviving biblical manuscripts, is largely an overlooked matter in most of the canon research undertaken, and yet if biblical authority is connected to the books in which the teachings are found, clarifying the words of those texts is important. The very texts that are often cited in defense of Christian faith are critically important for understanding that faith, so we need to be clear on what the manuscripts that have survived antiquity actually say.

To highlight the problem text-critics face, we need to know that there are many thousands of Hebrew and Aramaic texts of the Hebrew Bible and Greek manuscripts of the New Testament along with many lectionaries and translations of those texts—and no two manuscripts are exactly alike. Of the approximately nine thousand Hebrew manuscripts that have been found, including those in the Dead Sea Scrolls and other finds in the Judaean Desert, no two manuscripts of the same book are exactly alike. I mentioned earlier that Emanuel Tov from Jerusalem estimated that there are more than nine hundred thousand variants or differences in the Hebrew scriptural manuscripts.

Similarly, there are between 5,740 and 5,750 surviving New Testament manuscripts containing one or more books, and again no two are exactly alike. Current text-critical scholars debate whether there are close to two hundred thousand or even four hundred thousand differences in those manuscripts, although one professor friend has suggested that there are only hundreds of variants in the manuscripts and not thousands. Whatever the precise case, everyone acknowledges that there are multiple variants in the manuscripts. The point here, of course, is that we do not have, nor can we reconstruct with certainty, the elusive "original manuscripts" (autographs), and the church has not had them throughout most of its history. If the manuscripts have to be perfect before they can be considered inspired by God, Christianity has had uninspired manuscripts throughout almost all of its life.

61. What do the most recent Greek New Testaments tell us about the *text* of the New Testament?

This question is about the continual study of textual critics and the recent editions of the Greek New Testament that they have been able to produce on which all translations of the New Testament are based. Text critics are regularly seeking to establish the earliest and most accurate text of the New Testament for the translators of the New Testament and churches today. For those who do not speak or write Hebrew, Aramaic, or Greek, the church is indebted to those who labor in their study of the ancient biblical manuscripts. While there is no perfect translation of the Scriptures used today and no two of them in the same language are the same, which translation is best? The answer to that question varies due to which audience the translators are producing the Scriptures for, whether in English or French, or German, or any other of more than two thousand translations today.

Although the task of textual critics is to arrive at the earliest and most accurate text of the biblical books—a highly complex and multifaceted field of inquiry—they regularly say that they are much closer now to the earliest text of the biblical writings than was possible previously. None, however, would claim that they have arrived at the original text of the biblical manuscripts.

There have been multiple editions of the Greek New Testament over the past five hundred years that regularly reflect a better text of the Bible than was possible before, and that task continues to this day with new editions appearing periodically. Like with the Hebrew of the Old Testament books, the Greek New Testaments have also experienced many changes over those 500 years. Most recently the 28th edition of the Nestle/Aland Greek New Testament, or *Novum Testamentum Graece* (often noted as NA[28]) has been published and a 29th edition is being produced. The United Bible Society has published five major editions of its *Greek New Testament* (UBS[5th]) and still another is on the way. Both of these editions now broadly agree on most of the text of the New Testament, but not completely. Michael Holmes has produced an edition of the Greek New Testament for the Society of Biblical Literature with more than five hundred differences from the NA[28] edition and UBS[5th] edition. Similarly, Tyndale House in Cambridge recently produced another *The Greek New Testament* with still more differences. These latest editions are all good, but none of them are perfect and more will likely be on the way. None of the text-critical scholars who worked on any of the Greek editions of the New Testament claim to have arrived at the elusive "original" text.

Why is what they do important to us? This is a "bottom line" question for churches today. The answer is that the texts they prepare are the ones used by translators of the Bible to prepare Bibles for us in our own language to use both privately and publicly in churches. Scholars who write commentaries regularly appeal to and depend on the latest editions of the Hebrew and Greek texts of the Scriptures. The texts of the Scriptures that the textual critics prepare are those used and taught in seminaries to prepare students and teachers of the Scriptures for their ministry. The goal for clergy and professors of Scripture is to know as best they can what Jesus or the writers of the New Testament actually said. Christian theology and core beliefs are rooted in the very words of Scripture, so a careful examination of them is essential for Christian faith. Pastors want to share with their people the precise meaning of the Scriptures that were written in the biblical languages and have also been translated carefully.

62. What ancient biblical manuscripts are involved in the preparation of the text of the New Testament for students and translators?

The text of the current Hebrew Bible (or Old Testament) and the text of the Greek New Testament are what we call "eclectic" texts, that is the editions of the Scriptures produced by recent textual critics who believe that they are the best and most accurate recoverable form of the ancient biblical texts. There is no single ancient text of the Hebrew Bible or Old Testament or Greek New Testament that is exactly like the current eclectic texts of the Bible that textual scholars have produced and on which all modern translations are based. By using several ancient manuscripts, the textual critics believe that they have established as accurate a text of the church's Scriptures as is currently possible and that these selected texts are now closer to the original texts of the Scriptures, i.e., the autographs of the authors, than was earlier possible.

The overwhelming majority of variants in the biblical manuscripts were unintentional and more accidental. Most of them are easy to correct from comparison with earlier manuscripts or others from the same period. The intentional changes to the biblical texts inserted by copiers or scribes are fewer in number and often were attempts to clarify a text that might have been unfamiliar to readers. This is when copiers and scribes used something like "in other words" to clarify to their readers or hearers what the text in question meant. Most of these intentional changes affirm orthodox positions and are well known to biblical scholars and many pastors as well. The intentional changes are not considered heretical, but advanced theological positions that were popular in the copiers' generations. Three examples here will show how some changes were deliberately made or included to affirm current orthodox theology. 1 John 5:7–8 is commonly called the "Johannine Comma" by scholars. The text that is found in the King James Version of the Bible clearly affirms the Trinity ("the Father, the Word, and the Holy Spirit"), but those words did not exist in the original text of 1 John and were inserted into it later. Those verses are not in any early Greek manuscripts and all current Bible translations regularly now have those words in brackets or in footnotes to make clear that they were added later to the text of 1 John. Another example: John 3:13b has an added part ("who is in heaven") that was intended to affirm the omnipresence of Jesus and his divinity. That, too, was in the King James Version, but is now regularly a footnote in modern Bibles. Our third example is 1 Cor 14:33b–36 in which a woman is commanded to be silent in church. This does not fit the context of 1 Cor 11:5 in which women were to prophesy with their heads covered. How can a woman prophesy with her head covered and mouth shut? This inserted passage in 1 Cor is like 1 Tim 2:9–12 in which women are not allowed to teach or have authority over a man. From the church's beginning on the day of Pentecost men and women were allowed to prophesy (see Acts 2:17–18 citing Joel 2:28). To prophesy meant to speak in the power of the Holy Spirit, to proclaim the word and will of God. It is clear from Acts 2:17–18 that women were given the same Spirit and the ability by God to serve in the ministry of the church as prophets or proclaimers of the will and word of God. Examples of women serving in leading roles in the churches can be found in Paul's writings, as we see in the roles of Phoebe, Priscilla, Lydia, Junia, Euodia and Syntyche, plus other women Paul lists in Rom 16. Thus, 1 Cor 14:33b-36 does not fit Paul's own views of women prophesying or in leadership in the church. This passage is now in brackets in several contemporary translations and while some changes to ancient texts are sometimes unclear, the reason for this inserted and intentional text is obvious and comes from a later scribe or copier who hoped that if it was believed to have come from Paul it would have continuing implications for Christian ministry and women's roles in the churches.

63. What books were in the church's ancient scriptural manuscripts?

The most important aspect of the ancient biblical manuscripts is what was in them, both the individual form of the texts in them and specific books included. The nonbiblical books in the manuscripts are often ignored by canon scholars, but several surviving manuscripts contain writings that were not later included in the Bible but functioned like Scripture for some churches.

In 2003, the Institute for New Testament Textual Research in Münster, Germany, the official registry of biblical manuscripts, listed 5,735 Greek manuscripts of the New Testament, but more have been added to that number since then and more will likely be added in the near future from new finds in museums and libraries that have not yet been catalogued or new finds from archaeological sites yet to be excavated. The latest number of New Testament *papyrus* manuscripts (the oldest collection of manuscripts dating from the second to the sixth or seventh centuries) now stands at 117 and that may also change. The number of *majuscule* (or uncial) manuscripts, which are capital-lettered manuscripts without spaces between the words, and copied on animal skins (the next oldest collection, dating from roughly the fourth to the tenth centuries), now stands at 310. There are 2,877 *minuscule*, or lower-case manuscripts with running letters (roughly from the eighth to the fifteenth centuries), and some 2,432 *Greek lectionaries* (selected portions of Scriptures that were read in churches) that are often listed but seldom considered in the textual evidence of any reading, even though they may date much earlier than some other biblical manuscripts.[13] According to Eldon Epp's analysis of the surviving manuscripts, there are 2,361 that contain Gospels or fragments of them, 792 that contain letter(s) or fragments of Paul's letters, 662 that contain Acts and the Catholic or General Epistles or fragments of them, and 287 containing the book of Revelation or fragments of it.[14]

Hurtado and also Epp provide listings of Christian manuscripts (and their number) containing biblical texts in the second and third

---

13. Metzger and Ehrman, *Text of the New*, 50.
14. Epp, *Perspectives on New Testament*, 505.

centuries.[15] Hurtado notes that the transition from the second to third century up to the present is quite remarkable. These texts (mostly fragments), as well as other ancient Christian texts, are often not clearly distinguished from the biblical manuscripts and they were largely found in Egypt. These include the following books:

> *Old Testament*: Genesis (8), Exodus (8), Leviticus (3), Numbers (1), Deuteronomy (2), Joshua (1), Judges (1), 2 Chronicles (2), Esther (2), Job (1), Psalms (18), Proverbs (2), Ecclesiastes (2), Wisdom of Solomon (1), Sirach (2), Isaiah (6), Jeremiah (2), Ezekiel (2), Daniel (2), Bel and Susanna (1), Minor Prophets (2), Tobit (2), and 2 Maccabees (1).

> *New Testament*: Matthew (12), Mark (1), Luke (7), John (16), Acts (7), Romans (4), 1 Corinthians (2), 2 Corinthians (1), Galatians (1), Ephesians (3), Philippians (2), Colossians (1), 1 Thessalonians (3), 2 Thessalonians (2), Philemon (1), Titus (1), Hebrews (4), James (3), 1 Peter (1), 2 Peter (1), 1 John (1? = P9 or P.Oxy. 402, possibly fourth or fifth century), Jude (2), and Revelation (5).

> *Christian Apocryphal Writings*: Gospel of Thomas (3), Protevangelium of James (1), Gospel of Mary (2), "Egerton" Gospel (1), Gospel of Peter (2, possibly P.Oxy 2949 and P.Oxy. 4009), "Fayum" Gospel (1), Acts of Paul (3), Correspondence of Paul and Corinth (1), Apocalypse of Peter (1), Apocryphon of Jannes (1), and Apocryphon of Moses (1).

> *Other Christian Writings*, some with an element of doubt about them (?): Shepherd of Hermas (11), Irenaeus, *Against Heresies* (2); Melito, *Paschal Homily* (1); Melito, *On Prophecy?* (1); Melito, *Paschal Hymn?* (1), Tatian, *Diatessaron?* (1); Odes of Solomon (1), Julius Africanus, *Cesti* (1); Origen, *Gospel Commentary* (1) Origen, *Homily* (1); Origen, *De Principiis* (1); Sibylline Oracles (1); Theonas, *Against Manichaeans?* (1); and some unidentified theological texts (3) unidentified eschatological discourse (1), other unidentified homilies and letters (2); a Jewish and Christian dialogue (1); prayer texts (3); Hymn to the Trinity (1); and several exorcistic/apotropaic[16] texts.

---

15. Hurtado, *Earliest Christian Artifacts*, 19-24; Epp, "Issues in the Interrelation," 495-569; Epp, *Perspectives on New Testament*, 14-17.

16. Apotropaic (Greek = *apotropaios*, "turning away") is a reference to exorcisms or turning away from evil. Some ancients believed that one who is apotropaic has the power to turn away from evil or misfortune.

Examples of several ancient Jewish and Christian manuscripts are in the appendix at the end of this volume. That collection of examples reflects both amateur and professional hands in copying the church's Scriptures, including a few texts that were popular for a time but not eventually included in the church's biblical canon. It is not always easy to distinguish the biblical from the nonbiblical texts. The appendix concludes with an example from a modern printing of the Greek New Testament. More recent publications of the Greek New Testament are available from the Nestle/Aland 28th edition, the United Bible society 5th edition, as well as the Holmes, Society of Biblical Literature edition, and the more recent Tyndale edition. These are readily available to students, scholars, and interested readers.

We will now focus on other important factors that enable us to see both the stability of the faith transmitted in churches for centuries and also some of the impreciseness that the humanity of Scripture reveals in the midst of Scripture's transformative message for people of faith.

CHAPTER 5

More Christian Artifacts

Translations, Lectionaries, Hymns, and Church Councils

THE ANCIENT ARTIFACTS THAT are the subject of this chapter clarify many important questions and issues about the formation of the Bible and the church's desire to make the Christian proclamation of its gospel available to as many people as possible despite difficulties in translations that aimed at communicating the church's message and mission.

64. Why are the earliest translations of the Bible important? What can be learned from them about the formation of the Bible?

The early Jewish Christians were anxious to proclaim their message throughout the Greco-Roman world and beyond, but the people they sought to reach with their message about Jesus the Christ did not, for the most part, know Hebrew or Aramaic, but most could communicate in Greek, even if as a second language. Some, however, did not know Greek, so the practice of translating the church's Scriptures into other languages became common so that the people they wanted to reach could understand the message of and about Christ in their own language.

Jesus most often spoke Aramaic, and he could also read the Hebrew Scriptures and likely was also able to communicate in Greek with gentiles in Galilee and in the Jerusalem area. While the early missionaries took their message to the people mostly in Greek, the most common language spoken throughout the Greco-Roman world in the first century, by the end of the second century they did not hesitate to translate their sacred texts into other languages.

All of the New Testament writings were produced in Greek, and the words of Jesus were translated into Greek very soon after the church began. All of the Gospels told his story in Greek. The translation of the Hebrew Scriptures into Greek began around 283–280 BCE when the Pentateuch was translated into Greek to make the Hebrew Scriptures available to Greek-speaking Jews in Alexandria, Egypt, and that became the primary language in which Jews throughout the Greco-Roman region around the Mediterranean Sea could read and hear their Scriptures.

All of the Hebrew Scriptures had been translated into Greek by around 130 BCE, though that date is uncertain. The legendary story of that first translation is reported in the Letter of Aristeas (ca. 130 BCE). It spoke of some seventy-two translators working independently of each other and yet they came up with exactly the same translation of the Torah/Law (Pentateuch). That translation was thus believed by many Jews to have divine approval, and it could not be changed. As we saw earlier, its name was subsequently abbreviated as the LXX or the "Seventy," most likely by the Christians who made use of that Greek translation for their own first Scriptures (later called the Old Testament), and it was the most cited version of the Jewish Scriptures in the New Testament. With this precedent, the notion of providing translations of the church's Scriptures was also important to the first Christian missionaries as they went to multiple locations sharing their message, not only in Greek, but soon also Latin and Syriac, and eventually also in other languages. The early Christians freely translated their Scriptures into several languages, too, eventually including Syriac, the Syriac Peshitta, Old Latin, the Armenian translations, and others.

These translations provide many important lessons in the history of the origin of the Bible. While some early translations have been lost, the ones that survived let us know which books the recipients had and accepted as sacred Scripture. They also aid textual critics in piecing together the earliest possible text of the New Testament writings.

At the end of the second century several Latin translations of LXX manuscripts were produced and Tertullian regularly cited or quoted them. The early Latin translations were often inaccurate, and they often included several of the disputed or apocryphal books. At the end of the fourth century Augustine expressed his disappointment with the quality of many of the Latin translations by would-be but inferior translators as follows:

> Those who translated the scriptures from Hebrew into Greek can be counted, but the Latin translators are out of all number. For in the early days of the faith, everyone who happened to gain possession of a Greek manuscript and thought he had any facility in the two languages, went ahead and translated it. (Augustine, *Doctr. chr.* 2.11.16.36)

He goes on to say how poorly some of those translations were.

Given the complexity and expense of producing a translation, it is generally assumed that when the New Testament books began to be translated, those writings were highly valued and recognized for their liturgical, catechetical, and missional value for the churches. In other words, given the complexity of making a translation, the translated texts were likely recognized as authoritative texts not unlike Christian Scripture, if not already called Scripture by the time the writings were translated (and if they were not yet called Scripture, the translated texts were certainly well on their way toward scriptural recognition).

65. What are some of the earliest and most important translations of the New Testament?

The early Christian translations of both the Old and New Testament Scriptures are a primary resource for textual critics and current translators in preparing the earliest recoverable text of their Scriptures. What the early translators likely thought was that their translations were sacred literature. And the Christian communities for whom the translations were prepared received them like a collection of sacred texts, that is, at the very least something like Scripture.

The following early translations have considerable significance for understanding the development of the Christians' Bible.[1]

1. *Syrian Versions.* For several centuries the New Testament did not include the so-called Minor New Testament Epistles (2 Peter, 2–3 John, and Jude) and Revelation, but Tatian's *Diatessaron* (or *Gospel of the Mixed*) and 3 Corinthians were included in their scriptural

---

1. For a more complete description of these translations, see Metzger, *Bible in Translation*, 25–51.

collections. Eventually, after several centuries, as the Greek texts had greater influence in Syria, the *Diatessaron* and 3 Corinthians were excluded, and the Minor New Testament epistles were eventually added. It took longer, however, to include Revelation (seventh to eighth century). The surviving ancient manuscripts have an interesting history in several Syrian versions and reflect considerable diversity for centuries. The most important of these include: (1) The *Old Syriac* version, containing only the four canonical Gospels preserved in two fragmented manuscripts from the fourth or fifth centuries, but the original translation probably dates from the end of the second or beginning of the third century. The eastern church fathers who used this translation often also refer to Acts and the letters of Paul. By the end of the second century CE some Jews had translated the Hebrew Scriptures into Syriac, and it became known as the Syriac Peshitta ("common") translation. After their conversion to the Christian faith, the translators of the Peshitta also included the New Testament writings.[2] The Syriac Old Testament translations generally included all the Tanak books, with an unusual order, including the Book of the Women containing Ruth, Esther, Judith, and Susanna. (2) The Peshitta (or *Syriac Vulgate*, designated Syrp) likely comes from the beginning of the fifth century and contains twenty-two New Testament books (it omits 2 Peter, 2 and 3 John, Jude, and Revelation). (3) The *Philoxenian* version, perhaps produced in the early sixth century, was also known as the *Harclean Version* because of a later revision by Thomas of Harkel in the early seventh century. For the first time in this translation the Catholic Epistles and Revelation were added to the Syrian churches' collection of Scriptures. (4) The *Palestinian Syriac* version (ca. fifth century). Only a few fragments of these translations still exist, and they include the Gospels, Acts, and several (not all) of the letters of Paul.

2. *Latin Versions*. By the end of the second century, several Latin translations of the LXX manuscripts were produced and Tertullian regularly cited or quoted them. As noted above, the early Latin translations were often inaccurate and included, along with the Hebrew Bible's texts, several disputed apocryphal books.[3] The following information highlights the variety of books besides the

---

2. Metzger, *Bible in Translation*, 26–29; Weitzman, *Syriac Version*, 1.
3. Metzger, *Bible in Translation*, 30.

Hebrew Bible's books found in the Latin translations. Because of considerable confusion in existing Latin translations, Jerome produced a new translation. He, along with others, also translated the Old Testament Scriptures directly *from the Hebrew* (ca. 390–404) and not the Greek LXX, and he did not recognize the scriptural status of the disputed or deuterocanonical books. After that *Codex Amiatinus* (ca. 700 CE), the pandect Latin Bible, and most other translations following it, included several but not all the deuterocanonical or apocrypha books.[4] The most important of these translations are: (1) The *Old Latin* versions (perhaps late second to early third century). There were several Old Latin manuscripts produced during the third century and later that fall generally into two categories: African (especially from the Carthage and Hippo areas) and European versions. In the surviving fragments, portions of the four canonical Gospels, Acts, and portions of Paul's letters survive, along with a few fragments of Revelation. It may be that Tatian (ca. 170) used an Old Latin version of the Gospels for his *Diatessaron*, but he may also have used a Greek text that was translated into Syriac. (2) The *Latin Vulgate* version produced by Jerome in the late fourth and likely early fifth centuries in Palestine (Bethlehem). The surviving copies of this version contain the whole Bible but, besides the New Testament writings, there are two codices (*Codex Dublinensis*, ca. eighth century and *Codex Fuldensis*, ca. sixth century) that contain the apocryphal letter of Paul to the *Laodiceans*.

3. *Coptic Versions*. Around the late third or early fourth century, Coptic translations began appearing that included some six dialects (Sahidic, Boharic, Achmimic, sub-Achmimic, Middle Egyptian or Oxyrhynchite dialect, and Fayyumic). Most Tanak/Hebrew Bible books were included along with several disputed books. In the beginning of the third century, the Coptic versions in the Sahidic and Boharic dialects are the most important among the various manuscripts that have survived, and the contents of these versions include the four Gospels, Acts, and the Pauline Letters.

4. *Gothic Versions* (ca. middle to end of the fourth century). The earliest manuscripts of this version include four Gospels, some Pauline letters, and a portion of Nehemiah 5–7.

---

4. Liere, *Introduction to the Medieval*, 4–15.

5. *The Armenian Versions* (late fourth and early fifth centuries). The fifteen hundred or more copies that have survived date from the eighth century and later and some have all of the New Testament writings, but others are missing various New Testament books. It is interesting that 3 Corinthians is also in their New Testament writings. By the fifth century, the Old Testament and New Testament were translated from the Syriac versions. The Armenian Old Testament Scriptures included several of disputed books including the History of Joseph and Asenath, the Testaments of the Twelve Patriarchs, the Book of Adam, the History of Moses, the Deaths of the Prophets, Concerning King Solomon, A Short History of the Prophet Elias, Concerning the Prophet Jeremiah, the Vision of Enoch the Just, and the Third Book of Esdras (= chapters 3–14 of 4 Ezra).[5]

6. *The Georgian Version*. It is possible that the origin of this version goes back to the fourth or fifth century, but its oldest surviving manuscripts dates from the ninth century. It contains the four Gospels, Acts, and the Catholic Epistles. Near the end of the tenth century, the book of Revelation was translated and added to the collection.

7. *The Ethiopic Version* (now in the Ge'ez language and it began as early as the fourth or as late as the seventh century). Most of the surviving manuscripts of this version date after the thirteenth century and currently it is not possible to know how much of the New Testament was initially translated into this language in its earliest stages since only partial manuscripts have been discovered. This version is the largest known Bible containing more than eighty books and its New Testament includes not only the twenty-seven books of the New Testament but also Sinodos, 1 Clement, the Book of the Covenant, and Didascalia. Rufinus noted that the mission to Ethiopia began during the reign of Constantine (*Hist. eccl.* 11.9), but the contents of the Ethiopian Bible are puzzling since the eighty-one books that comprise it show considerable fluidity in the surviving manuscripts. It is difficult to find the same eighty-one books in each. Ethiopian Christians were isolated from the rest of Christendom for almost a thousand years and their Old Testament may date from the fourth and fifth centuries and reflect an early Syrian canon. Besides the Tanakh books, their Old Testament includes the Prayer of Manasseh, Jubilees, 1 Enoch, 2 Ezra and Ezra Sutuel, Tobit, Judith, Esther with

---

5. Hovhanessian, "New Testament Apocrypha," 1–6, 63–87.

additions, 1–3 Maccabees, Ps 151, Daniel with additions, Baruch, Epistle of Jeremiah, Wisdom, Sirach, and Pseudo-Josephus. The orders or sequence of these books in translation also vary in the surviving collections and Bibles.[6]

There were several other translations,[7] but the above shows that various books besides the Hebrew Bible books and the twenty-seven books of the New Testament were often included and that a few books we know from the Old or New Testament were not included in some early and later translations.

The examples in canon lists, citations, manuscripts, and the translations testify to the continuing fluidity for centuries in the books welcomed in these translations. Nonetheless, there is considerable overlap in these collections. The ancient Old Testament translations regularly included the Hebrew Bible books but often differed on the other books included in them.[8]

An important point here is that these New Testament translations do not always contain the same books even though they often overlap in terms of the Gospels and some letters of Paul. Most also include several other New Testament writings. Only one of the translations contains all of the New Testament books, but it contains other writings besides. Except for Jerome's *Latin Vulgate*, very few of the translations appear to have been well prepared, and Jerome did not improve on the translations of the apocryphal or deuterocanonical texts in his translation, nor did he think highly of several of the New Testament writings in his translation of them. His Vulgate is not an even treatment of all of the books it translates. Some of the difficulties with these early translations had to do with the problem of translating the many nuances of the Greek into other languages. Metzger and Ehrman explain that not only were incompetent translators involved in the preparation of many of these translations, but they also show that there were features of the Greek syntax that are not easily transferred to another language. For example, they explain, "Latin [unlike the Greek] has no definite article;

---

6. These can be seen in Metzger, *Bible in Translation*.

7. Other later and less important translations for our purposes include the Arabic versions from the eighth century to the nineteenth century, the Sogdian (or Middle Iranian) version, which dates from the ninth to the eleventh century, and the Old Church Slavonic version during the ninth century, which was important especially for the Bulgarians, the Serbians, Croats, and eastern Slavs.

8. Metzger, *Bible in Translation*, 38–51.

Syriac cannot distinguish between the Greek aorist and perfect tenses; Coptic lacks the passive voice and must use a circumlocution. In some cases, therefore, the testimony of these versions is ambiguous."[9]

66. What can ancient translations of the Scriptures tell us about the history and development of the Bible?

The implications of the survey of the early translations are considerable. The church in antiquity never claimed that only the Greek translation of the Hebrew Scriptures was important or that the Greek alone was an inspired text of the New Testament, but rather affirmed that all other translations were also inspired and useful in the expanding church. The Syriac Peshitta was surely Scripture to Syriac-speaking Christians who welcomed and used the Peshitta in their worship and instruction. They did not conclude that their Scriptures were less inspired than those used by Greek-speaking Christians. The Ethiopian and Coptic Christians had their own translations of the Scriptures, and both recognized them as divinely inspired. This is not unlike Christians today who welcome as Scripture popular new translations in English or French or German and read them in their churches. The variations in the quality of these modern translations are obvious to scholars and all of them are clearly not produced with equal skill but bookstores still sell them.

What bearing does the concept of translation have on the inspiration of the Bible? Does the notion of inspiration apply only to the autographs or original texts of the Bible (which we no longer have)? Does inspiration apply to copies of the biblical manuscripts and to translations of them, all of which contain mistakes of one sort or another or at least have variants within the manuscripts they used for their translations? That raises questions also about current translations of the Bible that are based on an eclectic Greek text of the Scriptures that does not exist in any single surviving ancient manuscript. This is not an argument to abandon any views on the sacredness of the biblical books. On the contrary, historically churches have affirmed the Bible and continue to believe that God still speaks to the followers of Jesus through a variety of translations. However, some of those translations are clearly better than others and the ancient churches agreed that the inspiration of their Scriptures does not reside in any one translation. Remarkably, the notion of the authority of

---

9. Metzger and Ehrman, *Text of the New*, 95.

Scripture was not significantly affected in the ancient churches despite fluidity in the biblical texts they possessed and in the multiple translations along with the challenges associated with them.

67. What are lectionaries and what can they tell us about which Scriptures were read in the ancient churches?

Lectionaries are the selections of Scripture that were and still are read in synagogues and churches. The practice of reading selected passages from the Jewish Scriptures was common in the time of Jesus and the early Christians followed that practice in their churches. It would have been next to impossible, for example, to read the whole of Isaiah or Jeremiah in one setting in a synagogue service or in a Christian service as well. It would also be difficult to read a whole Gospel in one church worship service due to the length of Matthew or Luke or John. Mark could be done, but it also would have taken considerable time in a worship setting. We see Jesus reading a portion of Isaiah in Luke 4:16–21 and interpreting it for the synagogue congregation. He was reading a lectionary text. The early Christians followed this long-established practice.

These lectionaries are helpful because they let us know which Scriptures were impacting the life and faith of the ancient churches. The evidence for what specifically was read in those churches is not as clear until the fourth and fifth centuries, but such lectionaries were read early on, as we will see below in Justin's description of a church worship service (1 Apol. 67).

While occasionally whole books were read, especially the smaller letters or minor prophets, most often the lectionaries were selections from the Law (Pentateuch), Prophets, Gospels, and Epistles. There is no doubt that Scriptures were read in worship, but the specific texts read are indicators of the specific texts that impacted early Christianity. J. W. Miller has observed that the Scriptures known to the Orthodox Christians in the East were almost always from lectionaries in the liturgies that were read in the churches. He argues that the common persons in churches knew their Old Testament Scriptures only partially from the selected texts in the lectionaries that he calls the "Prophetologion" and claims that the whole Old Testament was seldom known to all the churches throughout the whole Byzantine period and, Miller concludes, this was likely for three reasons: (1) the difficulty and cost of producing a complete collection of the Scriptures, which "ensured that few exemplars of such scope were produced in antiquity; (2) low literacy rates would have prevented most of the people from being familiar with all of the church's Scriptures; and (3) the familiarity and accessibility of a complete Old Testament text, as in the case of Isaiah or Jeremiah or Deuteronomy, would not have been possible to most since the circulation of such longer texts would have been prohibitive, thus they did not circulate freely in antiquity.[10]

This is similar in the surviving New Testament manuscripts, namely, there is little evidence that the full scope of the church's Scriptures were widely known in local churches throughout the Byzantine period and certainly only a few copies of both Testaments in the fourth and fifth centuries (Sinaiticus, Vaticanus, and Alexandrinus) existed at that time. Most of the surviving manuscripts from that period do not contain all of the biblical books or even most of them, as we will see. The accessible Scriptures at that time consisted largely of the lectionaries that were read in churches. The lectionaries that were circulating in the churches in antiquity are therefore the best representatives of the sacred books known in many of the ancient churches. Unfortunately, little attention has been paid to the role that lectionaries had in the formation of the church's Scriptures.[11] The ancient Christian scholars might well have known and had access to all the books that now comprise the church's Bible, but certainly the average minister or priest, to say nothing of laypersons, would not have seen or even known all of the church's Scriptures until centuries later. They might well have had lectionaries passed around of favorite passages, but likely not the whole of all of the books recognized as Scripture.

The overlooked lectionaries are among the most under-examined entities that informed the churches in their worship and instructional gatherings in antiquity.

The church's roots in Judaism make it understandable that early Christians would have followed the practice of their Jewish siblings reading selected readings of Scriptures in the synagogue gatherings on the sabbath (as we saw in Luke 4:16–21 and Acts 13:15). The lectionaries were often accompanied with interpretations, when possible, along with the implications of the sacred texts reflected by those who were able to interpret them.

---

10. Miller, "Prophetologion," 55–75.

11. This is carefully discussed in Schmidt, "Greek New Testament" and in Scanlin, "Old Testament Canon."

This practice among Jews was less common in Jewish temple worship, which focused mostly on sacrifice and the singing of psalms, than it was in synagogues. The practice of a regular reading of Torah or Pentateuchal texts and the *haftarah* (a conclusion of a biblical lesson), and the practice of including a pericope or short text from the Prophets was common in the synagogues on the sabbath in the time of Jesus (cf. also Philo, *Spec. Laws* 2.60–62; and Josephus *J. W.* 2.289–92; *m. Meg.* 3.6). Because the early Jewish Christians followed the pattern of the synagogue in their gatherings, they also read scriptural texts in their gatherings and that tradition carried on subsequently in the gentile Christian worship gatherings.

In the second century Justin described in his *1 Apol.* 67 a typical gathering of Christians on the Sunday and listed the activities that regularly took place in their meetings. That description mentions the regular reading of the "memoirs of the apostles" (the Gospels) "or" the writings of the prophets (the Hebrew Scriptures/Old Testament writings) as long as time allows or permits. They did not read all of them on one occasion but rather, like the Jews, read a selection. There are multiple examples of reading of selections of the Scriptures in synagogues in late Second Temple Judaism and in ancient Christianity.[12]

While these recognized scriptural texts were regularly read in churches from their beginning, their contents only become clearer and more specific from around the middle to the end of the fourth century, especially in Constantinople and other churches in the East.[13] Hopefully scholars will begin to give more attention to lectionaries as they consider the multiple influences that gave rise subsequently to the specific books that were included in the church's Bible.

68. How important were the early Christian hymns for advancing the church's faith and reflecting which books were included in the Bible?

Along with the summary creeds read in churches and observed above, often an overlooked area of influence in the transmission of the early core

---

12. For useful summaries of the lectionaries, see Levine, *Ancient Synagogue*, 135–51; and those in early Christianity are summarized in Rouwhorst, "Bible in Liturgy," 822–42; and Levine, "Bearing False Witness" 118–19, 249–50, 759–63.

13. A helpful summary of these valuable resources is in Rouwhorst, "Bible in Liturgy," 822–42.

Christian teachings and traditions as well as the Scriptures adopted are the early Christian hymns and spiritual songs. Like today and throughout the history of Christianity, the songs sung in various church liturgies have long advanced the transmission of the church's core beliefs with calls for appropriate responses among believers to the message of the hymns. The church's hymns and spiritual songs regularly affirmed the essence and significance of the Christian faith for most believers especially for those who were illiterate and could not read the Scriptures. The same could also be said of much of the art employed in Christian buildings, monasteries, chapels, and the like. They regularly told the story of the church's key teachings and events, and they proved especially helpful to the laity for understanding the primary teachings of the church by those who could not read. Christian hymns and spiritual songs were also common in churches from their beginning (e.g., Eph 5:18–20; Col 3:16; Rev 4:8, 11, 5:9–10). Everyone could understand the images, both young and old, and the core message they intended to present, whether with symbols of the cross, a fish, a boat, or other well-known images of the early churches that regularly appeared in their worship along with the early Christian hymns and spiritual songs. With such imagery in song and art, it was not long before non-literate persons in the church could understand the primary teachings of the church.

At the heart of the early Christian faith was a proclamation primarily about the identity and significance of Jesus for bringing God's salvation to humanity, and that was advanced by proclaiming a core collection of his teachings, actions (miracles), and fate (death and resurrection), all of which had implications for Christian belief, mission, and lifestyle. These core beliefs were transmitted in the church's core traditions, creeds, but also in worship through the church's hymns and spiritual songs. That practice remains the same to this day and Christian hymns and worship songs regularly extol the activity and love of God for the salvation of humanity and even the mission of the church. Long before the scope of the church's Scriptures was settled, early Christian beliefs were known not only in the New Testament writings and creedal affirmations at baptisms and serving the Eucharist or Holy Communion, but advanced in their hymns and spiritual songs. These were present in the early churches even before there were any Christian Scriptures to read in the churches. Although those songs were never on the same level of authority as the church's Scriptures, once the latter had been written, most of the early songs did transmit the core Christian beliefs. As we saw earlier, the early church beliefs and sacred traditions were circulated in churches orally well before there were any written New Testament writings. The music accompanying these activities regularly affirmed for church laity the core elements of their Christian faith. Interestingly, in Pliny's letter to the emperor Trajan, who was asking what he should do with Christians, Pliny says to Trajan that "they met regularly before dawn on a fixed day to *chant verses* [singing] alternatively among themselves in honor of Christ as if to a god" (Pliny the Younger, *Letter* 10.96.7).

While it is popular in some churches today to say that their core doctrines do not come from the hymn book but from the Bible, that was initially not the case when there were no recognized New Testament Scriptures for any church. Along with a command for those filled with or led by the Spirit to proclaim and teach the essence of the Christian faith (Matt 28:20; Acts 6:42), the early Christians were reminded that being filled with the Spirit eventuates into "singing psalms and hymns and spiritual songs" and "singing and making melody to the Lord in your hearts" as well as "giving thanks to God at all times and for everything" (Eph 5:18–21; cf. also Col 3:16). Examples of songs of praise and affirmation of faith can be seen, for example, in Luke 1:46–55; Phil 2:6–11; and Rev 4:8, 11; 5:9–10, 12–13.

This is not unlike what we find in the Old Testament. Singing in worshipful gatherings was not invented by the early Christians but inherited from their Jewish siblings who regularly sang in their times of worship and various gatherings as we see in the spontaneous songs in Exod 15:1–18 and Judg 5 and in songs sung in worship (e.g., Pss 22, 45, 57–59, 75, 80; cf. also Pss 30 and 68) or in songs of lament (e.g., Pss 12, 44, 74, 79; cf. 2 Chr 35:25). The Psalter was largely intended to be sung, though the original melodies have been lost. Those psalms continue to be sung in churches but with different melodies and that has continued throughout the history of Judaism and Christianity. Singers were always prominent in temple worship (1 Chr 15:16–28) and included both instruments and vocal praise (Ps 150:3–5; 2 Chr 5:13). When the Jews returned from Babylon, the singers were with them (Ezra 2:41; cf. Neh 7:1; 12:27–47). The additional song later inserted between Dan 3:24 and 3:25 was also well known in antiquity despite not being included in the Hebrew Bible but only in the LXX.

The point is that if the books considered were contrary to the faith that was conveyed in the hymns of the churches, those books would not likely have been included in the church's scriptural canon. The faith that is expressed in the church's earliest hymns reflects the theology of the early Christians and the books that reflected that faith were among those that were selected for inclusion in the church's New Testament.

69. Were there ancient examples of hymn books in early Christianity that told the story of Jesus?

Yes, of course. Most of those collections have not survived antiquity, but there are several examples of such collections of spiritual songs in early Christianity. The oldest known collection of Jewish-Christian hymns is the Odes of Solomon (*c.* 100–125 CE), a collection of some forty-two hymns. For a time, these songs were even cited as Scripture in some early churches, as we see in Lactantius, tutor for Constantine's son in the early fourth century, who is the last known church father to cite these Jewish-Christian hymns as Scripture, especially Ode 19.6 (see Lactantius, *Inst.* 4.12.3). The author of these hymns was not Solomon, of course, but the author used that designation to say that Jesus was the new Solomon and wise like Solomon. Odes 1, 5, 6, 22, and 25 were translated in the gnostic text Pistis Sophia (with other parallels in Odes 11, 24, 30, 34, and 39), causing some scholars to suggest that it was a gnostic collection of odes, but in the Odes there is no denying the role of God in creation and that collection also affirms the humility of Christ (Ode 41.11–16), the humanity and incarnation of the Messiah (Ode 33.5–11), that he was crucified (27.1–3; 42.1–2), and was raised from the dead (8.5–6; 41.12; 42.11–13).[14]

Songs were listed among some scriptural collections and that was not unusual in early Christianity before there was a Bible. As we saw above, since songs and hymns were common in the Hebrew Scriptures earlier, the early churches followed that tradition. For example, P72 (ca. late third or fourth century), besides Jude and 1–2 Peter, also contains Ode 11 of the Odes of Solomon. Also, an eleventh- or twelfth-century discovery at the Laura Monastery on Mount Athos contains besides New Testament books also a collection of psalms and odes (m. Gregory 1505). The links between songs and Scripture in early Christianity were strong.

---

[14]. For a discussion of the Odes and their temporary scriptural status, see McDonald, "Odes of Solomon," 108–36.

70. Did ancient *local* church councils influence the formation of the Bible?

Because there were local church councils that deliberated the scope of the church's Scriptures, it is likely that the church councils of the most influential churches had an impact on other churches, not only in local regions, but also in the rest of the Roman Empire. For instance, the church council at Rome (382) clearly influenced the decisions on the scope of the Scriptures for churches in Carthage (397 and 419 CE). The larger churches at Rome, Antioch, Ephesus, Constantinople, and Alexandria would surely have had an influence on smaller churches in rural locations. From the church's beginning its leaders have deliberated current issues affecting the churches, as we see in the first church council—in Jerusalem, home of the mother church for a time—which determined how to welcome the gentiles into the church without requiring their obedience to the Jewish Law and circumcision (Acts 15). There were also several *local* church councils (e.g., Acts 13:1–2), but here the decisions were all local ones that affected the churches and many of the decisions by local councils are unknown, though some are known.

There was no general or *ecumenical* council for all churches that discussed the scope of the Christian Scriptures, but several *local* church councils did make such decisions. While it is tempting to say that the Council of Trent (1546) was ecumenical and applied to all churches regarding the books in the Bible, it did not include the Orthodox churches in the East or the Protestants in the West. Only the local councils or synods produced lists of scriptural texts that could be read in local churches, and the earliest records of those decisions come from the middle to late fourth century. Their significance is seen in the fact that it appears that, for the most part, the decisions made by local councils about the books in the New Testament match the twenty-seven books now in all church Bibles (Orthodox, Catholic, and Protestant) and that this canon was *largely*, but not completely, determined in the middle to late fourth century at the earliest, though with some disagreements later on, largely over the acceptance of James, Hebrews, 2 Peter, 2–3 John, Jude, and especially Revelation (along with disagreement over some Old Testament books, such as Ecclesiastes, Song of Songs, Esther).[15]

---

15. For more detailed information on this, see McDonald, *New Testament*, 2:265–318.

71. Was there an early church council that rejected the status of the Shepherd of Hermas?

Although Tertullian (ca. 200) mentions earlier church councils that deliberated and rejected the Shepherd of Hermas (see below), he is most likely only speaking of the local church councils in Hippo and Carthage near his home. It is difficult to find evidence for rejecting that book at that time since it continued to have a long life for centuries well into the late fourth century and was welcomed as Scripture by several church fathers. It was also included later in Codex Sinaiticus (ca. 375–400 CE). The point here is that no one should suggest that Tertullian had in mind council decisions that were true for *all* churches in the Greco-Roman world in his generation. There is no evidence for that, or indeed for the councils he mentioned. Several local church councils later list the books that had greater receptivity and approval circulating among churches in the regions represented at the councils, indicating the books' catholicity or widespread reception in churches. The Shepherd of Hermas was included in some of those lists. And the Muratorian Fragment and Athanasius' *Thirty-Ninth Festal Letter* (367) both encourage private reading of the Shepherd.

To emphasize a point made earlier, since none of the first seven *ecumenical* councils deliberated the scope of the church's Scriptures, the local decisions on the matter were not reflective of the perspectives of all churches. Tertullian (c. 200) indicated that "every church council" rejected the Shepherd of Hermas, calling it an "adulterous" book because it allowed forgiveness after repentance and baptism (*Pud.* 10) and for its focus on adultery and immorality (see also *Pud.* 20 and *Or.* 16). However, he was still speaking only of local churches in his region and not for all churches throughout the Roman Empire. Tertullian focused on the repeated repentance after sexual offences, and condemned the Shepherd of Hermas as follows:

> I would yield my ground to you, if the scripture of "the Shepherd," which is the only one [book] which favors adulterers, had deserved to find a place in the Divine canon; *if it had not been habitually judged by every council of churches (even your own) among apocryphal and false (writings)*; itself adulterous and hence a patroness of its comrades; from which in other respects, too, you derive initiation; to which, perchance, that "Shepherd" will play the patron whom you depict upon your

(sacramental) chalice, (depict, I say, as) himself withal a prostitutor of the Christian sacrament. . . . I, however, imbibe the scriptures of that Shepherd who cannot be broken. . . . But, even if pardon is rather the "fruit of repentance," even pardon cannot co-exist without the cessation from sin. So is the cessation from sin the root of pardon, that pardon may be the fruit of repentance. (*Pud.* 10; emphasis added)

It is interesting that Tertullian indicates that before his time the Shepherd was already called "Scripture" by several church fathers. His concern over repeated repentance and pardon, which he believes is allowed in the Shepherd, is likely not only a statement in his post-Montanist conversion perspective, which was far more restrictive than the practice of the church more generally, but also a recognition that the Shepherd was widely welcomed as Scripture despite his assertion that it was rejected by "every church council" as apocryphal and false writing.

It is not clear which councils Tertullian had in view, but his comment most likely reflect the views of the Hippo and Carthage regions and not those found elsewhere in that period. Since there are no surviving records of those church councils that clarify which sacred texts were welcomed as Scripture and which were not, it may be unwise to guess what their decisions might have been. There is no other evidence that Shepherd was widely rejected by that time (not even in the Muratorian Fragment; ca. 375–400 CE).[16]

Surprisingly, Tertullian accepted the scriptural status of 1 Enoch, because it was cited by Jude. He contended that Jude accepted it as Scripture and so did he (see Jude 14; cf. his *Cult. fem.* 1.3). One can only wonder about what other books were deliberated at that time and what decisions, if any, came from council decisions. To support his arguments against Shepherd, Tertullian acknowledges that all early church councils supported his rejection of its scriptural status, but again, what those councils in the early third century decided is unclear and no record of their decisions has survived. It may be that Tertullian was speaking with hyperbole or perhaps he was speaking about decisions made at Carthage, which had regular (almost annual) church councils. Tertullian may have welcomed the Shepherd as Scripture *before* his Montanist conversion and because of their strictness in morality, he rejected it because it appeared to him to offer forgiveness or pardon of sins after

---

16. For a more detailed examination of the Muratorian Fragment see McDonald, *New Testament*, 2:274–305.

the initial repentance of sins and baptism (Shepherd 31:2–7). Because of this, Tertullian argued that it "favors adulterers."[17]

Charles E. Hill claims that Tertullian's reference to "every council of churches" rejecting the Shepherd supports his conclusion that the Muratorian Fragment canon list, which also rejects it, was written at or around the time of Tertullian.[18] The problem with that position, of course, is that no records of any local church councils at that time exist and none that are known from that time that dealt with the scope of the church's Scriptures. All known church councils at that time were local and those best known for making such decisions about the books that could be read in churches date from 360 (Laodicea) and thereafter. Also, the most recent dating of the Muratorian Fragment places it in the middle to late fourth century,[19] but more will be said about the date of the Muratorian Fragment in chapter 6 below.

It would be strange if the Shepherd had been widely rejected by the time of Tertullian, since other church fathers from approximately the same time had welcomed it *as Scripture*. For example, Clement of Alexandria regularly cites it as Scripture (e.g., *Strom.* 2.1, 9, 12; 4.9; 6.15 and more than seventeen times). Irenaeus introduced the Shepherd as Scripture when he wrote, "Truly, then, the scripture declared" (*Haer.* 4.20.2 citing Shepherd 2; *Sim.* 1, using *graphe* ["Scripture"]; cf. also *Haer.* 2.20.2; cf. *Mand.* 1.1). Origen (see *Princ.* 1.3.3 and 4.1.11) acknowledges the Shepherd, as Scripture, though he acknowledges that some despise it. He describes it as "divinely inspired" and connected its author with the Hermas mentioned in Rom 16:14. While it was later excluded from scriptural or canonical lists, as in the case of Athanasius' *Thirty-Ninth Festal Letter* in 367, it was nevertheless allowed to be read in private. The Shepherd was later included in the late fourth-century *Codex Sinaiticus* and also included in the Latin list inserted in *Codex Claromontanus* (Dp), along with Acts of Paul and the Revelation of Peter. There is an obelus posted beside these books that could mean that those texts may not have been in the initial listing or that they were for private reading only, but that is not clear. Shepherd was also included in the fifth-century *Codex Alexandrinus* along with 1–2 Clement. So, it appears that there was no

---

17. For more on the use and recognition of the Shepherd in early Christianity, see Osiek, *Shepherd of Hermas*, 1–7.

18. Hill, "Truth Above All Demonstration," 56–69.

19. Rothschild, *Muratorian Fragment*; Rothschild, "Muratorian Fragment as Roman," 55–82.

universal rejection of Shepherd at the time of Tertullian. Indeed, there is no clear evidence that any other councils made any decisions about the scope of the church's Scriptures near the time of Tertullian. Also, Tertullian himself, in the quote above, acknowledges that the Shepherd was called Scripture by others *at that time* (ca. 200). The only known widespread doubts about the Shepherd come from much later.

72. What are the most important ancient church councils that dealt with the scope of sacred Scriptures that could be read in churches?

The earliest known church councils that dealt specifically with the books that could be read in churches are the following:

1. Council of Laodicea, canons 59–60 (*c.* 360, but possibly later in origin): Canon 60 was most likely inserted later, and it does not accept Revelation. That council acknowledged as Scripture all the books of the Old Testament to be read in churches. It also included Baruch. Its New Testament approved all of the books of the New Testament except Revelation.

2. Council of Rome (382), which is also repeated later in the *Decretum Gelasianum* (496): it includes all of the books of the Hebrew Bible, but also Wisdom, Sirach, 1–2 Esdras, Tobit, Judith, and 1–2 Maccabees, probably also is unclear about the additions to Daniel and Esther, and Baruch and the Epistle of Jeremiah. This decree of the Council of Rome (CE 382) on the canon of Scripture took place during the reign of Pope Damasus I (CE 366–384).

3. The Councils of Hippo (393) and Carthage (393, 397) were likely influenced by the council of Rome in 382 and include all of the books in the Hebrew Bible but also Wisdom of Solomon, Sirach, Tobit, Judith, 1–2 Esdras, and 1 and 2 Maccabees. Its New Testament includes all of the books of the New Testament and, by the council at Carthage in 419 CE, attributes Hebrews to Paul, but it also includes reading The Passions of the Martyrs in the churches.

4. Trullan Synod (691) and Seventh Ecumenical Council (787): affirmed earlier eastern canons of local synods that welcomed various disputed books. They did not mention Cyril of Jerusalem, who

rejected the deuterocanonical books. None of the ecumenical church councils made any decisions on the scope of the church's Scriptures.

5. Council of Trent (1546): it welcomes as Scripture all of the books in the Hebrew Bible, but also 1–2 Esdras, Tobias, Judith, Wisdom, Sirach, Baruch, 1–2 Maccabees, plus additions in Daniel and Esther. Its New Testament includes all the books of the New Testament and no others. After listing these books, that council also concludes,

> If anyone does not accept as sacred and canonical the aforesaid books in their entirety and with all their parts, as they have been accustomed to being read in the Catholic church and as they are contained in the old Latin Vulgate Edition, and knowingly and deliberately rejects the aforesaid traditions, let him be anathema. Let all understand, therefore, in what order and manner the council, after having laid the foundation of the confession of faith, will proceed, and who are the chief witnesses and supports to whom it will appeal in conforming dogmas and in restoring morals in the church.

Remarkably, long after earlier church councils rejected the scriptural status of some books, some churches were still reading them, even centuries later. This lets us know that church council decisions on the scope of the biblical canon did not always speak for all churches, but only a limited number of the churches at that time and it is not clear whether all the churches those councils addressed agreed with the councils that constructed canon lists, nor is it clear whether those churches were even aware of those decisions. As noted earlier, no ecumenical council speaking for all churches addressed the issue of the biblical canon or which Scriptures to be read in churches. When fourth- and fifth-century church councils met and decided which books could be read in churches, they clearly did not settle the case for all churches throughout the Greco-Roman world. In other words, the council decisions did not determine the reading practices of all churches.

As late as 800 to 850 CE, a list of accepted and rejected books was produced in the name of Nicephorus. It concerned decisions made at earlier church councils, but it seems that the rejected books were still being read centuries later. This list is called the *Stichometry of Nicephorus*, and it lists the accepted books and even counts the number of lines in each, but it also lists the writings that were not to be read in churches, some of which were considered heretical. This list emerges hundreds of years after the decisions it reflects were taken! Why the need to repeat the list if no one was still reading the rejected texts?

The *Stichometry of Nicephorus* identifies the Old Testament books, including all of the Hebrew Bible books except Esther, but then lists the disputed books that are mostly in the LXX. It then accepts all the books of the New Testament except Revelation, which it lists among the disputed (*antilegomena*) or rejected books and includes in that category the Revelation of John, the Revelation of Peter, the Epistle of Barnabas, and the Gospel of the Hebrews. That extensive list then identifies the Apocrypha of the Old Testament, including Enoch and fourteen others, and then lists the New Testament apocryphal books, including the Didache, the Shepherd of Hermas, and eight others.

Again, the striking thing about the *Stichometry of Nicephorus* is that it mentions books that were rejected books more than four hundred years earlier by local church councils. That suggests that council decisions were not always followed in the ancient churches, especially regarding the collection of Christian writings that could be read in churches.

73. Did the first ecumenical council at Nicea in 325 CE settle the issue of which books would be in the Bible?

The short answer is no, but that view has been commonly and wrongly asserted for many years. That council did not even deal with the question of which books could be read in churches, the notion of a biblical canon, instead focusing on the pressing issue of identity of Jesus, a matter that was dividing some churches. Many authors over the years have made the claim that the scope of the Bible was settled at the Council of Nicea—a view popularized in Dan Brown's popular book *The Da Vinci Code* in 2003 (later made into a movie in 2005)—but such claims are clearly wrong. We know of the decisions that were made at Nicea because they have been preserved, along with the decisions of the rest of the seven ecumenical councils. And *none* of them dealt with the question of which books could be read in churches.

However, after that ecumenical council there was greater agreement on the identity of Jesus and that agreement made it possible *later* to recognize the books that agreed on the identity of Jesus established at Nicea for a majority of churches. It is important to appreciate that it would have been difficult to establish a *Christian* biblical canon for the churches without broad agreement on the identity of Jesus.

Although no decision was made on the scope of the Bible at Nicea, the full scope of the New Testament would be hard to imagine without the decision at Nicea on Jesus' identity. After Nicea, however, we begin seeing several canonical lists identifying the church's sacred Scriptures. Some of the canon lists emerged from local councils beginning with the Council at Laodicea in 360, then the Council of Rome in 382, and the Councils of Hippo and Carthage in 393, 397, and 419. A major list of the Scriptures that were canonical and could be read in the churches was sent out to the churches by Athanasius, bishop of Alexandria, in 367 in his famed *Thirty-Ninth Festal Letter* letting them know when to celebrate Easter that, but also identified the canonical Scriptures that could be read in churches (see earlier discussion of this text) but also those that could be read privately and those that should be shunned altogether.

Against my claims above, one might appeal to the fact that, later, Jerome, who did not attend the Council of Nicea, claimed the Book of Judith was welcomed by those at the Council. There are, however, questions about the veracity of that comment. In his subsequent *Prologue to Judith*, he makes a similar comment, which most scholars of canon and church history conclude was probably *not* written by Jerome but rather by someone else. This is supported by the fact that Jerome created a canon list in which he did not include Judith. In his acknowledged writings, Jerome rejected all of the deuterocanonical books (including Judith), though he did find some value in reading a few of those books. So it seems likely that Jerome never made any claims about Nicea welcoming a book as Scripture.

In the next chapter, I will focus on several particularly challenging questions surrounding the pseudepigraphical books. Many in the academy, the media, and the churches have shown considerable interest in those books in recent years and they warrant our attention.

CHAPTER 6

The Challenge of Authorship and Pseudepigrapha in Early Christianity

MANY RELIGIOUS WRITINGS IN antiquity were written without names attached to them and others were produced under false names. In what follows, the focus will be on the importance of authorship in early Christianity and its adoption of writings written in false names, and whether some of those books were included in the church's Bible.

74. Was authorship a determining factor in deciding which books to include in the church's Scriptures?

It is quite likely that authorship played a role in final decisions on the scope of the church's Scriptures. It is clear that this was not *initially* an important factor in the emergence of Christian writings since half of the New Testament was written anonymously. Understanding the growing importance of authorship in early Christianity is important for understanding the growth of the New Testament apocrypha, that is, pseudonymous or pseudepigraphal writings written under the name of Christian figures. Attitudes to authorship varied from the church's earliest days but by the time significant decisions about the boundaries of the Scriptures came into view in the fourth and fifth centuries authorship had become an important matter. Except for Paul's appeal to his readers by insisting that he was an apostle and identifying himself in the introductions of his letters (see also 1 Cor 9:1), the importance of authorship varied in the church fathers. Perhaps even in Paul's time others used his name to advance their own views on circumcision or keeping of the Law and in his letters Paul wanted to make sure that his readers knew it was truly him who was addressing the issues his churches were facing. It is likely that Paul felt the need to set the record straight on what may have been written falsely in his name (Gal 1:20; 5:2; 6:11).

However, for the most part, the lack of focus on authorship in New Testament books suggests that initially the *content* of a writing was more important than its authorship. Ehrman contends that only nine of the twenty-seven New Testament books were written by their traditionally attributed authors. Most of those, he claims, were believed to be writings attributed to Paul.[1] While scholars debate this issue, it does appear that the importance of authorship grew after the first century, which was a period in which several New Testament writings were welcomed and circulated in many churches without reference to their authorship. It seems that only when the *content* of a writing was questioned did the matter of authorship emerge in church fathers' debates. Their assumption was that a *genuine* apostolic figure would not promote heretical teachings in churches.

The most important New Testament books, and those most cited, were the canonical Gospels, and all of them—along with Acts—were written *anonymously*. So too were Hebrews and 1–3 John, and when those writings first circulated the focus was on their content and not their authorship. By the end of the second century, when we begin to see names attached to them (i.e., Matthew, Mark, Luke, John), it appears that several pseudonymous writings in the names of apostolic figures had begun to emerge and *this* is the time that authorship became a major issue in the church fathers.

Pseudonymous writings did not initially appear to be a problem. What mattered most was whether the content was orthodox, advancing the core beliefs and teachings of the churches. In the cases of the Gospels, it was the words and deeds of Jesus contained in them that were cited and that gave the texts authority, not the identity of their authors. Through most of the second-century citations of the Gospels their apostolic authorship was only minimally and broadly referred to, as in the case of Justin's speaking about the "memoirs of the apostles" that were read in churches (*1 Apol.* 64–67). It is only later that individual names

---

1. Ehrman, *Forged*.

are attached to each Gospels, as in the case of Irenaeus identifying each canonical Gospel by name (Matthew, Mark, Luke, and John). Initially attention was only drawn to the words and deeds of Jesus in Gospel citations, not the names of their authors.

While the authors of those books may well have been known to *some* early Christians, it did not appear to be important until the end of the second century. The words and activities of Jesus were considered to be the most important feature of the Gospels, not the identity of those who told the story of Jesus. Generally speaking, authorship initially was only important when dealing with heretical documents, as in the case of the Gospel of Judas (see Irenaeus, *Haer.* 1.31.1). While Paul regularly mentions his authorship in his recognized letters, that was not the case with the unnamed author(s) of 1–3 John.[2]

75. What New Testament books had a disputed authorship in the early churches?

The authorship of several New Testament books was questioned by some church fathers. These include the Pastorals (1–2 Timothy and Titus), Hebrews, 2 Peter, 2–3 John, Jude, and Revelation. Sometimes those books were not debated as much as ignored and not included in scriptural collections or canon lists. Current biblical scholars are divided over the authorship of the Pastoral Epistles, Ephesians, Colossians, 2 Thessalonians, Hebrews, 2 Peter, James, Jude, and Revelation and possibly others. Most contemporary New Testament scholars agree that some of the writings attributed to Paul were not produced by him, although they fit well within the orthodox tradition (especially the Pastoral Epistles). Furthermore, even if such letters are pseudonymous, they may well contain authentic Pauline teachings, words, or traditions (e.g., 1 Tim 1:12–15; 2 Tim 1:15–18; 4:6–8, 9–18; and possibly the tradition in Titus 1:5). It is difficult to find any theological argument to invent these words believed to be authentic or to attribute them falsely to Paul.

There are a number of reasons why scholars suspect that some of these New Testament letters attributed to Paul are not from Paul's own hand, including the fact that they do not include some of the major

---

2. We will see below the arguments for increasing awareness and concern over authorship of the biblical writings in the arguments of Jed Wyrick in his *The Ascension of Authorship*.

themes in Paul's recognized letters, such as the role of the Holy Spirit, the importance of reconciliation, and justification by faith. And the organizational structure appears more advanced in the Pastoral letters than in Paul's own letters. I. Howard Marshall may be correct when he concludes that the Pastorals, as they are now, were probably not written by Paul, but rather by someone who wanted to preserve Paul's words for a subsequent generation.[3] Again, there may well be some authentic Pauline sayings or teachings in the Pastoral Epistles, but what is more important is the practical contents of those books, which is what endeared them to later congregations and why they were welcomed among the church's Scriptures despite the questions over their authorship. Since the Pastoral Epistles are not included in the earliest known collection of Paul's letters—the papyrus document P46 (ca. 200 CE)—and it is not in the current fragmented Codex Vaticanus, some scholars contend that they were not included among Paul's writings by some church fathers. However, the orthodox messages in those books continued to have relevance for later churches and they achieved something of an "irresistible momentum." Which is presumably why they were not later rejected by the majority of churches.[4]

Regarding authorship of the book of Revelation, Eusebius expresses doubts about it in his *Ecclesiastical History* 3.25 and he later reports that Dionysius of Alexandria (d. 264) wrote an extensive and critical examination of the authorship of Revelation and concluded that the apostle John was not its author. Interestingly, however, Eusebius did not reject the scriptural status of Revelation (*Hist. eccl.* 7:25). There are some books that had become so popular and well received among many Christians that it would likely have caused an uproar if they had been rejected. Hebrews was one such book. It had a powerful message and warning for those considering leaving their Christian faith and returning to their former way of life in Judaism. Revelation by contrast was one of the most challenged books that eventually was included in the New Testament. Remarkably it is the only New Testament book that claims to be a revelation from God and yet it was one of the most disputed books in antiquity. To this day it is seldom included in church lectionaries and never read in Orthodox liturgical churches even though they include it in their Scriptures.

---

3. See the preface in Marshall, *Pastoral Epistles*.
4. See Stuckenbruck, "Apocrypha and Pseudepigrapha," 179–203.

There are several forgotten or ignored biblical books, and it is not unusual for many Christians today to adopt something like a "canon within the biblical canon." In other words, most Christians give priority to the Gospels and several letters of Paul but largely ignore Hebrews, most of the Catholic Epistles (except 1 John), and Revelation. This selectivity is also common in their use of the Old Testament. Although many Christians are familiar with Deuteronomy, Psalms, and Isaiah, few are aware of Leviticus, Numbers, Ezekiel, the Kings, Chronicles, and most of the Twelve minor prophets. Although John and Luke are popular New Testament books nowadays, along with the letters of Paul, several books in both Testaments are unfortunately ignored by many scriptural readers. There came a time when John became the most popular of the Gospels in churches, but Matthew was by far the most popular gospel in the early churches and was cited far more times than any of the others. Matthew and John were cited much more than Luke and Mark to start with, but that changes from generation to generation, depending on the needs and concerns facing Christians.

76. Since there was considerable debate in antiquity over the authorship of Hebrews, why was it finally included in the church's Bible?

Although Hebrews was not accepted by some churches early on, by the end of the second century most churches accepted it, despite uncertainty over its authorship, most likely because of its important and relevant message. As we observed, Eusebius acknowledged that some did not accept it, but its message was popular, and its canonical status widely accepted by the latter part of the fourth century, especially in the West. The biggest question was not its authorship, but rather its content. Tertullian thought that Barnabas wrote it (*Pud.* 20). Famously, after Origen examined Hebrews and claimed that much in it could have been from Paul, but the "style and composition" was not Paul's. He concluded that "who wrote the epistle, in truth God knows," but he did not reject it (Eusebius, *Hist. eccl.* 6.25.13–14).

Eventually Hebrews was attributed to Paul not unlike the later attributions given to other anonymous New Testament writings. This was perhaps because some name was later essential in churches, especially for Augustine in the late fourth century, but the *contents* of Hebrews is likely what carried the day and Hebrews remained among the church's sacred Scriptures. It had gained the "irresistible momentum" mentioned earlier. The majority of churches continued to welcome Hebrews despite uncertainty about its authorship. We see, for instance, that the church councils in Rome (382 CE) and Carthage (397 and 419) affirmed that it was written by Paul, though earlier there were questions about it at the council of Hippo in 393 CE.

Some canon lists do not include Hebrews, especially the Muratorian Fragment (late fourth or early fifth century—see arguments for its date below). Despite its lack of focus on the major themes in Paul's writings and the style and grammar were clearly unlike Paul's writings, it was eventually attributed to Paul when authorship became a critically important factor in the late fourth century. From the late fourth century on, it is often listed as the fourteenth letter of Paul, especially in Western churches. It was first attributed to Paul by the end of the second century in Alexandria, likely by the church father Pantaenus, and its future was largely secured thereafter. Although some churches in the West had serious doubts about its authorship, Augustine and Jerome accepted it, even though both had doubts about its authorship. Augustine was present, perhaps even in charge, at the Councils of Hippo and Carthage in 393, 397, and 419 when disputes over the authorship of Hebrews eventually gave way to acceptance of its authorship by Paul. Hebrews was included in the books to be read as Scripture and by 419 it was included without question among the letters written by Paul.

It is likely that attributing Hebrews to Paul saved its place in the biblical canon, but since it was written anonymously in the first century when authorship was not yet a prominent issue in churches, there was a clear move to welcome it in the church's Scriptures because of its content, and authorship became a means of making that happen. Initially it had widespread acceptance without questions or awareness of authorship but when authorship became more important to the church fathers, especially Augustine in the late fourth century, it slowly became common to attribute it to Paul. By the end of the fourth century all New Testament writings were attributed to specific authors, but that was not initially the case. There was a time in the early churches when anonymity and content were more important than authorship.

77. Did the early Christians welcome and produce pseudonymous writings as Scripture?

Some Christians did. Recently, Bart Ehrman made what was considered a controversial claim that the early Christians *knowingly* accepted pseudepigrapha and included of some it in their New Testament.[5] Many current scholars dispute the authorship of several New Testament writings and while some of those writings were written anonymously, they question whether the names later attached to several New Testament writings are authentic. The Gospels, Acts, Hebrews, and the three letters attributed to John the apostle were all written anonymously, so, even if some or all the authorships later attributed to them were mistaken, it is unclear whether they would have been included in the New Testament without the names attributed to them. Given that they were originally anonymous, it is also unclear whether they should now be called pseudepigrapha, that is, written under a false name.

However, some of the texts whose authorship is disputed were not anonymous but named their purported authors. Some biblical scholars question the authorship of 2 Peter, Jude, James, 2 Thessalonians, the Pastoral Epistles, Colossians, and Ephesians. As we saw earlier, pseudonymous writings were common in the Greco-Roman world and in late Second Temple Judaism. Many of the pseudonymous writings were written and circulated widely among the early Christians before authorship was a factor for most church fathers. Many of the earliest Christians were illiterate or unable to do a careful study of the ancient texts circulating among them in the names of well-known prophetic and apostolic names. The majority of the earliest church fathers did not have the skills or sufficient manuscripts to make informed decisions about authorship. Even if they had access to multiple manuscripts, they were generally unable to distinguish between authentic writings and those falsely attributed to prophets, apostles, or other well-known figures of antiquity. As authorship became a more important matter for leading church fathers by the end of the fourth century several were able to assess more critically the authorship of writings circulating among them as Christian Scripture. For Augustine authorship was an essential factor in determining the canonical status of books in the church's Scriptures. By then several church fathers rejected writings falsely written in the pseudonymous names in biblical history, as in the case of Enoch noted earlier. Augustine insisted

---

5. Ehrman, *Forged*.

on knowing the authorship of the biblical books and recognized that there were two kinds of writings, namely "those written by authors and those ascribed to God speaking through them" (*Civ.* 18.38). He likely thought he was following the rationale of the Jews, who maintained that writings ascribed to authors prior to the time of Moses, as was the case with 1 Enoch, should not be considered Scripture.

Augustine acknowledged that while there were some useful things in 1 Enoch and that it was cited by the apostle Jude (Jude 14), there were nonetheless many fables in it, such as the giants, that could not be verified, so Enoch had to be excluded from the canon. He went on to conclude that apocryphal writings in the names of prophets, such as Enoch, were like those written in the names of apostles and both had to be rejected. He wrote,

> So that the writings which are produced under his [Enoch's] name and which contain these fables about the giants . . . are properly judged by prudent men to be not genuine; just as many writings are produced by heretics under the names of both other prophets, and, more recently, under the names of the apostles, all of which, after careful examination, have been set apart from canonical authority under the title of Apocrypha. (*Civ.* 15.23, *NPNF* 2:305).

Wyrick has shown that Augustine's notion of canonicity depended significantly on the ability to ascribe correct authorship, or it was determined to be a forgery.[6]

78. Should churches welcome biblical books written in a false name?

It has long been apparent to many biblical scholars that some biblical books were likely not written by the author(s) to whom those books were later attributed. As we saw above, such matters were not initially of great significance unless those writings promoted heretical teachings. For example, while Hebrews was later attributed to Paul and was likely welcomed into the New Testament canon *later* because it was attributed to Paul, many in the early church (most notably Origen) did not believe that Paul wrote it. Several church fathers guessed possible authors, but eventually it was attributed to Paul, despite the fact that the major themes

---

6. Wyrick, *Ascension of Authorship*, 353–67.

in Paul's acknowledged writings are not in Hebrews and the style of Hebrews is considerably unlike Paul's writings. Paul's letters were eventually arranged by their size, beginning with the largest, Romans, and ending with Philemon, the smallest. Hebrews, however, was generally placed after Philemon, demonstrating continuing uncertainty over its authorship (see the councils of Hippo and Carthage in 397).[7]

As we observed above, Hebrews was written anonymously when its authorship was not a major issue, and it continued to be cited by the early church fathers because it had a powerful message for those facing difficulties or persecutions and who were considering departing their Christian faith to return to their former religious traditions (Judaism). Its message was well established in churches when authorship was not an issue, and it continued to have a powerful message for subsequent generations. As a result, as I noted earlier, it had acquired what Loren Stuckenbruck called an "irresistible momentum" in the churches and could not be deleted from the church's Scriptures.

The Book of Revelation was attributed to John the apostle, but even in antiquity its authorship was doubted because it was so different from the welcomed Gospel of John and 1 John. Dionysius of Alexandria (ca. fl. 260–264) studied it extensively and concluded that John the apostle did not write it. Nevertheless, he did not reject its message (Eusebius, *Hist. eccl.* 7.24–25). Eusebius gave considerable space to Dionysius's expressions of doubt about the authorship of Revelation (see the story in *Hist. eccl.* 7.25,1–9), but he, too, did not reject its content. Although it was clearly written by someone named John (Rev 1:1–4), its authorship was doubted, yet it appealed to some in the early churches and its place in the church's Scriptures was finally assured by attributing it to John the apostle. It was also the most contested New Testament book, with many questioning its scriptural inclusion early on, and it took centuries before it eventually gained approval in most churches. The point here is that some writings whose authorship was later questioned nevertheless continued to have an important message for churches and were not eventually always rejected. The welcomed content of several writings with doubtful authorship led to the inclusion of those writings, as in the case of the Pastoral Epistles. The "irresistible momentum" noted earlier—grounded in their content and usefulness in churches—seems to be the best explanation for the continuation of books whose authorship was disputed. It

---

7 By contrast, P46, the earliest known collection of Paul's writings, placed Hebrews after Romans and before the Corinthian letters.

may well be best for churches today to focus on the content of the biblical writings whose authorship was questioned in antiquity and ask whether unquestioned authorship is an important criterion for acceptance.

Questions about the disputed books often ignore the important contribution they made to early understanding of Christian faith. The church, and also Judaism of late antiquity, regularly welcomed books whose authors were unknown (e.g., Judges, Samuels, Kings, Chronicles, many Psalms, and others). The disputed books in the New Testament often reflect core beliefs and sacred traditions that circulated in early Christianity. There remain for some scholars debates over the authorship of various New Testament books. Perhaps it is best to conclude that these writings had long proved themselves to be useful to the churches and so they remain a valuable part of our New Testament. While authorship eventually became an important factor to the later church fathers, the fact that several of those texts remained in the New Testament is primarily because of their orthodox content.

79. Does reference to 1 Enoch in the New Testament reflect its scriptural status?

As was mentioned earlier, the character of Enoch is first mentioned in Gen 5:18–24 and there is a lengthy history of texts about him. He is mentioned in Heb 11:5 and especially in Jude 14 as one who "prophesied saying." Jude then goes on to quote the pseudonymous text of 1 Enoch, which is also cited multiple times in the early church fathers as Scripture. The act of prophesying is, after all, at the heart of Jewish and Christian notions of Scripture.

Some church fathers tried to figure out how the text of 1 Enoch survived when there was a flood on the earth during the time of Noah and it was concluded that somebody got a copy of that book brought into Noah's ark! So, it survived. Currently, no one thinks that the Enoch of Gen 5:18–24 wrote 1 Enoch. The text was likely produced over many years, beginning around 250 BCE and concluding perhaps around 40 BCE.[8] Even the later church fathers who eventually rejected it did not

---

8. Of the five tractates that make up 1 Enoch, most scholars agree that the tractate called the *Watchers* was probably the earliest part of 1 Enoch and portions of it could have been written as early as 300–250 BCE while the latest, the *Parables*, was likely written perhaps by 40 BCE. Some scholars think that parts of the *Parables* could have been written as late as 40 CE. Enoch continued to be a popular book in the early churches well into the third century and is still included among the Scriptures of the Orthodox Ethiopian Christians.

believe that Enoch wrote it. Nevertheless, it is a very helpful work, for it has some valuable information in it that is useful for understanding several New Testament texts.

By and large, by the fourth century, most church fathers had rejected 1 Enoch as Scripture, but before that 1 Enoch was highly respected and received as Scripture by many leading church fathers. That raises the question of whether Jude should be included in our New Testament since he accepted it as Scripture. Many churches in the East, especially Syria, rejected Jude, as did Martin Luther in the Reformation era. Most, however, accept it.

One can suppose from the multiple copies of 1 Enoch discovered at Qumran and its citation *as Scripture* by several early church fathers that it was a favored book and circulated among several early Christians for centuries and continued to be read for centuries in churches even after it was rejected by some church councils. The popularity and sacredness of this book both in Judaism of late Second Temple and early Christianity is unquestioned.

The Old Testament prophets often began their prophecies saying something like "The word of the LORD came to me, saying" (e.g., Jer 1:4; cf. Joel 1:1; Zech 1:1). The term "prophet" was used in reference to sacred prophecy whether orally proclaimed, as in the case of Elijah, or in writing, that is, *as Scripture*. Of course, the Scriptures of the Jews and first Scriptures of the early Christians were commonly known as "the Law [or Moses] *and the Prophets*." Like Jude citing 1 Enoch 1:9 and saying that Enoch prophesied, multiple early church fathers well into the third century also accepted 1 Enoch as Scripture. The considerable influence of 1 Enoch in antiquity was seldom in doubt and its acceptance as Scripture by many early church fathers is well known. Some samples of the extensive Christian citations of Enoch as Scripture in an authoritative manner in the early centuries include the following:

1. Epistle of Barnabas (ca. 70–100 or 130–150 and possibly as late as 140, Alexandria) 4:3 cites Enoch using "as it is written" (*gegraptai*); 16:4–6 (which is a summary of 1 En. 106:19–107, esp. 91:13; cf. also 1 En. 89:56–74).

2. Apocalypse of Peter (ca. 100–110, possibly Egypt) 2–8 (1 En. 108:7–9; 106:2, 10; 61:9–11; 53:3).

3. Justin Martyr (ca. 100–165,), *1 Apol.* 2.5 (cf. 1 En. 7; 8:9; 15:8, 9).

4. Athenagoras (fl. ca. 170–180, Athens), *Leg.* 24, 25 (cf. 1 En. 6, 7, 13:5; 15:3, 8, 10; 60:15–21).

5. Minucius Felix (second or third century, North Africa), *Oct.* 26 (1 En. 8; 15:8–12; 16:1; 19:1).

6. Irenaeus (c. 130–200, bishop of Lyons), *Adv. Haer.* 1.2.1 (1 En. 10:13–14); 1.8.17 (1 En. 7:1; 8:1); 4.16.2 (1 En. 12:4–6; 13; 14:3–7; 15; 16); 4:36.4 (1 En. 10:2); 4.58.4 (1 En. 7:1); 5.28.2 (1 En. 15:3; 99:7; 19:1); 5.5.1, plus 1.15.6 (1 En. 8:1; cf. 10:8); *Adv. Haer.* 4.36.4 draws on 1 Enoch re: angelic rebellion. *Adv. Haer.* 4.16.2 (cf. 1 En. 12.13, 6, 10). See also 4.36.4 where Irenaeus understood Gen 5:21–24 and 6:1–4 in light of 1 Enoch.

7. Clement of Alexandria (c. 150–215), *Ecl.* 2.1, 53; 3.456 (1 En. 19:3); 3.474 (1 En. 8:2–3); *Strom.* 3.9 (1 En. 8; 16:3).

8. Tertullian (c. 160–225, Carthage), *Apol.* 22 (cf. 1 En. 15:8, 9); *Cult. fem.* 1.3.1 (1 En. 8:1, 3); 2.10 (1 En. 8:1); *Idol.* 4, 15 (1 En. 19:1; 99:6–7); 9 (1 En. 6; 14:5), 15; *Virg.* 7 (1 En. 6; 14:5; see also *An.* 50).

9. Hippolytus (c. 170–236, Rome), *Antichr.* 43–47; *Or. adv. Graec.* (cf. 1 En. 22:3; 21:1).

10. Origen (ca. 185–254, Alexandria and Caesarea), cites Enoch as "Scripture" (*Princ.* 1.3; 4.35). There are many more citations of 1 Enoch listed in McDonald, *Old Testament*, 1:360–65.

80. When was 1 Enoch finally rejected in early Christianity?

The circulation of 1 Enoch in the Judaism of late antiquity and in early Christianity suggests that it was welcomed as a Scriptural text in early Christianity well into the third century CE. The last prominent church father to cite it as Scripture was Origen (ca. 230–240 CE), though eventually and shortly thereafter he rejected its scriptural status. Not all Christians did the same, but by the mid-third century most church leaders concluded that 1 Enoch was not Scripture and so it was not listed among their scriptural writings. It nevertheless remains in the Orthodox Ethiopian Bibles *as Scripture*. Recent scholarship has shown that it had considerable value for understanding late Second Temple Judaism (i.e., Judaism before 70 CE) and early Christianity.

Perhaps some Christians now are hesitant to acknowledge that there may an element of truth in some ancient books that were not included in the Bible and perhaps they also worry that reading them might affect the authority of the books recognized as Scripture. However, several well-known nonbiblical books, such as the Didache, 1 Clement, and others, aid in our understanding of the early church and often bring clarity to some portions of the New Testament. In them we often gain a better understanding of the Jewish notion of the anticipated coming Messiah before and during the time of Jesus. They show us that some Jews were looking for a messianic figure to come and establish the kingdom of God and destroy the occupying Roman army on Palestinian soil. We also gain a better understanding of the meaning of the title Son of Man, Jesus' most common self-designation in the Gospels.[9] These documents are also often helpful in clarifying the social concerns the people were facing when Jesus came among them and they fill in some of the historical background. For example, we find the origins of Hanukkah in 1 Maccabees as well as the transitionary history from the emergence of the Greek dominance of Palestine. The apocryphal and pseudepigraphal writings were written largely after the end of the Old Testament period (Ezra–Nehemiah and Malachi) and *mostly* before the emergence of early Christianity. Jesus likely knew or read some of that literature or was informed by some of its teachings circulating orally in Palestine in the first century.

Also, in the Old Testament times the land of Israel was populated largely by agrarian communities but in New Testament times more people were living in cities. The lifestyles and everything changed during that "intertestamental" time. Awareness of this literature aids our understanding of Judaism and early Christianity enormously.

In sum, most Christians do not accept 1 Enoch as Scripture, even though it served as Scripture for some early followers of Jesus, but most thoughtful Christians do accept it as an aid that grants us a more informed understanding of the New Testament Scriptures when they were written.[10]

We will now focus on the emergence of *Christian* apocryphal texts and some related issues in early Christianity.

---

9. "Son of Man" is only found on the lips of Jesus in the canonical Gospels (over eighty times), but only once in Acts. 1 Enoch helps clarify to us that this designation was much more than a reference to simple humanity. It was a reference to a messianic leader, even if Enoch was that figure in the *Parables of Enoch* portion of 1 Enoch.

10. John Collins, Craig Evans, and Lee McDonald discuss how best to understand the literature that did not make it into our Bibles in their *Ancient Jewish and Christian Scriptures*.

CHAPTER 7

Early Christian Apocrypha, the Muratorian Fragment, and Scriptural Authorship

THE AREAS OF THIS chapter are among the most debated of those related to the New Testament canon formation. They deserve careful attention to grasp how they relate to our primary focus.

The attention given to Christian pseudonymous religious texts in antiquity has grown considerable in recent years and it can only be introduced here with accompanying contemporary responses. Most of the writings discussed here were attributed to well-known New Testament persons (often Peter, John, and Paul, but others also) and often produced in the similar New Testament genres (namely gospels, acts, epistles, and apocalypses or revelations).

The Muratorian Fragment is also central to current debates on the formation of the New Testament canon and many appeal to it as a second-century document to argue for an earlier date for the formation the New Testament.

Finally, we will focus some more on the importance of authorship in early Christianity and when it becomes a factor for determining the scope of the Christian Scriptures.

81. What are the *Christian* apocryphal books and how were they welcomed in antiquity?

There are many writings that fall into the category of Christian apocrypha, and they had a long history over many centuries in some ancient churches. They began to emerge after the recognition of the authority of apostolic writings in the latter half of the second century and continued well into the seventh century, and in some cases even beyond. Most were written in popular apostolic names and the genre common to the New Testament (gospels, letters, acts, and apocalypses) and were welcomed as Scripture in some churches that believed in their apostolic origin and authority (e.g., the Gospel of Peter in the Rhossus church discussed earlier; Eusebius, *Hist. eccl.* 6.12.3–6). *At least* eighty such books were produced that were not later included in the New Testament and *probably many more* than that (some scholars do not include the gnostic writings among this collection).[1]

Of the three most popular apocalyptic books circulating in early Christianity—The Apocalypse of John (Revelation), The Apocalypse of Peter, and The Shepherd of Hermas—only the first was eventually recognized as Scripture, and that likely because John the apostle was believed to be its author. The Shepherd of Hermas was quite popular in churches, so much so that more copies of it have survived antiquity than all the New Testament books except for the Gospels of Matthew and John. The apocryphal Acts of Paul and Thecla was also quite popular for centuries in some churches. The apocryphal gospels and acts, too, were in circulation in some churches for centuries, but most gradually ceased being cited after the church established a fixed collection of writings that formed the Old and New Testaments. After the boundaries of the biblical canon had become clearer many of these documents were lost or ceased being copied. However, numbers of these texts have been found in modern times—in caves or garbage dumps or in recently discovered boxes of undocumented ancient texts found in some European libraries or museums—and published. It is likely that even more will be found in some newly discovered cave or garbage dump, or in some as yet undocumented old texts still stored away in some museums and libraries in Europe and the Middle East.

---

1. For more examples of these writings, see the works by Elliot, *Apocryphal New Testament* and by Burke and Landau, *New Testament Apocrypha*.

82. What is the Muratorian Fragment (MF) and is it a fake document?

The Muratorian Fragment (likely dating from 375–400 CE) was found in the Ambrosian Library in Milan, Italy, in 1700 and published in 1740. It is named after its founder, Lodovico Muratori. It includes a fragmented list of New Testament books and others not included. In previous publications I have referred to the MF as the "Achilles' Heel" of New Testament canon formation because many New Testament scholars consider it a late-second-century list of the church's Scriptures and regularly assume that it reflects common beliefs about the scope of the New Testament at end of the second century.

The MF is a poorly written Latin text included in a seventh- or eighth-century Latin text that contains several writings of famous church fathers Ambrose, Eucherius, and Chrysostom (all well-known and influential late fourth- and fifth-century church fathers). It also contains a list of New Testament writings that strangely also includes near its end and before the Book of Revelation the apocryphal or deuterocanonical book Wisdom of Solomon that the author says was "written by the friends of Solomon." It then says, "We receive only the apocalypses of John and Peter," noting that "some of us are not willing the latter be read in church" (lines 70–72). The Shepherd of Hermas (lines 73–78) is rejected for public reading but encouraged to be read. Earlier it says that Jude and two letters bearing the name of John are "counted" in the "catholic" church (Latin = *catholica*) (see lines 68–69). The author also mentions the "catholic church" (62–63 and 69), a designation largely unknown before the fourth century.[2]

Until recently, most scholars who examined this ancient text concluded that it was written either in the late second or early third century, but more recently a growing number of scholars date it in the late fourth or early fifth century. Some scholars debate whether it was originally written in Greek or Latin.

There are several problems with dating this text in the late second or early third century and I will summarize them here. The major arguments against a second-century date include:

---

2. For more detailed research on this fragment see McDonald, *New Testament*, 2:274–304 and especially more detail in Rothschild, "Muratorian Fragment as Roman" and Rothschild, *Muratorian Fragment*.

1. If it was a late second- or early third-century document, it has no known parallels until the late fourth and early fifth centuries.

2. The listing of the Wisdom of Solomon among New Testament writings has its only parallels in the late fourth century (see Eusebius, *Hist. eccl.* 5.8.7–8; Epiphanius, *Pan.* 76.22.5) and putting a deuterocanonical or apocryphal text among New Testament books is puzzling to contemporary scholars.

3. The reference to Hermas as the brother of Pius, the bishop of Rome (lines 75–76) is only found elsewhere in the late fourth century (lines 73–76). Rothschild observes that this "fraternity legend" is only found elsewhere in the *Liberian Catalogue* (*Liber Pontificalis*, ca. 352–366 CE), in Pseudo-Tertullian's *Carmen adversus Marcionitas* (ca. 325), and in the *Letter of Pius to Justus of Vienne* (ca. fourth century).[3]

4. Also, if the "fraternity legend" is correct, it would place the writing of the document more in the middle of the second century (ca. 140–161) and not at the end, as most scholars who want an early date claim, and that is far too early for the heresies listed, which are late second century. It is also highly unlikely that Hermas was the brother of Pius of Rome.

5. The reference to the "Cataphrygians" (line 85) is not a second-century designation for the Montanists but rather was only beginning to be used to refer to the Montanists in the fourth century, as we see in Eusebius, (*Hist. eccl.* 3.3.6). They were called Montanists until the early part of the fourth century when that began to change and then both designations were beginning to be used, as we saw in Eusebius.

6. The reference to Miltiades as a heretic (line 82) is also strange since he was praised by Tertullian for his apologetic debates against heretics (*Val.* 5). Much later, Eusebius praised Miltiades for his opposition to the gnostic teachings and writings (*Hist. eccl.* 5.17.1, and 5, see also 5.16.3). Only in the late fourth century and thereafter was he associated with heretics or spoken of disparagingly.

7. The reference to the rejected Epistle to the Laodiceans falsely attributed to Paul (lines 64–65) most likely refers to a rejected book that was written around the fourth or fifth centuries and was soon condemned by the church fathers. That is where all of the references to

3. Rothschild, "Muratorian Fragment as Roman," 55–82.

it are found. The MF text is never referred to in the second century by any church father. Tertullian mentions a letter from Paul that Marcion called Paul's Letter to the Ephesians by that name (noted earlier), but he knows that Laodicaeans was Marcion's name for Ephesians (*Adv. Marc.* 5.11, 17). There is no evidence in antiquity saying that the Letter to the Ephesians was pseudonymous or falsely written in Paul's name. The letter in question is likely a fourth-century document when it is first mentioned and rejected.

8. The multiple references to "catholic" (lines 62–63, 66 and 68) is also strange for a second-century document since there are no references to the "catholic" church in the second century and it is much more at home in the fourth century and thereafter.[4]

Rothschild concludes that the MF is a fraudulent text dating from the fourth century but writing as if it were a second century document where it is first cited by Chromatius of Aquileia (*Tract. Matt.*, Prologue: esp. §§2, 3, 5, 6, 11. ca. 398–407). Again, the MF has no parallels or citations in the second century and no one else speaks about a canon list of *Christian* Scriptures until the middle to late fourth century CE.

In Athanasius's famed *Thirty-Ninth Festal Letter* in 367, he concludes his comments about apocryphal texts circulating in churches and adds that those who produce fabricated texts to lead astray the ignorant and simple people will find the judgment of God. He writes,

> They have fabricated books which they call books of tables, in which they shew stars, to which they give the names of Saints. And therein of a truth they have inflicted on themselves a double reproach: those who have written such books, because they have perfected themselves in a lying and contemptible science; and as to the ignorant and simple, they have led them astray by evil thoughts concerning the right faith established in all truth and upright in the presence of God.

The MF reflects a fourth-century context when pseudonymous texts were circulating that tried to convince readers that they were created earlier in order to get their views more widely accepted. The MF was likely produced to look like earlier second-century documents to persuade simple readers that the author's list was much earlier than the fourth century. We

---

4. See McDonald, "Forming Christian Scriptures"; but especially Rothschild, "Muratorian Fragment as Roman," and her *Muratorian Fragment*.

have fourth-century evidence that such activity was taking place and that it was condemned when discovered.

83. Is the Muratorian Fragment a useful document for understanding second-century Christian thought about Christian Scripture?

Given what was shared above, the answer is no. Scholars who date this document in the late second or early third centuries conclude that the early church fathers dealt with the issues of second-century heresies by establishing a biblical canon of the books that could be read in churches. That makes some sense, but it assumes thinking about a fixed collection of writings that could be read in churches and such a notion has no support from that time period and no parallels in church history. It is well known by church historians that the second-century churches responded to the heretical movements of their day not by establishing a biblical canon of sacred Scriptures, but rather by affirming a "canon of faith" that was circulating in churches and regularly was called the "*regula fidei*" or "rule of faith." No one in the second century spoke of a biblical canon of the church's Scriptures. Those scholars who claim that the church fathers responded to the heresies in the second century by creating a biblical canon have trouble finding anyone else who was thinking that way at that time.

84. Were the biblical authors aware that they were writing sacred Scripture?

There is no evidence for this in the New Testament texts, and in fact there is evidence that it was not the case. Nonetheless, this notion has become popular among several recent New Testament scholars who claim that the authors of the New Testament literature were consciously aware that they were writing sacred Scripture. Although the New Testament authors likely believed that they were led by the Spirit when they wrote, that, as we saw, was not the same as knowing that they were writing sacred Scripture. As I have noted earlier, the early churches did not limit inspiration or the filling of the Holy Spirit to those who wrote Scripture. Probably the scriptural authors believed that they were led by the Spirit to say or write what they did and so what they were writing was true. But does that mean that they were all consciously aware of writing sacred Scripture? As we saw earlier in our discussion about inspiration, being led by the Spirit did not always eventuate into the writing of Scripture and it obviously does not mean that those who wrote were consciously aware of writing Scripture when they wrote. If they were all conscious of writing Scripture one would think that they would say so once in a while, but they never do. The closest New Testament author to come close to saying anything like that is the author of Revelation and there was little recognition of the scriptural status of that book for centuries, indeed, it was the last one to be universally welcomed in the New Testament.

Those who claim that the New Testament authors were aware of writing Scripture when they penned their books offer many unconvincing arguments, and I address some of them here.[5] If Paul thought that he was writing Scripture, why did he distinguish what he said from what Jesus said (1 Cor 7:10–12)? He was clearly making the strongest case for his position saying that it came not from him, but from the Lord, and then he goes on to say what he thought and he made it clear that it was from him and *not from the Lord* (7:12). Further on in 7:25, he acknowledges that he has "no command of the Lord" on his own position but he offers his own "opinion" (Greek = *gnōmēn*) on what he is saying and then concludes in 7:40 that "*I think*" (*doko* from *dokeo*) "I have the Spirit" in what he has said to the Corinthians. It is not, "I know this for sure." So, here and in 7:25 there is also a level of uncertainty in his comments.

In 2 Cor 11:17–18, Paul is boasting about his past to show that he is not inferior to other apostolic figures (see also 1 Cor 9:1), but then says that *what he is speaking is not according to the Lord (kata kyrion)* but rather acknowledges that such boasting is foolish and that he was speaking "according to the flesh" (*kata sarka*) (11:18). It does not seem that Paul is consciously aware of writing Scripture when he says that he was speaking "according to the flesh" and "not according to the Lord." Can speaking or writing "according to the flesh" ever be equivalent to writing sacred Scripture? If Paul was aware of writing Scripture, one would think that somewhere in his letters he would say so, but he does not, and it even took churches almost a hundred years later to begin to call his letters Scripture despite their being read in churches almost from the time he wrote them (Col 4:16–17).

---

5. For more examples, see Collins et al., *Ancient Jewish and Christian*, 106–19.

Paul's appeal to a command of the Lord over his own teaching is similar to his reference in 1 Cor 14:37 where Paul lets his readers know that what he is saying about a particular subject is not on his own thinking, but that it came but *from the Lord*. Paul wants to strengthen his teaching here by saying to those who might doubt him that they must know that what he is saying is coming for the Lord Jesus himself. Why say that if he was not wanting to make clear to his readers that they should know that this teaching came from the Lord and not just Paul himself and so it must be followed as a command from the Lord? The point is that he does not make his own comments equal to those of the Lord (Jesus).

There are, of course, other examples that suggest that Paul was not consciously aware of writing Scripture and being filled by the Spirit in what he wrote. In 1 Cor 1:14 he says, "I did not baptize anybody else except Crispus and Gaius," but then later corrects himself saying, "Oh! I did baptize the household of Stephanus" (1:16). When writing to the Galatian Christians, Paul was very angry with those who were undermining his mission to the gentiles who were telling them that they must be circumcised and keep the Law. He says in anger, "I would that those who have deceived you would castrate themselves" (Gal 5:12). He is using angry and unusual language here. I think that if Paul thought he was writing Scripture, he might well have used better language, but he did not.[6]

Paul often cites biblical authors and employs the usual designations when introducing scriptural texts with "as the Scripture says," or "it is written," but there is no place where he or any New Testament author uses those designations for their own writings. Nor do any of them say, "I am writing sacred Scripture." If they were consciously aware of writing Scripture, we should anticipate having at least one New Testament author making that claim.

Scholars who claim Paul was aware of writing sacred Scripture when he wrote often confuse his references to *revelation* with his own writings. For Paul, that *revelation* was the gospel that he *preached* earlier to his readers that is summarized in 1 Cor 15:3–8: that gospel was "according to the Scriptures," but he does not say that the letters he wrote to the churches were sacred Scripture, even though they were recognized as such by later second-century church fathers. Paul distinguishes his letters from the gospel he preached and reminded his *readers* that he had *proclaimed* the revelatory message, the gospel, to them and they *heard* and

---

6. For a discussion of this, see Collins et al., *Ancient Jewish and Christian*, 106–19.

received it. But he does *not* say that his letters are always equal to that revelation. He only reminds his readers in his letters of what the essence of the revelation was that he received and gave to them and that it was from the Lord (Gal 1:11–12). In other words, for Paul the gospel he preached was not the same as the letters that he wrote. What he *proclaimed* and the Galatian Christians *heard* was the revelation he had received from the Lord and delivered to them (Gal 3:1–3).

Affirmations of the sacredness of Paul's letters came later in the second century but not in the first century even though his letters were read in his churches along with others. Again, like all New Testament writings, Paul's letters were used and functioned like Scripture before they were called Scripture in the second century. Paul believed that he had *proclaimed* a divinely inspired revelation from God to the churches, but he did not equate that with his own letters.

In the next chapter, I will next address some commonly-asked faith questions about biblical and historical questions that I have dealt with earlier, including how faith engages with the complexity of canon formation.

CHAPTER 8

Christian Faith and the Bible
Some Practical Faith Questions

THE FOLLOWING QUESTIONS FOCUS on some of the bottom-line issues that many Christians face as they hear scholars and others make comments about the history of the biblical texts that have implications for how one thinks about the Christian faith and its Scriptures. Hopefully the questions and responses below will also be an encouragement to seekers who are considering embracing the Christian faith.

85. Can historians affirm Christian beliefs about the inspiration of the Bible?

This question requires some comments about the nature of historical inquiry, and then how it affects our understanding of the formation of the Bible. Historians *as historians* deal with the reality of the past and sometimes their research aids our understanding of the biblical message and the context in which it was written. However, such critical inquiry has self-imposed limitations. The development of critical historical inquiry emerged during the Renaissance and Enlightenment eras and since then historians limit their inquiry to human activity or events that affect human activity. They do not deal with extra-mundane activity such as the activity of God in human history. They seek instead to understand humanity in its social environment, and their explanations are always rooted in the natural field of cause-and-effect events that are explained by what is normal or natural or common in human existence. Historians do not deal with divine activity except to say that certain events (which Scripture understands to be the work of God) did or didn't happen, and to try to explain said events with historical (natural) reasoning.

Many historians employ their own experience of reality as they try to make sense of the past, and since miracles—such as the resurrection from the dead—are not in their experience, they try to find other explanations for how stories about such claimed events could have emerged. That perspective is especially true today and sometimes is referred to as "positivistic" historical inquiry, an approach that developed mostly in the late nineteenth century. When natural historical explanations fall short of explaining human events, historians who deal carefully with such affirmations in history simply conclude that they do not have an adequate explanation, but they do not as historians conclude that God was involved in the remarkable or unique events in human history.

Historians who examine history bring with them some assumptions or principles, and that includes their own autonomy, that is, they do not accept authoritarian decisions or reports of previous historians or theologians but determine for themselves what the facts are, as best they can construct them. These "facts" are largely based on their own experience and assumptions about the world, namely:

- seeing the world as a closed causal-nexus—with no bolts from the blue, from beyond the world;
- employing analogy to interpret events (i.e., comparing historical reports of events to events we can witness today)—so whatever is unique, such as miracles and other divine activity, is without analogy and is beyond the historians ability to enquire into;
- and employing their own experience of reality, as well as of probability (in such-and-such circumstances, what is more probable?).

While it is historical to say that humans believed that Jesus was raised from the dead, the historian's own experience, assessment of probabilities, and the lack of modern analogies for such events often leads them to prefer non-miraculous explanations for the appearance of such a belief, whether in psychological categories or simply that those who claimed to see the risen Christ were mistaken. Because many followers of Jesus were executed for their proclamation about the risen Jesus (suggesting that they *genuinely believed* Christ had been resurrected), historians can only say that those persons *reported* encountering the risen Jesus, but not that Jesus was *actually* raised from the dead or is now in heaven.

The historical principles just noted are quite common today, underpinning the metaphysics of historical inquiry, and as such historians do not deal with resurrections from the dead nor affirm God's activity in the death of Jesus *for the forgiveness of sins*. Neither do they embrace miracles (Jesus walking on water, his miracles of healing, and his resurrection), which are unique and without parallel. Historians deal with *what is probable* in life or *what has analogy* and not with the unique. Whatever is unique cannot be examined by them unless they think they can discern a more probable explanation for such reported unique events.

While some events happened only once in history, including some remarkable events, they are accounted for in the social context of humanity. Miracles are different. Since ordinarily it is not probable that someone who was crucified on a cross would be raised from the dead after three days in a tomb, such reports are not usually considered "historical" reports. If Jesus appeared to his disciples after crucifixion, then, the historians may suggest that he did not actually die, because in the historian's experience dead people do not rise from the dead. While we have many examples of crucifixions in antiquity, what other examples do we have of any who died for the sins of the world?

At the heart of Christian faith from its beginning there was a belief that Jesus of Nazareth, the church's Christ/Messiah and Lord, was crucified on a cross for the sins of the whole world and that he was buried, but soon after that his tomb was empty, and he appeared to his followers as one who was raised from the dead. Historians can find parallels to the arrest of Jesus as a threat to religious authority and even to his crucifixion on a cross, but they cannot affirm *as historians* that his death was for the sins of the whole world. That is a faith statement that *cannot be historically verified*, but it is verified by faith for those who do not have a limited view of what is possible in history. I will return to that below. Similarly, historians can affirm that it is possible that the tomb in which Jesus' body was placed was empty by the Sunday, but they could also suggest that either his disciples or his enemies stole the body. They can even argue historically that the tomb in which he was buried was empty after a short time (two to three days), and that his closest followers believed that he had appeared to them, and that they believed that he was raised from the dead, but they have no ability *as historians* to affirm that he was raised from the dead.

An empty tomb on its own is not enough for faith. Mary Magdalene saw the empty tomb and thought someone had moved the body of Jesus from there—until the risen Christ appeared to her (John 20:11–18). The early church fathers did not root their faith in the empty tomb but in the appearances of the risen Christ. And even a seeming appearance may not be enough. Some of the disciples even doubted after an appearance from the risen Christ to them (Matt 28:17). In the historians' experience and in light of principle of probability, it is easier for many historians to believe that someone stole the body of Jesus than to argue that he was raised from the dead, an event that would have no parallels in their experience. Their own experience and the principle of probability says that there simply *must* be an explanation other than resurrection, even if it either eludes them to be specific about it or they are sometimes pushed into creating fanciful explanations.

In regard to the formation of the Bible, historians *in their capacity as historians*, cannot say that God was in the process of the origin, development, and recognition of the church's Scriptures. Christians, however, do make that claim. Yet how do Christians know that God was involved in the process of canonicity? Those who claim to have had an encounter with God through the proclamation of the good news about Jesus believe that they have an answer beyond what historians can assess or even destroy.

So, the answer to the question above here is *no*. Historians cannot *as historians* affirm the core beliefs of the church about its faith or about divine inspiration of the Bible and its origins. That is beyond the historian's scope of inquiry, but that does not mean that the church's affirmation of the activity of God is wrong. There are elements of faith that are real and yet beyond historical critical inquiry. Much of what I have been doing in this small book is showing what credible historians can affirm about the Bible, but meanwhile Christians historically have affirmed the inspiration of the Bible and its importance for Christian faith, but that is a faith conclusion rooted in one's encounter with God through faith, and billions of followers of Jesus throughout history affirm the reality of their experience with God.

86. Was God involved in the writing of Scripture and the formation of the Bible?

The answer is yes, if we are speaking from the perspective of faith, but not if speaking from the perspective of historical critical inquiry since historians cannot address questions of divine activity. Christians have long believed that God inspired their Scriptures and often cite biblical support for that position, as we have seen above, but the belief that God prompted the biblical authors to write what they believed was a revelation of the will and proclamation of God is beyond historical investigation and historical scholars can only say that this was a popular belief in early Christianity and Judaism of late antiquity. However, such affirmations are not beyond the faith experience of Christians who order their lives in accordance with the will of God and their Scriptures. A historian *as a historian* cannot make such affirmations. Many affirmations from faith are believed to be true, but they cannot be proved by current positivistic perspectives of historical inquiry. That, however, does not mean that such affirmations are untrue. Christian faith believes that there is a reality that is beyond the historian's inquiry.

While the above question is not one that historians can answer, they can aid considerably in Christian understanding of much of what is in the Bible. For instance, a believer cannot know who the Pharisees, Herodians, Essenes, or other groups were by faith, but faith can be enhanced by the work of historians who can answer those kinds of questions and clarify the historical context in which early Christian faith was born. That context can be understood better through historical research. These and many other questions can be answered by the historians who have added greatly to our understanding of the Christian faith, but historians cannot address the fundamental questions of our faith, such as who God is, what the will of God is, whether Jesus had a special relationship with God, or whether he had an essential role in the salvation of humanity. But these kinds of questions are answered in the Bible and by faith for those put their trust in God and welcome Jesus as their Lord and Christ. Those matters are not for the historian to answer one way or the other but are discovered in the context of faith within the community of faith.

The above comments often appear to believers to challenge their Christian faith, but that is not the case. Christian faith makes genuine and important affirmations that go beyond historical inquiry and the result of that is a new empowering and even transforming experience with God and a sense of God's forgiveness and hope beyond the grave.

There is clearly a point beyond which historians as historians cannot go. They can affirm with considerable certainly that Jesus of Nazareth was crucified on a cross by the Romans around 29–30 CE, but they have no means to affirm that he died for the sins of the world or that whoever believes in him will have eternal life. The major tenets of Christian faith affirm that God was in the processes that led to the death and resurrection of Jesus as well as the formation of the Bible. Historians have no ability to say credibly what happened in the resurrection of Jesus or speak about how God was and is involved in the history of the development of the church or in its development of a biblical canon. This does not mean that the church has to be silent on such matters. The followers of Jesus are not limited to the historical-critical restrictions of inquiry and regularly affirm that God was involved in a group of prophets and apostles in producing the church's Scriptures and in the real historic events of the Christian faith.

Christians are not locked into the methodological restrictions of historical inquiry that limit historical knowledge to explanations referencing natural cause-and-effect events, the historians' experience, analogies to other historical events that can be reasonably argued, or to other similar non-unique explanations. Historians do not deal with God but limit themselves to human activity in its social environment.

Those Christian apologists who want to prove the resurrection of Jesus historically, affirming the historical validity of Christian faith, often do not understand how historians do history nor the constraints on their discipline, especially the underlying metaphysics of how historians do historical inquiry. Christian faith does not and cannot restrict itself to the limitations of the historian, which in practice ignore (or even deny) the presence of God in history. Christian faith is inextricably bound to history but acknowledges that there is *a reality beyond the scope of the historian's craft*. Christian faith is rooted both in history, for Jesus lived and died in Palestine in the first century CE, but also in the activity of God that is beyond historical inquiry.

As both a historian and theologian, I can argue credibly that Jesus lived and died in Palestine in the first century and was crucified and buried, even that the tomb was empty after Jesus was buried in it, and that within a few short days the church emerged believing that God had raised Jesus from the dead. Those are very credible historical statements that are essential for an understanding Christian faith, but faith is also rooted in God, who is inaccessible to the historian's gaze, and in the risen Christ. The reality of God and divine activity is *not* beyond faith and biblical faith affirms that divine activity happens in history.

A response to the above question is important because it also relates to many of the critical issues concerning the formation of the Bible that we have focused on throughout this book. Can Christian faith relate to God's activity in history and still be intelligible to unbelievers and historians in a sophisticated world with its many scientists and historians who follow a craft that in practice denies or ignores the theological issues that are central to Christian faith? Fortunately, Christians are not limited to the historian's method, though many persons who claim to be followers of Jesus have tried to limit the scope of their faith to what can be argued by historical research. I would say to them that they do not have to be silent on the issues that are central to their faith. From the church's beginning there was a transformative faith that brought courage and even boldness to a band of believers who were willing to give their lives to make the Christ they followed available to all. They saw something in Jesus that transformed them and gave them hope for the future. Any historian can affirm that the early followers of Jesus believed that he was sent from God with the mission of being the Messiah whom they had hoped would come. Indeed, the first followers of Jesus were not silent about their beliefs and eventually laid down their lives to proclaim him and the reality of their faith in him. The historian, as a historian, cannot prove that they were right in their assessment of Jesus, or affirm that Jesus of Nazareth had a special relationship with God and was sent by God to initiate the kingdom of God, but the followers of Jesus can affirm it!

87. Is there subjectivity in biblical faith and can it ever be based on rational logic, history, and science?

Yes, of course, there is considerable subjectivity in faith, and *faith cannot prove to unfaith that it is anything more than faith*. Christian faith is rooted in the biblical call to obedience to God and submission to that call which comes through the proclamation of the gospel about Jesus. That submission and obedience to that call has led countless millions to a faith that has been transformative in their lives. That faith is "merely" subjective in the eyes of the non-believer, but not to those who have found faith in Christ.

There is a reality that goes beyond objective historical data, which does not acknowledge God or divine unique activity in humanity.

Luke Timothy Johnson has shown the importance of the experience with God in Christian faith and he emphasizes the significance of a person's experience with God through Christ, in New Testament times and today.[1] Christians from the beginning have chosen the path of faith in the God who reveals himself in the proclamation of the good news, or gospel. That experiential aspect has been central to Christian faith from its beginning. Historically the church has affirmed the importance of faith in the God who comes to us in his Son and who continues to come to us in his written word, but because God and the activity of God is beyond the area of inquiry for historians, those who emphasize their experience of God are often accused of being "subjective," which is a bad term to those who want to root faith in science and history.

Well-meaning Christian apologists often appear to be fearful of Christians "slipping" into a subjective proclamation of their faith rooted in their personal experience, one that cannot be examined objectively by historians or scientists. It is personal and is anchored in the revelation of God in the church's proclamation rather than in what we can prove historically. While such well-intended persons mean well, they often ignore the importance of faith, and the fact that God had to reveal his *revelation* to human beings who could not arrive at it on their own. If they could achieve that through their own scholarship, it would be something like a salvation of works, which the Christian community historically rejects as unbiblical. They also tend to ignore or minimize the role of the Spirit in their biblical inquiry, but that too is essential to Christian faith. Christian faith does not deny the activity of God in events in history.

Of course, if one could prove that Jesus never existed or that he was not crucified or that the resurrection did not occur, that would be devastating to Christian faith. Christian faith is always connected to history. But no one seriously argues any more that Jesus never existed or that he didn't die on a cross. Such views were promoted and became popular for a short time during the discovery of the Talpiot tomb in Jerusalem promoted by a popular Canadian journalist named S. Jacobovici. He claimed that Jesus had survived the crucifixion, had married Mary Magdalene, and together they had a son, and that their bones were found in a first-century ossuary. That fanciful notion was demonstrably

---

1. See his very important earlier study: Johnson, *Religious Experience*.

proven to be false. Jewish and Christian scholars argued at length in Jerusalem in 2008 that this journalist's assertions were bogus and nonsense.[2] Forty-nine out of fifty scholars, both Jews and Christians, came to that conclusion with only one scholar suggesting that the proposal was even "possible." My point is that *if* such claims could be proven, that *would* disturb Christian faith. This is not unlike the famous Gospel of Jesus' Wife that caused another alarming stir in Christianity a few years ago before it was seen to be a forgery. Because Christian faith is rooted in history, critics will likely continue to be around for a long time seeking to find ways that undermine Christian faith. Christianity cannot be reduced to timeless truths, for faith is rooted in time and space, so Christians must be interested in history as well as faith and faith cannot ignore the incidentals of historical inquiry, which sometimes do not fit fanciful notions about the activity of God.

Christians should never fear being "subjective" or deny that they have a faith perspective on God's activity in history. That faith is transformative, as Saint Paul discovered: he once persecuted the followers of Jesus but was himself transformed by an experience that took place on the Damascus Road, an experience that is beyond historical inquiry (Acts 9:1–22; cf. 22:1–16). Attempts to explain away Paul's experience in terms of a meltdown of some kind induced by his feelings of guilt for the persecution of Jewish Christians do not hold water. Neither do arguments to the effect that the original disciples' psychological conditions led to their view that Jesus *must* still be with them (a belief they framed in terms of Jewish resurrection beliefs), despite their having no evidence for such a conclusion. Paul claimed that his experience was of a personal encounter with the divine Lord, a revelation of the risen Christ who came him. Paul subsequently became one of the most influential early followers of Jesus. Now, no historian can plausibly deny the remarkable transformation of Paul and all that he went through in his encounter on the Damascus Road and following, but historians cannot conclude that he had a divine experience.

Some Christian apologists may be surprised to find that faith in the Christ who comes to those who hear the message about him is more compelling to people than current philosophical arguments from the

---

2. Among the fifty papers is McDonald, "Burial of Jesus," but see conclusions of the scholars in the whole volume Charlesworth, ed., *Tomb of Jesus?* Jewish and Christian scholars brought forth conclusive evidence against the argument that the Talpiot tomb is where Jesus was buried with his wife and son.

apologists. Some apologetic scholars often say that they "believe" what the Bible says. But as Paul long ago wrote, "One believes with the heart and so is justified and confesses with the mouth and so is saved" and he later says, "Faith comes from what is heard and what is heard comes from the word of Christ" (Rom 10:10, 17). Christian apologists rightly have good responses to the critics who question the historical roots of the Christian faith but they should be cautious about suggesting that Christian faith can be demonstrated historically. That, as mentioned already, would lead to a salvation by works that ignores the role of divine revelation and the role of the Spirit in the Christian proclamation. Salvation cannot be reserved for the smartest among us who has figured out historically the foundations of Christian faith. Of course, the New Testament does not teach a salvation of works nor one that minimizes the faith of the average person, people who do not have the skills to investigate their faith and their Scriptures at the academic level of scholars. That is a dangerous path that has been around for a while, going back to the second- and third-century gnostics who tolerated the simple and poorly educated but raised themselves to a higher level of approval in their esoteric knowledge and awareness of God.

Again, Christians should not be against historical-critical inquiry because it often advances our understanding of the historical context of Christian faith and the many historical and social issues facing churches from their beginning. But faith also recognizes that historical inquiry has limitations, and faith can never be based on the ever-changing arguments of historical scholars who inquire into Christian origins. It is important to be open to learning something new when new discoveries present themselves, but faith can never be rooted in the ever-changing results of historical or scientific inquiry. Faith ultimately grows in a reception and practice of biblical faith, obedience, and hope.

Since the above question is also related to God's actions in the formation of the Bible, I conclude that those theologians who argue for God's activity in the formation of the biblical canon regularly do so *theologically* based on their presuppositions, but not on any presuppositionless historical data. Most Christians believe that the Bible is inspired by God, and their Scriptures have their origin in the activity of God, but they cannot *prove* its inspiration to a critical historian who does not share their assumptions about the existence of God or divine activity in Jesus the Christ. That does not mean that Christians should abandon their beliefs about God's activity in the canonical processes, but only that secular historians cannot affirm divine activity in that process. There are always limitations on what reality historians can address given their self-imposed limitations noted above. In the New Testament, God reveals himself in his Son and faith in him comes by hearing the proclaimed word of Christ (Rom. 10:17)—"Blessed are those who have not seen and yet believe" (John 20:29). Faith is never by sight. Even though apologists provide valuable information that shows that the historical roots of Christianity are credible, they cannot prove to the unbeliever or historians that the activity of God was in those roots.

88. Do the variants or differences in the surviving New Testament manuscripts affect their scriptural status?

As we saw at the end of chapter 1 in question 26, there were many variants in the surviving Hebrew Bible and Christian Old Testament manuscripts and these are often troubling to new students of the church's Scriptures. Along with the positions and data noted earlier in regard to the Old Testament manuscript variants, I broaden here that discussion to expand Christian perspectives. When readers begin learning about the formation of the Bible the question about the variants or differences in the surviving biblical manuscripts is often asked. When readers become aware of the numerous variants in the New Testament biblical manuscripts, which run well into some hundreds of thousands, many can understandably become quite concerned. When, for example, they read the New Testament Gospels' reports of the same teachings (sermon on the Mount) or events (death and resurrection narratives) and realize multiple differences, the question arises about which one can be trusted or even can any of them be trusted? This is not unlike the differences noted earlier in the "mysterious numbers" in the Hebrew Bible's Kings and Chronicles when telling the same story and not unlike the many thousands of variants in the texts of the biblical manuscripts, such as how the Gospel of Mark ends, whether at 16:8 or 16:9–20, or which version of Jesus' sayings is the correct one as in the case of John 3:13 or John 7–8.

A major obstacle to overcome has to do with common beliefs in many churches that God divinely inspired the Bible and therefore the Bible must be perfect. That notion is often rooted in a popular syllogism, namely:

1. God is perfect;

2. God inspired the Bible;

3. so the Bible is perfect.

There can be no imperfections in an inspired Bible. If such believers find what appears to be an imperfection in our biblical manuscripts, it is not uncommon for them to offer fanciful explanations that have little support or contend that they were not there when the biblical authors wrote the "original manuscripts" (autographs). This comes from the notion that a perfect God who inspired the Bible must have inspired the authors to write perfect "original manuscripts" (the autographs), and those have not survived. Any errors belong to flawed copies, not the flawless originals. Since none of those autographs have survived, this is only a belief that cannot be backed up with what is "perfect." But if God intended the church to have a perfect Bible, and went to the lengths of inspiring one, why did God not preserve it for the church, and why not inspire a perfect interpretation of the Bible? Thus far no one argues for the latter, so . . . .

Another syllogism that is seldom considered is the well-known adage that to err is human and since the Bible was written by humans, then the Bible must have errors. The problem with both syllogisms is that neither is based on the data of the Scriptures themselves or their historic transmission. Biblical scholars acknowledge that there are many problems, variants, and differences in the manuscripts that have survived.[3] What appears to be missing in the discussion is the implicit denial of the humanity of the authors of Scripture when we insist upon a flawless Bible. While the imperfection of humanity, including that of Scripture's authors, is quickly seen in the biblical stories (Peter most notably, but also David, Paul, and others), it is often claimed, without any biblical support, that their humanity was divinely suspended while they were writing inspired Scripture.

It is well-known that over the years God continues to use weak and frail human beings to accomplish the divine will and mission in the world. Years ago, I was invited to a luncheon to hear Billy Graham speak to about a thousand clergy and he freely admitted that he sometimes made mistakes or errors in judgment, yet no one in the history

---

3. For collections of examples of such variants or problems in the manuscripts that survive, see Beegle, *Scripture, Tradition, and Infallibility*; Achtemeier, *Inspiration and Authority*. See also McDonald, *Forgotten Scriptures*, 201–21; and Licona, *Why Are There Differences?* and his more recent *Jesus Contradicted*.

of Christianity has preached the gospel to more people or had greater results than he had. There is no record that God suspended the humanity of the authors of Scripture when they wrote their sacred texts, nor do the biblical authors themselves make that claim, and yet God has used those sacred texts whose humanity is often clearly present in order to transform the lives of millions of people.

While the Bible is a primary authority for Christians today and it is regularly read in all church services, we must still remember that Jesus said that *he* was the final authority (Matt 28:19) and he never transferred that authority to the Bible or to anyone else. In a real sense the Bible is a *derived* authority that points its readers to the final authority—*God!* God used human beings to write the divine message God wanted to convey and their humanity sometimes shows.

There are also things in the Scriptures that are "gospel," that is, those are the things that are foundational and essential for Christian faith, such as that God is creator of the heavens and the earth, that Jesus the Christ died for the sins of humanity and so on, but there are also some things that are sometimes called "culture," such as women wearing covering over their heads or keeping most of the Old Testament laws that were meant for the Jews, but most of the 613 commands in the Old Testament are not for the church (Lev 12–15). There are principles in both Testaments that are essential for all of God's people (e.g., Mic 6:8; Mark 8:34–36; Gal 3:28 and many more). Many commands need to be understood within the ancient cultures in which they were written, commands that are no longer as relevant or essential, such as "wives be subject to your husbands" or "slaves obey your earthly masters." Some things in the Scriptures need to be followed even today, such as the imperative to live a moral life and the call to advance the Christian mission, but some things are less clear. Hence, it is important to examine the Scriptures in terms of what is "gospel," and thus necessary for Christians in all times, and what is "culture," which may not be true for all times. Most Christians agree that there are some things Scripture teaches that are no longer necessary for the churches to follow, but some biblical admonitions are "gospel" and are essential for Christian faith (Rom 10:9; John 3:16) for all time. Paul and later Justin Martyr and others recognized the limits of some Old Testament laws for gentiles or all Christians. Even Paul himself, who lived by the Jewish Law (Acts 16:3; 18:18; 20:6, 17; 21:26–27; 1 Cor 9: 19–23), acknowledged the limited adherence to those laws required of gentile followers of Christ.

As we will see in the next chapter, divine use of imperfect individuals is well known in the church, past and present, and many such individuals have had an important impact on the history of the church. Both the divine inspiration of the Scriptures and the humanity of those who penned them will be explored below, but for here even casual readers will often see the different reports of the same stories in the Bible. Occasionally some problems are not easily resolved, yet Christians often thank God for the Scriptures that have led to the transformed lives of those who follow their teachings. The biblical books can be both inspired by God and produced by humans who were led by the Spirit and whose humanity was not suspended in the process.

The importance of the Bible for the church today must not be underestimated. More than any other writings in antiquity it points us to the final authorities for our faith, namely God, his Son Jesus the Christ, and his Holy Spirit. It declares to us who God is and the will of God for his people, but it also identifies who Jesus is and what he has done for the salvation of humanity. While it is often suggested that the Bible was an essential book for the church, there was a time (several centuries in fact) when the early church did not have a Bible. They had some Scriptures, of course, but generally not a complete Bible. They were clearly influenced by some books from the Old Testament, but even that part of the Bible was not settled for Christians for centuries. When the church was born (Acts 2), they had *no* New Testament writings at all. The church today is blessed to have a complete Bible, but the formation of the New Testament took centuries to develop and to this day churches still do not agree on the scope of their Old Testament. This is not to deny the value of the Bible for churches today but only to say that the earliest followers of Jesus did not have what we possess and yet they survived initially with the church's proclamation, their limited Old Testament Scriptures, the creedal summaries of their faith, baptismal and eucharistic affirmations, and the hymns. They faced many challenges from within their communities and from without by the authorities, but they survived and even grew in number.

89. Can the church survive without a Bible?

Yes, of course, and the church did precisely this for several centuries after it was born. But the value of the Bible for churches today cannot be underestimated. The church at first existed with only *some* Old Testament writings and the oral traditions about Jesus circulating in the congregations. The early followers of Jesus recognized the importance of their Hebrew Scriptures (most often translated in Greek for them) but their Old Testament, like the Jews' Hebrew Scriptures, was not complete or fixed when the church began. As the Christian writings were being produced, they were regularly read in churches and some of them, especially the Gospels, were read in an authoritative way as soon as they were circulating in churches. That, of course, is because they focused on the Lord of the church, Jesus the Christ. But the earliest followers of Jesus did not have the Gospels until between the 60s to the 90s CE (Mark most likely was the first Gospel written and John likely the last).

It took centuries for the ancient churches to recognize several of their New Testament Scriptures and also to form the Bible as we now have it. Most of the early churches only had partial collections of the Christian Scriptures that they later called their New Testament. Most often those collections included only one or sometimes two of the Gospels and a few letters of Paul plus another book or two. Of the surviving scriptural papyrus manuscripts only fourteen had more than one book in them. No doubt some of the Jewish Scriptures and some of the early Christian writings that were later called Scripture were read in churches from their beginning, but it took the churches over a hundred years before acknowledging *some* of the New Testament writings as Scripture. In the third and early fourth centuries during the widespread persecutions of the churches, many churches had their sacred texts confiscated and destroyed, but the church's core faith continued and even survived in those times despite having their property and Scriptures taken from them and destroyed and often suffering painful persecutions to martyrdom. What allowed the early churches to grow and prosper without a Bible is that from their beginning they had a proclamation that inspired them, creeds that reminded them of a summary of their core beliefs, teachings from their church leaders that encouraged them, hymns that blessed and inspired them, and long-standing affirmations at their baptisms and eucharistic meals (communion). While the earliest followers of Jesus did not have a Bible, what they had reminded them of the core elements of their faith, their mission, and guidelines for moral conduct.

No one would suggest that churches should abandon their Bible or question its value for advancing Christian faith. It is an overwhelming treasure for people of faith. Without the Bible, we would have much less clarity on the identity of God, Christ, and the mission of the church. While we do not know the full scope of the first Scriptures in the time of Jesus or shortly after that, we are well aware that Jesus cited the Hebrew Scriptures and likewise so did the New Testament authors (in Greek mostly). The church was born with some Scriptures, but not yet with a Bible like those present today. Jesus as Lord and Christ was always at the heart and center of authority in early Christianity. Whatever Jesus said settled the matter in question. He was and is the Lord of the church and all authority is derived from him (1 Cor 7:10–12; Matt 28:19; Rom 10:9; Phil 2:6–11). The writings produced closest in time to him came to comprise the New Testament with a few possible exceptions noted earlier, and churches with a full Bible have always been grateful to have this treasure among them.

90. What is the value of studying the Bible in its historical and social context?

It is quite common for persons inside or even outside of the church to see many documentaries about biblical personalities and subjects on their television sets that regularly discuss Christian faith from a historical perspective and often reference the various books that were not included in the Bible. Such programs often raise questions about many biblical teachings and their historic traditions. The information coming out in current documentaries, popular magazines, and media presentations, often lead to confusion for some Christians, especially when discussing the origin of the Bible and the faith affirmed in it. However, the best place to begin to examine historic Christianity is in a careful study of the Bible itself and also the history of its formation. Such a study can offer careful responses and affirmations of the value of the Bible for Christian faith today and answer many of the questions that have been raised in popular media.

A careful historical study of the Bible and what the early churches believed from their beginning to the time when church leaders focused on which sacred books should be read to the people in their churches to inform them of their faith and mission. The questions in chapters 7 and 8 call for an encouraging word to readers who come to the Bible from conservative traditions. The bottom line is that the Bible offers a rule and guide for those who read or hear its message and seek to follow it. Several early church fathers sought to answer which books properly inform the faith and mission of the church and give guidelines for living faithfully for the God who has brought forgiveness to them in his Son, Jesus of Nazareth, the Christ and Lord. If we get too caught up with the questions of academics, including this one, we might miss this closing point. The Bible is only a biblical *canon* if we believe its message and welcome and seek to live according to its teachings. That is when the Bible becomes a canon or rule of faith for the church. If it does not function that way for us, then it is simply a collection of ancient religious writings that may be interesting to read but have little value for those who read it. If we accept the Bible as canon, we accept its authority and its message for our faith and life. If it is not canonical (authoritative) in our faith and living, it is not a biblical canon at all.

91. What are the most important ancient sources for investigating the origin and formation of the Bible?

There are many ancient texts that have been listed above and others that are critically important to arrive at a well-informed understanding of the origin of the Bible. The following is not a complete list, but they are some of the more important ancient sources for a careful inquiry of the emergence of the biblical canons.[4] Here are the most important ancient resources for this study.

A. Primary Ancient Sources for the Study of the Old Testament/Hebrew Bible Canon

The following ancient sources are commonly cited by modern biblical scholars investigating the origins and development of the Old/First Testament or Hebrew Bible. This list is not exhaustive, but the items listed here are centrally important and should not be ignored. Any conclusions regarding the origins and development of the Old Testament canon must take account at least of the following:

1. 2 Kgs 17:13; Ezra 9–10 and Neh 8–9: the reading of the law of Moses, and writings that were authoritative in the fifth century BCE.

---

4. A focus on the most important issues and the debates related to the formation of the Bible are in McDonald and Sanders, eds., *Canon Debate*. I have added more issues in the more recent two-volume work *The Formation of the Biblical Canon* (2017).

2. Sir 49:8–10: Ezekiel, Job, and the Twelve Prophets. See also the context in Sir 44:1—50:25, the "praise of famous men." Is the focus in this passage on sacred literature or holy men?

3. Prologue to Sirach: three groupings of sacred literature. The third group is imprecise, and none of the literature within the groupings is specifically identified.

4. 1 Macc 1:54–57: the destruction of the Jewish sacred writings under the Seleucid tyranny.

5. 2 Macc 2:13–15: Judas Maccabeus's recovery and collection of Jewish sacred writings. The identity of these writings is not clear.

6. 4QMMT: see 6ab–28b, but especially C9–12 (perhaps ca. 150 BCE). This is a very difficult text to discern because of its corruption, but it does describe three or four vague groupings of sacred writings.

7. Letter of Aristeas §308–11 (ca. 110–100 BCE): the origins of the LXX. Only the Law of Moses is mentioned in this tradition.

8. Philo, *Contempl.* 3.25–28 and *Mos.* 2.37–40: three or four categories of sacred writings among the Therapeutae (probably Essenes) in Egypt roughly just before the ministry of Jesus.

9. Luke 11:49–51: Jesus' reference to the martyrs in the Old Testament beginning with the first (Abel) and concluding with the last (Zechariah). Was 2 Chronicles the last book in the Old Testament in Jesus' canon (see 2 Chr 24:2–24) or simply the last martyr mentioned in the Old Testament Scripture? Does this passage suggest a closed biblical canon in the time of Jesus that began with Genesis and closed with the last book in the Writings (*Ketuvim*), namely, 2 Chronicles? This is highly unlikely due to the place of 2 Chronicles in several manuscripts, especially in the Aleppo texts, and due to the repetition of the closing verses of 2 Chronicles in Ezra 1 (which shows that Ezra was written after 2 Chronicles).

10. Luke 24:44: a reference by Jesus to the Law, Prophets, and "psalms." Does "psalms" refer to the whole of the Writings, or does it refer only to the book of Psalms, or simply to some of the psalms? Did the later term "fifths" (Heb. = *hāmîšîôt*), which was used by the rabbinic sages of the second century CE of the book of Psalms and also of all of the Writings, refer to the whole of the Writings in the time of Jesus? Were the "psalms" equal to the later designated Writings?

11. Jub. 2.23-24 (as cited by Epiphanius, *Mens.* 22, ca. 380 CE). Is this the original form of the text, or is it the Qumran or Ethiopic version of the text? Did the original form refer to a twenty-two-book biblical canon?

12. Josephus, *C. Ap.* 1.37-43 (ca. 90 CE), mentions a three-part, twenty-two-book biblical canon. Are the books in each of the three categories of his list identifiable and are they the same as the later and more clearly defined collection called the Tanak? Also on prophecy, see *C. Ap.* 1.8.41; *Ant.* 13, 311-13; *B. J.* 6, 286; 6, 300-9. Did Josephus believe that all prophecy had ceased from the time of Artaxerxes and therefore all Scripture or prophetic writing ended by ca. 400 BCE? Did he view his writings as "inspired"?

13. 4 Ezra 14.22-48 (ca. 90-100 CE), describes the divine translation of ninety-four holy books—twenty-four plus seventy others. This is probably a reference to the sacredness of the apocryphal and pseudepigraphal literature besides a twenty-four-book collection of Hebrew Scriptures. Why would many of the early Christians include this book (4 Ezra) in their sacred collections?

14. Mishnah, completed under the direction of Rabbi Judah Ha-Nasi (ca. 200-210 CE). There is not much focus on a biblical canon and very few references to the Hebrew Scriptures. See m. Yad. 3.2-5 and 4.6 on which books "defile the hands."

15. b. B. Bat. 14b-15a (ca. middle to late second century CE). This is the first reference in Judaism that specifically lists by name the twenty-four books of the Hebrew Bible. It is not clear how representative this list was of mainstream Judaism at that time.

16. Several references in the rabbinic literature indicate a conflict over the place of some books in their sacred collection. On Song of Songs, see m. Yad. 3.5 and b. Meg. 7a; on Ecclesiastes see m. Yad. 3.5 and b. Shabb. 100a; on Ruth see b. Meg. 7a; on Esther see b. Sanh. 100a and b. Meg. 7a; on Proverbs see b. Shabb. 30b; on Ezekiel see b. Shabb. 13b, Hag. 13a and Men. 45a.

17. The church fathers' references to the Old/First Testament Scriptures:

    a. Justin, *Dial.* 100.1; *1 Apol.* 28.1 and 67.3; *Cohort. Graec.* 13 (pseudo-Justin?).

b. Melito's list of Old Testament Scriptures, see Eusebius, *Hist. eccl.* 4.26.12–14.

c. Irenaeus, *Haer.* 2.27.2; 3.3.3; 3.11.8; 3.12.15; 3.14.1–15.1; 3.21.3–4; 3.17.4. See also Eusebius's reference to the biblical canon of Irenaeus in *Hist. ecc.* 5.8.1.

d. Clement of Alexandria, *Strom.* 7.20. In *Hist. ecc.* 6.13.4–8 and 6.14.5–7 Eusebius gives what he claims is Clement's scriptural canon.

e. Origen, *Ep. Afr.* 13; cf. Julius Africanus, *Hist. Sus.*. Eusebius, in *Hist. ecc.* 6.25.3–14, indicates that Origen added the books of the Maccabees (as "outside books") to the Hebrew Bible that he knew from contacts with Jews in the third century CE. On his New Testament, see Eusebius, *Hist. ecc.* 6.25.3–14.

f. Tertullian, *Marc.* 4.2.2,5; *Prax.* 15; and *Praescr.* 32, 36. On Marcion's view of the law and what he did to Luke's Gospel, see *Marc.* 1.29; 4.2; and 5.18.1; *Praescr.* 38.7; *Cult. fem.* 1.3.

g. Eusebius, *Hist. eccl.* 3.3.1–5;3.25.1–7, for his own biblical canon, and compare with 5.8.1; 6.14.; 6.24–25; 7.25.22–27.

h. Jerome, *Prologus in Jeremiam, In libros Salomonis (Chromatio et Heliodoro), In Danielem prophetam, In Ezram, In librum Tobiae, In librum Judith, Comm. Isa.* 3.6.

i. Other church fathers referring to the Old Testament Scriptures in the fourth–fifth centuries include Athanasius (*Ep. fest.* 39); Cyril (*Catech.* 4.33–36); Rufinus (*Symb.* 38); Epiphanius (*Pond.* 22–23; *Pan.* 8.6.1); Hilary of Poitiers (*Prologus in libros Psalmorum* 15); Augustine (*Doct. chr.* 2.13).

18. Canonical lists of the fourth and fifth centuries from both the East and the West.[5]

19. Cairo Geniza. A careful reading of selected texts from this collection of recovered documents in Cairo, Egypt indicates that several writings were deemed sacred among the Jews in Cairo in the eighth and ninth centuries CE, and considerably earlier in some instances. Non-sacred writings were also included in this collection because they contained sacred names and therefore caution is needed in any evaluation of their status within that community.

---

5. See especially Gallagher and Meade, *Biblical Canon Lists*.

20. What holds some of these passages together are texts that united portions of the Old Testament literature. Some of these texts include: Deut 34:1–12; 2 Chr 36:22–23; Prov 25:1; Ezra 1:1–4; and Mal 4:4–6. When were these passages added to tie some larger sections or books of the Old Testament together?

B. Primary Sources for the Study of the New Testament Canon

The following ancient sources are those most often cited by modern scholars investigating the origins and development of the New/Second Testament. Again, this list is not exhaustive, but the items listed here are certainly centrally important for drawing conclusions about the origins and development of the New Testament canon.

1. Apostolic Fathers (writers who, for the most part, followed the writers of the New Testament). Passages that show use of New Testament literature and in some cases recognition of the authority of those writings: (1) 1 Clem. 13.1–3; (2) Barn. 4.14; (3) Ign. *Phld.* 5.1–2; 8:2; (4) Poly. *Phil.* 2.2–3; 3.2; 6.3; 7.1–2; 8.2; 12.1; (5) 2 Clem. 2.4–6; 14.2.

2. Reference to the authority of Jesus' words in early gnostic teaching (Ptolemy, *Flor.* 3.5–8; 4.1, 4; 7.5, 10).

3. Justin's use of New Testament writings to support Christian teaching and worship (Justin, *Dial.* 28.1; 65.2; 84.4; 100.1–8; *1 Apol.* 66, 67).

4. Writings that mention Marcion's limited collection of New Testament Scriptures (*Marcionite Gospel Prologues*), Tertullian, *Marc.* 4.2–5; Adamantius, *Dial.* 2.18; Eusebius, *Hist. eccl.* 6.12.3–6.

5. Irenaeus on heresies and the use of Scripture (*Haer.* 1.26.2; 2.27.2; 2.28.2; 2.35.4; 3.2.2; 3.3.1–3; 3.4.1–2; 3.11.8–9; 3.14.1; 3.15.1; 3.17.4; 4.15.2; 4.29–34).

6. Origen's awareness of New Testament literature (*Comm. Matt.* 15.3, which shows a Marcionite use of Matthew, and *Hom. Jes. Nav.* 7; and see also *Princ.*).

7. Discussion of Scripture, tradition, and authority in the church (Clement of Alexandria, *Strom.* 1.20, on the value of philosophy for understanding God's truth; see also 7.16).

8. Gnostic beliefs and errors (see Irenaeus, *Haer.*, all of book 1, but also 3.3.1).

9. Second-century reference to Paul's writings as Scripture (2 Pet 3:15–16).

10. Reference to Paul in scriptural-like manner to argue his case in Athenagoras, *Res.* 18 (see also 7–8), ca. 180 CE.

11. Theophilus's calling on Autolycus to reverence the Scriptures and then citing Rom 2:7, 1 Cor 2:9, and Rom 2:8–9 (*Autol.* 1.14 and 2.9, 14, 22).

12. Tertullian's discussion of Marcion's editing of Luke and Paul (*Marc.* 1.29; 4.2; 5.18.1; 5.21; and *Praescr.* 32, 36, 38.4–7; *Prax.* 15).

13. Sources that may refer to earlier collections of Scriptures in the second century (Hippolytus, *Haer.* 8.19.1).

14. Discussion and description of the burning of sacred books during the Diocletianic persecution (303 CE) in *Gesta apud Zenophilum* and *Acta Saturnini* 18.

15. Passages in Eusebius that list or discuss Christian writings: (1) his own perspective (*Hist. eccl.* 3.3.1–5; 3.25.1–7); (2) Papias's preference for oral sources over written sources (3.39.4); (3) Martyrs of Lyons and Vienna (5.1.3–63); (4) the Montanists (5.14–19); (5) on persecution and burning of sacred books (8.5–6); (6) on Irenaeus's New Testament canon and LXX collection (5.8.1–15); (7) on Origen's Old Testament and New Testament canon (6.24–25); see also Rufinus's translation of *Hom. Jes. Nav.* 7; (8) on Clement of Alexandria's collection of divine names (6.13.4–8; 6.14.1–24); (9) on why Serapion rejected the Gospel of Peter (6.12.1–6); (10) Dionysius's perspective on Scripture (7.25.22–27); (11) on Constantine's role in the churches and his ordering of fifty copies of Scriptures (*V. C.* 2.2–4, 34–3, 65, 68).

16. Other important primary references include:

    1. Epiphanius, *Haer.* 5 and 76; *Mens.*

    2. Filastrius, *Haer.* 40

    3. Council of Hippo, Canon 38

    4. Council of Carthage, Canon 47

    5. Council of Laodicea, Canons 59, 60

6. Jerome: *Prologus galeatus; Epist.* 50 *ad Paulinum; Commentaria in Matthaeum; Epist. Dard.* 2; *Vir. ill.* 5–10, 15, 17, 36, 41, 63, 81, 135

17. Some of the more important New Testament canonical lists are as follows:

   1. Eusebius, *Hist. eccl.* 3.25.1–7 (ca. 303–325) from Palestine/Western Syria

   2. Catalogue in Codex Claramontanus (ca. 303–367) from Alexandria, Egypt

   3. Cyril of Jerusalem, *Catechetical Lectures* 4.33 (ca. 350) from Palestine

   4. Muratorian Catalogue (ca. 375–400) from the West

   5. Athanasius, *Ep. fest.* 39 (367) from Alexandria, Egypt

   6. Mommsen Catalogue (365–90) from Northern Africa

   7. Epiphanius, *Pan.*76.5(374–77) from Palestine/Western Syria

   8. *Apostolic Canons* (ca. 380) from Palestine/Western Syria

   9. Gregory of Nazianzus, *Carmen de veris scripturae libris* 12.31 (383–90) from Asia Minor

   10. African Canons (ca. 393–419) from Northern Africa

   11. Jerome, *Epist.* 53 (ca. 394) from Palestine

   12. Augustine, *Doct. chr.* 2.8.12 (ca. 396–97) from Northern Africa (see also 2.3.1)

   13. Amphilochius, *Iambi ad Seleucum* 289–319 (ca. 396) from Asia Minor

   14. Rufinus, *Symb.* 36 (ca. 400) from Rome/Italy

   15. Pope Innocent, *Letter to Exsuperius*, bishop of Toulouse (ca. 405) from Rome/Italy

   16. Syrian catalogue of St. Catherine's (ca. 400) from Eastern Syria

   17. The collections in the following important biblical manuscripts:

       Codex Vaticanus (ca. 331–350) likely from Alexandria/Egypt; *Codex Sinaiticus* (ca. 331–350) from Alexandria/Egypt; *Codex Alexandrinus* (ca. 425) from Asia Minor; *Syriac Peshitta* (ca. 400) from Eastern Syria

CHAPTER 9

Inspiration and the Bible

AMONG SOME OF THE most debated issues in current Christianity, especially among evangelical Christians, has to do with the inspiration of the Bible. It has become a divisive issue for many Christians and will be the focus in what follows.

92. What is meant by "inspiration" and how is it applied to the Bible?

"Inspiration" is a Latin translation of the Greek word *theopneustos*, which is found only once in the Bible, in 2 Tim 3:16. It literally means "God-breathed" or "divinely breathed." The Latin church fathers translated it in 2 Tim 3:16 as "divinely inspired." In that context, Scripture is divinely breathed (or "inspired by God"). The dominant assumption in churches is that the Scriptures had their origin in the activity of God and did not come from human initiation, but in God alone. In the context of 2 Tim 3:15–17, the passage has the LXX translation of the Hebrew Scriptures in view. Since in the context of 2 Timothy the Jews in the diaspora regularly used the Greek translation of their sacred texts and not the Hebrew. Later the designation "inspired" (or "inspiration") was also applied to all the church's Scriptures.

Inspiration (*theopneustos*; or "God-breathed") was not only used in antiquity in reference to sacred Scriptures, but also of all texts that were believed to truly convey the Christian message, as well of individuals who spoke or wrote the truth of God. Gregory of Nyssa (*Apologia hexaemeron*, ca. 330–95) describes Basil's (ca. 330–79 CE) commentary on the creation story and claims that his work was inspired and that his words even surpassed those of Moses in terms of beauty, complexity, and form, saying that it was an "exposition given by inspiration of God . . . [admired] no less than the words composed by Moses himself." This is quite remarkable since the text in question is compared to the church's Old Testament Scriptures, that is, the words of Moses, and Gregory of Nyssa thought Basil's words were superior to Moses' words! This reference obviously does not make a qualitative distinction between biblical texts and later ecclesiastical texts.

From these and many other examples, the early church fathers who used this term did not limit inspiration to their Scriptures or even to literature alone. In his *Dialogue with Trypho*, Justin Martyr argues that "the prophetical gifts remain with us even to the present time. And hence you ought to understand that [the gifts] formerly among your nation [Israel] have been transferred to us" (*Dial.* 82, ANF; see also *Dial.* 87–88). He was speaking of the present prophetic gifts and not just those of the past or only of Scripture. The early church fathers did not confine inspiration to an already past apostolic age, as we saw in arguments against the Montanist controversy in the latter third of the second century (see Eusebius, *Hist. eccl.* 5.14–19). The traditional assumption that the early Christians believed that only the canonical writings were inspired is not demonstrable from the available ancient evidence. Also, the rabbinic notion that "when the latter prophets died, that is, Haggai, Zechariah, and Malachi, then the Holy Spirit came to an end in Israel" (t. Sotah 13:2), was simply not shared by the early church fathers, the primary interpreters of the church's core teachings.

Among the most common biblical texts cited in support of the belief that God initiated the emergence of the church's Scriptures is 2 Pet 1:20–21, which emphasizes that no prophecy or Scripture "ever came by human will, but by men and women moved by the Holy Spirit [who] spoke from God." Often Jesus' words in John 10:34 are mentioned in reference to inspiration since it states that the "word of God" came to individuals and "the Scripture cannot be annulled." That belief is widely attested in the church fathers in early church history, but there were still concerns expressed about the human element that was involved in the production of the church's Scriptures and how that can be understood in the Scriptures themselves.

93. Does inspiration assume a perfect Bible?

The assumption that the autographs (original manuscripts written by the biblical authors) were perfect is an assumption that is commonly held and is based on the belief that God inspired and gave rise to the church's Scriptures, so they are perfect in every way. That common assumption is difficult to demonstrate when examining the biblical texts, as we saw earlier with the numerous variants in the biblical literature when comparing different texts dealing with the same story or event. The idea of perfect autographs produced by the biblical authors is commonly held by many Christians today and supports their faith about an inerrant or infallible Bible.

However, the familiar modern doctrine of biblical inspiration appears to deny the obvious humanity of those inspired to proclaim, teach, and write the truth and revelation that God gave to them as they were writing the Scriptures, and it assumes that their humanity was suspended while they were writing. It ignores the usual human imperfections, such as misspellings, sometimes poor grammar, and failure to complete sentences—all of which we find in the Bible—and such argument of suspension of humanity and proneness to error while writing Scripture is a statement of faith that cannot be demonstrated.

That view faces many challenges in the biblical text itself and often has to resort to fanciful ways of explaining away seeming imperfections. For example, the case of the number of times the cock crowed before Peter denied knowing Jesus. To smooth over the differences between the Gospels, some feel compelled to construct highly implausible scenarios in order for all the Gospel accounts to be literally historically accurate, but ironically these accounts actually conform to *none* of the Gospels. There are many other such examples. The other way to deal with the obvious flaws in the current biblical manuscripts is to say that the flaws were not there in the "original manuscripts," the autographs. Again, that is a faith conclusion that is not supported by any known evidence, because those autographs no longer exist, but it allows for some to maintain a belief in the existence at a past time of perfect original manuscripts. That view, as we saw, has roots in Origen and Augustine, but cannot be demonstrated.

Should one take a pen and paper with the goal of making a copy of the Bible, or even a book in it like Isaiah or Matthew or Luke, it would soon become obvious, after the lifting of the pen after every five or six letters, a common feature in ancient copying, that it was necessary to refill the stylus or writing instrument. That would turn into a very large amount of work and the variants of copying the same text hour after hour would surely lead to many variants or errors. Even with modern pens, such a project will take a considerable amount of time, and one will tire easily and perhaps skip a line or two or even misspell a word here or there in the process of depending on one's skill and memory of copying whatever text lies before one. It is easy to understand the multiple errors in the surviving biblical manuscripts. If we consider that there would be several breaks during the day for meals or a rest, and at the end of the day they were working using weak lamps, and they had to stop to get (or make) new pens for continuing the writing, one can easily imagine how many errors would occur in the simple copying of a single manuscript even by a literate amateur or a professional copier. Then imagine how many mistakes would occur in the preparation of thousands of copies of the Scriptures by hand. One can easily understand why there are no two ancient manuscripts that are exactly alike, even when copying the same book again and again.

Most of the mistakes or errors are easily corrected by comparing them with other manuscripts from earlier or even contemporary times. That comparison did not always happen in antiquity and copiers may not have had access to more than one manuscript from which to copy the text they were preparing for church use. Throughout the study of copying scriptural texts many variants or simple errors have been found in the surviving manuscripts. Like the Old Testament books that were written mostly in Hebrew with some Aramaic and subsequently were translated into Greek between roughly 280 BCE and 130 BCE, New Testament books were also hand copied often by amateur copiers, and no two manuscripts or copies of the Bible are exactly the same until Johannes Gutenberg's printing of the Bible with the newly invented printing press with moveable type in 1455–1456 in Mainz, Germany.

All of this is to say that there is no perfect Bible that was hand copied and the possibility of multiple errors in the long process of making a single copy of a larger manuscript makes the number of variants in the ancient manuscripts astronomical. It is clear that God did not see fit to preserve exact copies of the church's Scriptures. This suggests that there must be another way to speak about the inspiration of the Bible that despite the humanity obvious in the production and preservations of the biblical texts God continues to speak through it to the people of faith.

94. What is allegory and how was it used to affirm the inspiration of Scripture?

How did the ancient churches deal with the obvious humanity in the church's Scriptures? How did the church fathers deal with the apparent contradictions or errors in the Bible since Scripture was universally believed to come from the perfect God? How could they explain the many problems in the Scriptures and how could they understand the contribution of the human authors of them? Most of the church fathers affirmed that the Scriptures were perfect, but many also recognized the apparent historical errors in them. One of the common early means of affirming the inspiration of the perfect Scriptures was through the use of allegory, that is by spiritualizing the data of the Scriptures when there appeared to be a problem or to discern more than the historical data conveyed in the Scriptures, as in the case of unexplained numbers. For instance, in John 21:11 there is a mention of 153 fish without any explanation of that number, but with the use of allegory a deeper spiritual meaning could be discerned.

There were several available options for handling problem texts, namely: (i) one could try to give what some have called fanciful explanations that would harmonize them; or (ii) one could claim that the copiers of the Scriptures were careless in their work;[1] or (iii) one could argue that there were intentional changes made to the texts by enemies of the Christians; or (iv) one could argue that what was called an error actually revealed a deeper spiritual meaning that could be recovered through the use of allegory. It was argued that since the apostle Paul made use of allegory to reinterpret the stories of Sarah and Hagar (Gal 4:21–30), then it must be okay for church fathers to do the same. The best-known users of allegory were Origen and Augustine in the third and fourth centuries, but others also made use of it as well to address the more obvious differences and difficulties in the church's Scriptures.

The Greeks made use of allegory to deal with the obvious human errors in what they considered sacred texts, such as Homer's *Iliad* and *Odyssey*. How could the Greeks continue to welcome the iconic sacred texts without finding a way to interpret the unacceptable in them? They

---

1. Augustine answered the question about the problems in the church's Scriptures by suggesting that the autographs ("original manuscripts") did not have those problems (see below his *Letter* 82.34 to Jerome). That view has continued in some churches and is still quite popular to this day.

used allegory to discern the intended deeper spiritual meaning of challenging texts of sacred writings. One well-known interpreter of the Jewish Scriptures, mostly the Pentateuch, was Philo from Egypt (ca. 20 BCE–40 CE), who adopted the well-known method of interpretation, allegory, to deal with the anthropomorphic language in the Hebrew Scriptures, such as talk of the "hand of God," the "eye or God," and such like. God is not made in our human image and that had to be dealt with, so Philo used allegory to do that. Several early church fathers followed his example in order to address the obvious difficulties in the church's Scriptures and to find a deeper spiritual meaning in them.

Allegory appeared to be a common useful means of addressing the problems for several church fathers, beginning with Clement of Alexandria in the second century. Philo, Clement, and Origen were all from Alexandria and doubtless Philo was familiar to the early church fathers who lived there. They concluded that the historical problems in their Scriptures indicated that the texts had a powerful life-changing story to tell and it could best be told with allegory; that is, they recognized the human element in the sacred texts and some errors, but because God inspired the writing, it had to be perfect. The way they found to clarify the historical problems, such as we see in the Gospels, was with the use of a spiritual interpretation of those texts to bring out their deeper spiritual meaning (see multiple examples of this in Origen's *Comm. Jo.* 10, in which he points to many historical problems, and see also Augustine's lengthy writings on the *Harmony of the Gospels*). The apostle Paul's use of allegory (Gal 4:21—5:1) made it easier to justify using allegory to deal with difficult issues. Allegory was emphasized for a time but soon fell out of acceptance and more "reasonable" interpretations without allegory emerged, such as Chrysostom's claim that God condescended to human language with all of its problems to make clear the message of salvation.

In the third century Origen and later Chrysostom both saw the problems in the Scriptures and tried to address them. Both of them acknowledged that God "accommodated" the divine message to human language to make understandable to humans the message of God (Origen) or "condescended" (Chrysostom) to the language that humans spoke and understood to clarify to humans the essence of Christian faith and the salvation God had for humanity.

Chrysostom likened this to the incarnation of the Christ who came in human form to bring with clarity the message of God to humanity. This had some parallel, though not exactly, with the incarnation, namely for

God to communicate his will to humanity, he sent his Son in human flesh to tell the will of God and to bring the hope of forgiveness and eternal life. Again, the parallels are not exact, but the notion of God condescending to the language of humanity to communicate better to humans his will was thought important in early Christianity by some church fathers who acknowledged the historical problems in the church's Scriptures.

Modern scholars such as Paul Achtemeier, Dewey Beegle, Michael Graves, and Michael Licona have adopted something similar by acknowledging the humanity in the Scriptures but also acknowledging the divine message in them that is nonetheless transformative.[2]

95. Does inspiration involve divine "possession" of scriptural authors? Hellenistic, Jewish, and some ancient Christian perspectives.

This question takes us into a study of the ancient Greeks who believed that the best writings of antiquity, especially those of Homer (the *Iliad* and the *Odyssey*) and Hesiod, had divine origins and that the authors themselves were "possessed" by supernatural power when they wrote what was divinely dictated to them. Just as some classical authors made use of allegory to deal with the humanity of classical texts with errors or unpopular notions that tended to humanize God, so, too, did Philo, followed by some early Christians who employed it to deal with the issue of the humanity (including factual or moral problems) in the church's Scriptures.

But some also indicated that prophetic figures appear to have been possessed by the divine and could not act on their own. The following examples illustrate this. In Plato's response to Meno, he indicated that wisdom came from soothsayers and diviners who "utter many a true thing when inspired but have no knowledge of anything they say." And subsequently he asks, "May we, Meno, rightly call those men divine who, having no understanding, yet succeed in many a great deed and word." He adds that "we can say of the statesmen [who speak wisdom] that they are divine and *enraptured, as being inspired and possessed of God when they succeed in speaking many great things, while knowing naught of what they say*" (Plato, *Meno* 99 C, D; LCL. Emphasis added). Later he emphasizes to

---

2. See Achtemeirer, *Inspiration and Authority*; Beegle, *Scripture, Tradition, and Infallibility*; Graves, *Inspiration and Interpretation*; and Licona, *Differences in the Gospels* and his *Jesus Contradicted*.

Timaeus that the one who has the "gift of divination" does not achieve true and inspired divination "in his rational mind, but only when the power of his intelligence is fettered in sleep or when it is distraught by disease or by reason of some divine inspiration." He concludes that "it is customary to set the tribe of prophets to pass judgments upon these inspired divinations; and they, indeed, themselves are named 'diviners' by certain who are wholly ignorant of the truth that they are not diviners but interpreters of the mysterious voice and apparition, for whom the most fitting name would be 'prophets of things divined.'" (*Tim.* 71E, 72A; LCL).

Philo later indicated that sometimes inspired prophetic figures have passivity in mind saying, "If indeed the mind can ever be at rest; and the best form of all *is the divine possession* or frenzy to which the prophets as a class are subject" (*Heir*, 249; LCL. Emphasis added). He goes on to say that "a prophet (being a spokesman) has no utterance of his own, but all his utterance came from elsewhere, the echoes of another's voice." He then claims that the prophet is "the *vocal instrument* of God smitten and played by his [God's] invisible hand" (*Heir* 258–59; LCL; Emphasis added). Josephus also acknowledged the role of the prophet as largely a passive role, for the prophet is possessed without the ability to act on his own. Speaking also of the role of Balaam (Num 23:11) he said, "Such was the inspired utterance of one *who was no longer his own master* but was overruled by the divine spirit to deliver it" (*Ant.* 4.118; LCL; Emphasis added). He goes on to explain, "For the spirit gives utterance to such language and words as it will, whereof we are all unconscious" and adds "God is mightier than that determination of mine [Balaam speaking] to do this favor . . . [requested by Balak, Num 23:13]" (*Ant.* 4:119–121; LCL). The same could be said of Saul who was *possessed* by the spirit of God and prophesied until his "prophetic frenzy" ended (1 Sam 10:9–13). This may be similar to Acts 2:1–4 in which the apostles were "filled with the Holy Spirit and began to speak in other languages, as the Spirit gave them ability."

Justin, the second-century Christian apologist, contends that while the prophets spoke as it were "personally," they did not write by themselves, "but by the Divine Word who moves them." He notes that what the authors presented was not from themselves, but they came from the Holy Spirit "who descended upon them, chose to teach through them to those who are desirous to learn the true religion" (*1 Apol.* 36, 38; *ANF*). Athanagoras also indicated that the prophetic writings "of Moses or of Isaiah and Jeremiah, and the other prophets, who, lifted in ecstasy *above the natural operations of their minds* by impulses of the Divine Spirit, uttered the things with which they were inspired, the Spirit making use of them as a flute-player breathes into a flute;—what, then do these men say? 'The Lord is our God; no other can be compared with Him'" (*Leg.* 9, ANF).[3]

For some early church fathers, the one receiving a divine word was not conscious of what he or she was receiving. Those who interpreted their divine words, the diviners, were unaware of what they had said. This is not unlike the later Plutarch, the priest at Delphi who told of the oracles, young virgins, were able to sit over a cone in the temple of Apollo and gas fumes put them into a state in which they spoke unintelligible words they did not know, and prophets interpreted them for those seeking guidance in decisions they had to make.[4]

The notion of "possession" by the Holy Spirit in the production of the church's Scriptures minimizes the human involvement in their production and this was a common belief in both Hellenistic paganism and in Hellenistic Judaism (Philo and Josephus). Maximizing the divine origin of the church's Scriptures was sometimes accompanied by minimizing human involvement altogether. However, because the human element is clearly manifested in the Scriptures (different grammar, style, emphases, vocabularies, and different ways to tell the same story in both Old and New Testaments), some church fathers employed commonly known means from the Greeks (possession) to address the human issues in the church's Scriptures.

---

3. The classical texts are briefly noted with their implications for understanding Christian notions of inspiration in Beegle, *Scripture, Tradition, and Infallibility*, 124–49.

4. For an important discussion of this ancient practice at Delphi-Python, see Gunkel et al., "Plutarch and Pentecost," especially 72–82. See also Craig S. Keener's "Excursus on the Pythoness Spirits" in his discussion of the woman with a *pneuma pythona* in Acts 16:16–18 in his *Acts* (2014), 2422–29. He explains the background of the Pythonic oracles at the Temple of Apollo at Delphi and shows some parallels in early Christianity. See also his discussion of the coming of the Spirit in Acts 2:2–3 and some related parallels with manic (madness or frenzy) expressions when the Spirit of God comes upon a person and possesses that person. See also his in-depth discussion of possession in antiquity and the present on pp. 2435–64.

96. Was inspiration a criterion for including a writing in the New Testament?

Inspiration was not a criterion for canonicity, but rather a corollary. That means that while all Scripture was believed to be inspired by God, almost everything else believed to be true—whether in Scripture or in proclamation, either orally or written—was also believed to be inspired by God. Not all such "inspired" writings or teachings were included in the biblical canon. Ignatius of Antioch likewise claimed inspiration for his writings, and they were not included in the New Testament. In his doctoral dissertation at Harvard University, Everett Kalin argued convincingly that in the first five centuries everything that was written for the church and was considered to be true was also believed to be inspired by God. Whatever was not believed to be true was considered heretical and rejected. One of his points is that inspiration was not considered a criterion for canonicity, but rather whatever was considered sacred Scripture was *also* believed to be inspired by God, like other writings that were not later included in the Bible.[5] The Apostolic Fathers—texts such as 1 Clement, Polycarp's *Letter to the Philippians*, Ignatius's letters, Shepherd of Hermas, the Didache, and the Epistle of Barnabas—were not finally accepted as Christian Scripture but all were deemed valuable as edifying writings in many early churches. Athanasius and later Rufinus found several of these writings useful for developing Christian piety and dubbed them "readable" or "ecclesiastical" writings for private reading only. There were several popular writings that were orthodox but not included in the New Testament.

97. Was inspiration limited to the biblical authors?

The early church fathers believed that their Scriptures were inspired, but inspiration alone was not the basis for including those works in the New Testament canon. As we saw earlier, several ancient nonbiblical writers believed that they were inspired as they wrote. We cited above examples of Clement of Rome, who believed what he wrote in 1 Clement was inspired by God (63.2), and Ignatius, who claimed inspiration for his writing to the Philadelphians (Ign. *Phld.* 7.1–2).[6]

---

5. Kalin, "Argument from Inspiration"; and Kalin, "Inspired Community," 541–49.
6. For other examples, see McDonald, *New Testament*, 2:341–47.

Many church fathers agreed on most of the New Testament books but often disagreed on several others. Decisions about several texts were unclear and not unanimous, but in the words of Irenaeus, those books welcomed "were spoken by the word of God and by His Spirit" (*Haer.* 2.28.2; *ANF*). Inspiration appears to be more of an *after recognition* based on whether the truth that had been handed down through apostolic succession was widely perceived. Origen maintained that "the scriptures were written by the Spirit of God, and have a meaning, not such only as is apparent at first sight, but also another which escapes the notice of most" (*Princ.*, Preface 8; *ANF*). It is likely that Irenaeus was the first Christian to allegorize New Testament writings, a sign of their scriptural recognition. Thereafter, Origen and others felt free to allegorize their Scriptures because they were considered inspired of God. In his discrediting the so-called Doctrine of Peter, he says that he can show that it was not written by Peter "or by any other person inspired by the Spirit of God" (*Princ.*, Preface 8; *ANF*). This was based on what he discerned was heretical information in it. It appears that for him the recognition that a text is Scripture also recognizes that it is inspired. On the other hand, heresy and falsehood are not inspired by God. Inspiration was recognized when a text was believed to be in conformity with the church's core traditions passed on in the early churches. It soon became clear that the church's Scriptures were not the only ancient messages or words that were believed to be inspired by God.

From his investigation of the church fathers up to 400, Everett Kalin failed to turn up one example where an orthodox but noncanonical writing was ever called "uninspired"; such a designation appears to have been reserved only for heretical authors. He concludes, "If the scriptures were the only writings the church fathers considered inspired, one would expect them to say so, at least once in a while." He adds that in the early church inspiration applied not only to all Scripture, but also to the Christian community as a whole, as it bore a "living witness of Jesus Christ."[7] Generally only heresy was deemed uninspired because it was contrary to the church's proclamation. It would be more accurate to say that inspiration was not limited to the authors of the New Testament, but by the end of the second century some in the church were beginning to assume that inspired Christian Scripture ceased after the apostolic era. While the early church fathers did not restrict inspiration to scriptural

---

7. Kalin, "Argument from Inspiration" and his later "Inspired Community."

texts, any writings that were not considered inspired by God would not have been included in the church's Scriptures.

How did the early church fathers determine the inspiration of the New Testament writings? That question is difficult to answer since there are no ancient documents that clarify precisely what the characteristics of inspiration in ancient documents are apart from their faithful conveyance of the truth passed on in the churches. As noted already, that was true of teaching and preaching and other non-biblical orthodox texts as well. As a criterion for canonicity, inspiration played no *discernible* role until a document was later identified as sacred Scripture by many churches and it was deemed faithful to the church's core truth, or rule of faith (*regula fidei*) that was passed on in the churches from their beginning. It is not always clear why some writings were welcomed (2 Peter, 2–3 John, Jude, and Revelation) while other equally orthodox writings were not (1 Clement, the letters of Ignatius, the Didache, Shepherd of Hermas, Epistle of Barnabas, and others). In the case of the Didache, Clement of Alexandria concluded that it was Scripture and also said that 1 Clement, Shepherd of Hermas, and Epistle of Barnabas and other noncanonical writings were also "inspired" (see *Strom.* 1.100.4).

The problem the early Christians had in deciding what literature was inspired and should be included in their Scriptures demonstrates a lack of agreement on the meaning of inspiration and how to recognize it, but it also accounts for the variations in the books in various canon lists discussed above and in the surviving ancient biblical manuscripts. The belief in the ongoing prophetic ministry of the Spirit, that called individuals through the proclamation of the good news to faith in Jesus the Christ, was believed by the early church fathers to be resident in their community of faith and in their ministry, just as it was in the first century. They did not distinguish the filling of the Spirit to proclaim God's word from being led by the Spirit or inspired by the Spirit to write it. They believed that God continued to inspire individuals in their proclamation, just as God inspired the writers of the Old and New Testament literature. They believed that the Spirit was the gift of God to the whole church, not just to writers of sacred literature.

There never was any biblical, theological, or ecclesiastical argument in early Christianity that claimed that the Spirit ceased its activity in the church either at the completion of the biblical canon or at any point in its existence. F. F. Bruce rightly concluded that "inspiration is no longer a criterion of canonicity: it is a corollary of canonicity."[8] Metzger agrees saying, "While it is true that the biblical authors were inspired by God, this does not mean that inspiration is a criterion of canonicity. A writing is not canonical because the author was inspired, but rather an author is considered to be inspired because what he has written is recognized as canonical, that is, is recognized as authoritative."[9] Finally, Dunn rejects the notion that the canonical books are canonical "because they are more inspired than other and later Christian writings. Almost every Christian who wrote in an authoritative way in the first two centuries claimed the same sort of inspiration for their writing as Paul did for his."[10] Inspiration alone was never enough in itself to allow a writing to be included in the church's New Testament. Other criteria for the New Testament writings were more in view when those decisions were made, namely, as we saw above, their orthodoxy, widespread use, apostolic authorship, antiquity (closest to the time of Jesus), and the continuing adaptability of a text to address the current issues facing the churches.

Although there was widespread belief in early Christianity that God inspired the Scriptures, the understanding of the role of its human authors varied considerably in the churches. That issue was more complex, and it dealt not only with human participation in writing the church's Scriptures, but eventually how to deal with the problems of harmony in the Scriptures and what appeared to some as errors in the biblical texts. How are Christians to understand the role of human participation in the production of the Scriptures? Multiple attempts were made by the early church fathers to harmonize the Scriptures, as we see in Origen (*Comm. Jo.* 10) and Augustine (four books in his *Harmony of the Gospels*) in which he addresses some 150 such cases. Examples of what the early church fathers noted dealt with who slew Goliath (David in 1 Sam 17:48–52 or Elhanan in 2 Sam 21:19), or the location of the appearances of the risen Christ to the disciples (Galilee in Matthew and Mark or Jerusalem in Luke and John), how many times the cock crowed before Peter denied knowing Jesus, and so on. These problems were well known to several church fathers, who made several attempts to resolve them. An early explanation is that such passages had a dual interpretation: a historical one in which the variances in the biblical texts were clear, but these variances were the Spirit's way to provoke us to look below the surface and

---

8. Bruce, *Canon of Scripture*, 268.
9. Metzger, *Canon of the New*, 257.
10. Dunn, "Has the Canon," 578.

to seek the deeper spiritual meanings discerned through allegory. Others sought to resolve the problems by claiming that the disagreements were not present in the autographs of the Scriptures.

98. Did the early church fathers agree on what inspiration meant?

While from the church's beginning the followers of Jesus affirmed that their Scriptures had their origin in divine activity, and they all agreed that the Scriptures were inspired by God, *they did not all agree on what "inspiration" meant.* Nor did they agree on which books were considered Scripture and inspired by God, though there was considerable agreement among most churches on most of the books in their Scriptures. All believed that the Scriptures *that they recognized* had their origin in God's activity. Most often inspiration referred to the activity of God in conveying his identity, activity in human affairs, and his will for humanity. Inspiration was not a convenient term for addressing the scope of the Christian Scriptures and it was not an easy matter for the church leaders to work through multiple decisions over which sacred texts were Scripture. This of course, leads us back to the question, what did the early churches mean by "inspiration"?

Long ago, James Barr summarized what has often been understood about the role and place of inspiration in the history of the church. He wrote, "If we take a really strict old-fashioned view of inspiration, all books within the canon are fully inspired by the Holy Spirit, and no books outside it, however good in other respects, are inspired."[11] Traditionally many have thought that inspiration was a primary consideration for determining the canonicity of the biblical books, but as we saw earlier, the early church fathers believed that the role of the Spirit in their community of faith was not only related to books, but also to the church's continuing proclamation, teaching, and ministry. The extent that inspiration played a role in the canonization process is difficult to assess since it appears to have been applied in hindsight rather than seen in the initial writing of the document. No one that we know wrote a document and said to anyone, "Please add this to our scriptural collection." This suggests that our response to the question here begins first by examining how inspiration was applied in early Christianity.

11. Barr, *Holy Scripture*, 57.

Those who have examined the early church's understanding of inspiration regularly acknowledge that it is especially difficult to show conclusively that God inspired a biblical writer to write what later became recognized sacred Scripture, though admittedly, this is what the author of Revelation claims was true of the revelations he imparted (Rev 1:3, 9–10 and 22:18–19). I have shared above that the criteria most commonly cited in antiquity include widespread use in churches (catholicity), orthodoxy, antiquity (written closest to the time of Jesus), apostolicity, and adaptability, but the problem with adding inspiration to the above criteria is twofold. *First* is the difficulty of determining what is or is not inspired coupled with the lack of a definitive church definition of inspiration. *Second*, and more importantly, the early church never limited inspiration to its sacred writings, but rather extended it to everything considered theologically true, whether it was written, taught, or preached.

99. Can the church affirm the authority and inspiration of the Bible today?

Yes, of course. This is because the central teachings of the Bible continue to bring life-transformation for those who adopt the biblical call to follow Jesus as Lord. The message of the Bible continues to bring hope and peace with God and one another. Those who contend that the Bible is perfect and often offer fanciful explanations to explain away the human elements in the Bible ignore the reality of the church's Scriptures. It is possible to affirm God's activity in the origins of Scripture, but at the same time acknowledge the humanity reflected in the same Scriptures. Although many in antiquity and today deny or minimize human participation in the production of the biblical texts and contend that the apparent errors in Scripture were not in the biblical autographs, the defense of that position often ignores the reality of what is in the texts and the evidence for that position is not convincing. It is better to adopt something like Chrysostom's view that God "condescended" to humanity and employed human beings to communicate the divine message to human beings.

While his appeal to the incarnation of the Son is interesting and has some merit, there are obvious differences, namely, the widely accepted position that Jesus, the Son of God, did not teach or live falsely. That God condescended to the lives and languages of human beings to communicate his will and mission for the church can be illustrated with countless examples throughout history and in the Bible. God has always used humanity to tell his message to humanity. That was understood by Origen and later especially Chrysostom as well as others in church history and up until today. What is important here is that while the authority of God is affirmed in origin of the church Scriptures, the humanity in them that is obvious and cannot denied but must rather be acknowledged and affirmed. Doing so does not diminish the Bible's proclamation of the will of God for humanity.

100. What are some of the most important ancient sources that influenced Christian notions of biblical inspiration?

1. Key biblical texts: these include Ps 19:7–10, which affirms that the Law of God is perfect; Ps 119 is divided into twenty-two sections of eight verses, each and each beginning with a different letter of the Hebrew alphabet, reflecting the perfection of the divine law and precepts of God; Gen 2:7, which says that when God breathed into the nostrils of man, man (Adam) became a living soul, noting that here the breath/spirit/wind of God gives life; Ezek 37:1–10 speaks of the life of the dry bones when the divine breath came into them; John 3:5 emphasizes the necessity of being born of the Spirit; in John 20:21–23 as Jesus gave the Holy Spirit to the disciples, he breathed on them as they received the Spirit; Acts 2:1–4 indicates that when the violent wind came upon the apostles, tongues of fire came upon them and they were filled with the Holy Spirit; 2 Tim 3:15–17 indicated that all Scriptures (the LXX) were divinely-breathed or "inspired"; 2 Pet 1:20–21 contends that no prophecy comes from human will but through men and women moved by the Holy Spirit. This is not all the relevant texts, but these are some important ones that give a perspective on the understanding of sacred Scriptures in Judaism and early Christianity.

2. Classical/Hellenistic perspectives on inspiration:

    a. Aristotle (384–322 BCE) addressed the problems in the widely received poetic and sacred writings, especially Homer's *Iliad* and *Odyssey*, that were welcomed as divinely written documents, and he indicated how to address them (*Poetics* 25). See also Porphyry's *Homeric Questions* which deals with the same issues in the sacred texts of Homer and how to understand the difficulties in Homer's writings.

b. Plato (428–348 BCE), in response to Meno, indicated that wisdom came from soothsayers and diviners who "utter many a true thing when inspired but have no knowledge of anything they say." And subsequently he asks Meno, "May we . . . rightly call those men divine who, having no understanding, yet succeed in many a great deed and word?" He adds to that "we can say of the statesmen [who speak wisdom] that they are divine and enraptured, as being inspired *and possessed* of God when they succeed in speaking many great things, while knowing naught of what they say" (Plato, *Meno* 99 C, D; LCL. Emphasis added). Later he emphasizes to Timaeus that the one who has the "gift of divination" does not achieve true and inspired divination "in his [their] rational mind, but only when the power of his intelligence is fettered in sleep or when it is distraught by disease or by reason of some divine inspiration." He adds that for the one with that gift "it is not the task of him who has been in a state of frenzy, and still continues therein, to judge the apparitions and voices seen or uttered by himself; for it was well said of old that to do and to know one's own and oneself belongs only to him who is sound of mind." He concludes that "it is customary to set the tribe of prophets to pass judgments upon these inspired divinations; and they, indeed, themselves are named 'diviners' by certain who are wholly ignorant of the truth that they are not diviners but interpreters of the mysterious voice and apparition, for whom the most fitting name would be 'prophets of things divined'" (*Tim.* 71E, 72A; LCL).

c. Hellenism and the notion of divine dictation. When the belief emerged that Scripture came from God and every word was divinely inspired it was believed that whenever unreconcilable texts in the Scriptures became apparent it was clear that there must be a second deeper meaning in the difficulties that could be discerned through the practice of allegorizing those sacred texts. This was a Hellenistic invention that was adopted to bring harmony to their sacred texts, such as in Homer's *Iliad* and *Odyssey*. Philo, and subsequently several church fathers—beginning with Clement of Alexandria, Origen, and Augustine—found this interpretive methodology acceptable and useful to account for the difficulties in the Scriptures. Allegory was deemed most fitting and it appears that this is what the Hellenistic community believed and accepted. Philo (see below) also saw in the discordant human element merely an idol not unlike an instrument incapable of producing the document though bearing the human name. It was for him the musician (the divine) producing the welcomed product through the instrument (prophet).

d. Plutarch (c. 46–119 CE), a priest at Delphi, wrote about the inspired priestesses at Delphi called Pythian priestesses who sat over a cone in a cave in which gases rose and put them into a *possessed* state in which they spoke what was believed to be divine messages from Apollo. Those messages were subsequently interpreted by prophetic individuals. Plutarch's extensive writing on a variety of subjects also focused on the experience of possession and that those priests and priestesses who spoke at Delphi were unaware of what they were saying. Without the divine input they would not know anything. All of what they said came from God. See Plutarch, *Mor.* 410–436 and his *Plac. Phil* 5.2 and in *Vett. Val.* IX, 1.

e. Strabo (64 BCE–21 CE), *Geogr.* 9.3.5, describes the experience of the Pythian or Delphic priestesses who received breath from the cave fumes at Delphi that inspired them in "a divine frenzy who in an "enthusiastic spirit" (Greek *pneuma enthusiastikon*) = "utters oracles in both verse and prose.

f. Pliny the Elder (c. 23–79 CE) calls this experience of possession an intoxicating exhalation (*exhalatione temulenti*) (see his *Nat.* 2.95–208). This is like Acts 2:1–4. In his *On the Obsolescence of Oracles* 414 D-E, Pliny discusses the phenomena that comes when the divine *Pythones* enters the bodies of the priestesses and prompts their word, "employing their mouths and voices as instruments" (418C-D). He observes that when the oracles go their separate way, they lose their power and it only returns when they return, like musical instruments, and become articulate again when those who can put them to use are present (418C-D; and 431B). This condition is like one who is out of the body and allowing for mantic visions (Greek =

enthusiasmos) in which the divine breath enters the body and produces a condition of enthusiasm (432D).[12]

3. Judaism:

   a. Belief in prophetic *mania* is not often found in the early church fathers (except perhaps in Acts 2:1–4) but is rooted in the Old Testament (Saul in 1 Sam 10:6, 10; Balaam in Num 22:12, 22, 28; 23:16; 24:2; Balaam has word of the Lord put in his mouth and the Lord and angel of the Lord spoke. See also Num 11:25, 29).

   b. Authorship in ancient Judaism. Authorship of the Scriptures was not initially emphasized in the texts of the Hebrew Bible or in the Judaism of late antiquity, with the exceptions of the Hebrew prophets. There was a belief that all Scripture came from God and not primarily from human authors and therefore authorship was not that important initially. For a careful analysis of b. Baba Bathra 14b-15a in which authorship is minimized and "copying" is emphasized. Although there was little focus on authorship in Judaism of late antiquity and also in early Christianity, the belief was strong that God produced divine oracles and sacred writings that were transmitted by human figures. The recognized Scriptures of the early churches, given through prophetic and apostolic figures, were commonly believed to have come from God and to have been delivered through (or copied by) human agents. This is the earliest listing of the Jewish sacred Scriptures and it carefully acknowledges that the Scriptures came from God and were only "copied" (Heb. *kotev*)—not written or authored—by Moses or others, with the exceptions being the Psalms and Proverbs.[13] God through the Holy Spirit (most often) was the source of the sacred Scriptures and this notion of "thus says the Lord" is found more than four hundred times in the Old Testament. While later Christians in the fourth century emphasized the importance authorship of their Scriptures (especially Augustine), they often followed the Greek and Hellenistic Jewish practice (Philo) when initially there was little focus placed on human authorship and in early Christianity.

---

12. For a careful and more detailed discussion of this phenomenon, Plutarch, and the New Testament, see Gunkel et al., "Plutarch and Pentecost," 80–81.

13. For a careful analysis of b. Baba Bathra 14b-15a in which authorship is minimized and "copying" is emphasized, see Wyrick, *Ascension of Authorship*, 71–110.

Except in the cases of heretical documents the question of false authorship was seldom in focus. More than half of the New Testament was written anonymously and only later were names of authors attached. Prophetic or apostolic authorship was denied if a document was considered heretical, but otherwise authorship was not emphasized initially in the early churches, though the rule of faith was emphasized and writings that cohered to that sacred tradition were widely welcomed in churches.

c. Philo (Jewish scholar 20 BCE–40 CE). In his explanation of the testing of the translators of the Torah into Greek for the early stages of the Septuagint, Philo's acceptance of the Letter of Aristeas, emphasized the sacredness of the LXX translation in which the translators were separated when they did their work yet all of their translations came out exactly the same. He then says, "After standing this test, they at once began to fulfill their duties of their high errand. Reflecting how great an undertaking it was to make a full version of the laws *given by the Voice of God* where they could not add or take away or transfer anything, but must keep the original form and shape [of the law]" and subsequently he adds that as they were doing their translation "they *became as it were possessed, and under inspiration wrote*, not each several scribe something different, but the same, word for word, as though dictated to each by an invisible prompter" (*Mos.* 2.34, 38, LCL. Emphasis added). He goes on to praise the result of their translation reflecting his awareness of The Letter of Aristeas's mythical report (see sections 301–11).

Philo also cited the story of Balaam, who was commanded to prophesy against the Jews (Hebrews), but he could not do so. Philo saw what Balaam did as evidence that prophets could not speak on their own. He concludes, "For the prophet is the interpreter of God who prompts from within what he should say, and with God nothing is in fault" (*Rewards* 55). There are parallels and significant differences between the classic writers and Philo on those who received a divine word and wrote it. Elsewhere, he claims that the darkness that fell on Abraham (Gen 15:12) was ecstasy, saying: "Now 'ecstasy' or 'standing out' takes different forms. Sometimes it was portrayed as a mad fury producing mental delusion due to age or melancholy or other similar cause. Sometimes it is extreme amazement at the event which so often happens suddenly and unexpectedly. Sometimes it is passivity of mind, if indeed the mind can ever be at rest; and *the best form of all is the divine possession or frenzy to which the prophets as a class are subject*" (Heir 249; LCL. Emphasis added). He goes on to identify the four kinds of ecstasy and cites the story of Abraham (Gen 15:1–6 and 20:6–7) stating that "a prophet (being a spokesman) has no utterance of his own, but all his utterance came from elsewhere, the echoes of another's [God's] voice." He then claims that the prophet is "the *vocal instrument* of God *smitten and played* by his invisible hand" (*Heir* 258–59; LCL. Emphasis added).

On the question of divine possession, Philo tells the story of four different kinds of "ecstasy" in which prophecy takes place. Philo references Abraham who was a prophet (Gen 20:7), and says that "a prophet (being a spokesperson) *has no utterance of his own*, but all his utterance came from elsewhere, the echoes of another's voice" and adds that the 'God-inspired' person *is the vocal instrument of God, smitten and played by His invisible hand*. Thus, all whom Moses describes as just are pictured *as possessed and prophesying*." He adds that all who are prophetic figures "are under divine possession" (Philo, *Heir* 249–60; LCL. Emphasis added). See also *Moses II*.37 in which Philo advances, from the myth of the Letter of Aristeas, the notion of the divine translation of the Hebrew Scriptures into Greek without flaw. In this he affirms *divine dictation* of that translation (*Moses II*.31–43; LCL. Emphasis added). Elsewhere he refers to the *inability of the prophet to prophecy unless he is possessed by God* who imparts divine truth to him. He states, "A prophet possessed by God [Greek = *theoforetos*] will suddenly appear and give prophetic oracles. *Nothing of what he says will be his own*, for he that is truly under the control of divine inspiration has no power of apprehension when he speaks but serves as the channel for the insistent words of Another's [God's] prompting. For prophets are the interpreters of God, who makes full use of their organs of speech to set forth what he wills. These and the like are his injunctions as to the conception of the one truly existing God" (Philo, *Special Laws* 1:65; LCL. Emphasis added). Philo reflects the notion of divine dictation that minimizes the human influence in conveying the word of God.

d. Flavius Josephus (ca. fl. 37–100 CE). In his *Antiquities* 4.118, Josephus, speaking in reference to the divine origin of the prophecy given to Balaam, says, "Such was the inspired utterance of one who was no longer his own master *but was overruled by the divine spirit to deliver it.*" Balaam asks Balak, when challenged, whether "it rests with us at all to be silent or to speak on such themes as these, *when we are possessed by the spirit of God*? For that spirit gives utterance to such language and words as it will, *whereof we are all unconscious*" (*Ant.* 4.5.118–19; LCL. Emphasis added). He adds elsewhere that in contrast to other writings, the Jewish Scriptures (in Greek) had "no discrepancy in what is written, seeing that, on the contrary, the prophets alone had this privilege, obtaining their knowledge of the most remote and ancient history through the inspiration which they owed to God, and committing to writing a clear account of the events of their own time just as they occurred—it follows, I say, that we do not possess myriads of inconsistent books, conflicting with each other" (*C. Ap.* 1.37–38; LCL).

4. The Early church fathers and their perspectives:

   a. New Testament: 2 Tim 3:15–17; 2 Pet 1:19–21; John 10:35. These are among the most cited New Testament texts that argue for the inspiration and divine origin of the biblical texts. The notion of "God's in-breathing" issuing forth in "life giving" is manifest in Gen 2:7 and Ezek 37:1–10. Similarly, in John 20:21–23, as Jesus imparts his divine commission to his disciples, he breathes on the disciples, and they receive the Spirit that enables them to carry out that mission. The wind or divine breath comes upon the disciples in Acts 2:1–4 and they were "filled with the Holy Spirit" and enabled to communicate the message of God in other than their own languages.

   b. The early church and inspiration:

      1. Theophilus of Antioch (ca. 180 CE) believed that the Scriptures were inspired but so also were the human authors of those Scriptures. He asserts that "the holy writings teach us, and all the spirit-bearing [inspired] men, . . . that at first God

was alone, and the Word in Him" (*Autol.* 2.22; *ANF*). For him, inspiration involved "men of God carrying in them a holy spirit [*pneumatophoroi*] and becoming prophets, being inspired and made wise by God, became God-taught, and holy and righteous" (*Autol.* 2.9).

2. Clement of Rome (fl. 88–97 CE), the Epistle of Barnabas (130–150 CE), and the *Letters* of Ignatius (d. ca. 110 CE), and others speak of the divine inspiration not only of the earlier Christian writings of Paul and others, but also of their own writings. Inspiration in early Christianity was not for sacred texts alone, but for divine activity in advancing the gospel, whether through preaching or writing or divine acts. Metzger has offered several other ancient texts that demonstrate that inspiration was never a criterion for canonicity and that it was never limited to the church's Scriptures.[14] The author of 2 Clement believed that 1 Clement was an inspired document and cites 1 Clement 23.3–4 with the words "for the prophetic word also says" (*legei gar kai ho prophētikos logos*) (2 Clem. 11.2), the usual words that designate writings as Scripture and inspired. Barnabas 16.5 introduces a passage from 2 Enoch with the words "for the scripture says" (*legei gar hē graphē*). In a somewhat different light, Clement of Rome (ca. 95) told his readers that Paul's 1 Corinthians was written "with true inspiration" (*ep' alētheias pneumatikōs*) (1 Clem. 47.3), but later he also claimed the same inspiration for himself, saying that he wrote his letter "through the Holy Spirit" (*gegrammenois dia tou hagiou pneumatos*) (1 Clem. 63.2). Ignatius likewise expressed awareness of his own inspiration: "I spoke with a great voice—with God's own voice. . . . But some suspected me of saying this because I had previous knowledge of the division of some persons: but he in whom I am bound is my witness that I had no knowledge of this from any human being, but the Spirit was preaching and saying this [*to de pneuma ekēryssen legon tade*]" (Ign. Phld. 7.1b–2; LCL).

There is no evidence that the early church confined inspiration to an already past apostolic age or to a collection of sacred writings, even in writings that dealt with the

---

14. Metzger, *New Testament Canon*, 255–57.

Montanist controversy (see Eusebius, *Hist. eccl.* 5.14-19) in the latter third of the second century. The traditional assumption that the early Christians believed that only the canonical writings were inspired is not demonstrable from the available evidence. Everett Kalin concludes, "If the scriptures were the only writings the church fathers considered inspired, one would expect them to say so, at least once in a while."[15] He concludes from his study of Irenaeus, Origen, Eusebius, and other ancient fathers that *only the work of the false prophets mentioned in the Old Testament, the heathen oracles, and philosophy were deemed uninspired.*[16] Krister Stendahl summarizes the early Christian belief that inspiration played a role in early Christianity and in the biblical tradition thusly: "Inspiration, to be sure, is the divine presupposition for the NT, but the twenty-seven books were never chosen because they, and only they, were recognized as inspired. Strange as it may sound, inspiration was not enough. Other standards had to be applied."[17]

3. The notion of a prophetic individual being played like an instrument is seen first in Plato and later in Plutarch, but also later in Philo and Athenagoras. Greek scholars who recognized flaws in Homer's and Hesiod's writings, namely Pythagoras (582-507 BCE) and Xenophanes (570-480 BCE), made use of allegory to explain or cover up the weaknesses they saw in those sacred texts. Allegory was adopted by Philo of Alexandria to deal with perceived problems in the Pentateuch.

F. F. Bruce claims that Irenaeus was the first Christian writer to allegorize the New Testament writings because he was among the first to treat New Testament writings as unreservedly inspired. Irenaeus (ca. 180), for example, makes it clear that the Scriptures, even when they are not clearly understood, "were spoken by the Word of God and by His Spirit" (*Haer.* 2.28.2; *ANF*).[18] Several church fathers felt free

---

15. Kalin, "Inspired Community," 543.
16. See also Kalin, "Argument from Inspiration," 163, 168.
17. Stendahl, "Apocalypse of John," 245.
18. Bruce, *Canon of Scripture*, 267-68.

to allegorize the Scriptures because they were considered inspired of God and therefore perfect. Given Clement of Alexandria's praise of Philo, who made much use of allegorical interpretation, it is likely that he also made use of allegory at roughly the same time as Irenaeus. Origen made considerable use of allegory not only to deal with difficulties in Scriptural texts but also to find what he believed was the deeper and more spiritual meaning of scriptural texts. This practice was later employed well into the Middle Ages.

See also Justin's *Dialogue* 118 (PG 6:749), *Legatio pro Christianis* 9 (PG:905–7); and *1 Apol.* 1.36; in which he suggests something close to a dictation perspective on the origin of the prophetic writings. He writes, "When you hear the utterances of the prophets spoken as it were personally, you must not suppose that they are spoken by the inspired themselves [the prophets], but by the Divine Word [God] who moves them" (*1 Apol.* 1.36; *ANF*); see also the *Writings of Justin Martyr and Athenagoras* 2.35 (*ANF*). In his *Dialogue with Trypho*, Justin speaks of a priest named Joshua (= Jesus; see Zech 2:10–13; 3:1–2) who did not speak the revelation of God or prophecy on his own, but rather "the prophet had not seen him [God] in his revelation, just as he had not seen either the devil or the angel of the Lord by eyesight, *and in his waking condition, but in a trance at the time when the revelation was made to him*." He later adds that a priest in the days of Joshua made an announcement "of the things to be accomplished by our Priest, who is God, and Christ the Son of God the Father of all" (*Dial.* 115; *ANF*. Emphasis added). Again, for Justin, the word of the Lord does not come by human volition, but by God alone. Tertullian (ca. 150–220 CE) also makes a similar claim in his *Apology* 18, par. 2.[19]

4. Origen (185–254) focused on the problems of harmony in the biblical texts in his *Commentary on John*, books 1–10, but especially 10.14–18. He first seeks to find historical and philological answers to texts that could not be harmonized and then appeals ultimately to a second, allegorical sense.

---

19. Tertullian, *Apological Works*.

In his *Commentary on John* 10.3-10, 17-18, he goes into considerable detail trying to harmonize the canonical differences in Matthew's story of the triumphal entry in which two animals were selected, not one, as in Mark, Luke, and John (cf. Zech 9:9 cited in Matt 21:1-11; Mark 11:1-11; [not in Luke 19:29-39]; John 12:12-15; see also Origen's *Hom. Ezek.* frag. 6.1; *Cels.* 1.42; *De princ.* 4.9; PG 11; 360; *Comm. Ev. Mt* 15.3, PG 13:1257; *De princ.* 4.14, PG 11:372; *Cels.* 7.3-4; PG 11:1424-5; on allegory cf. *Commentaries and Homilies of Origen.*) In his *Contra Celsum*, Origen accuses Celsus of mixing up "things that are dissimilar [in the Gospels], and *incapable of being united*" [emphasis added], including the number of angels at the tomb of Jesus and the angel or angels that rolled away the stone covering the tomb of Jesus (*Cels.* 5.56, and also 57-58).

Examples of the fanciful harmonizations of the discrepancies in the church's Scriptures are seen in multiple examples provided by Origen's *Commentary on John* 10.1-30. He asks questions about the discrepancies in the Gospels when read literally and concludes that they must be "read spiritually and mystically" and goes on to use allegory to obtain the deeper "spiritual" meaning that he sees in the biblical texts (see especially 10.2-4). In another text responding to Celsus's criticisms of the Christian Scriptures, especially the Gospels, Origen writes, "Each of these occurrences might now be demonstrated to have actually taken place, and to be indicative of a figurative meaning [allegorical] existing in these 'phenomena,' and intelligible to those who were prepared to behold the resurrection of the Word."[20] Peter W. Martens likewise shows that Origen did not view the scriptural authors as passive instruments, as was widely accepted from the Greek notion of possession, but rather that they "actively and willingly participated in the writing of scripture" (see Origen, *Hom. Ezek.* 6.1; *Comm. Matt.* 12.40). He also points out that the Scriptures' intended message was the "advancing of the salvation of its readers."[21]

---

20. *Cels.* 56; *ANF.*
21. Martens, *Origen and Scripture*, 54-56 and 194-205.

Origen clearly recognized the human element in the production of the Scriptures, including what he believed were the obvious historical errors and contradictions in the Scriptures. He observed errors in the surviving manuscripts of both the Hebrew and Greek Old Testament and sometimes he preferred the Greek over the Hebrew (see his *Comm. John* 10). He had doubts about the historical truth of several biblical events in both the Old Testament and New Testament, such as the Genesis story of the tree of life in the Garden of Eden, and whether the devil could show Jesus all of the kingdoms of the world from a high mountain, or geographically he denied that the location of Bethany was by the Jordan river (John 1:28), and noted that the surviving manuscripts of both the Hebrew and Greek Old Testaments were sometimes in error (*Princ.* 4.3.5, 4.3.1; see also *Hom. Ezek. frag.* 6.1 dealing with contradictions in the Gospels; see also *Princ.* 4.3.5, 4.3.1, and *Hom. Ezek. frag.* 6.1 dealing with contradictions in the Gospels.)

5. Eusebius (260–340 CE), in his *Historia ecclesiastica* 1.7.1–17, shows awareness of the difficulty of harmonizing the genealogies of Jesus in Matthew and Luke. Noting the obvious differences, he cites the *Letter of Africanus to Aristides* (see *Epistle to Aristides* 1–6 in the *Extant Writings of Julius Africanus* 1.1–61). He was aware of the difficulties in Africanus's complex and often confusing argument that both texts were true despite their differences. Africanus's argument depends on following Jewish law where the brother of a brother who died without having a child could have a son through the wife of his brother and it would *lawfully* be the son the dead brother though *biologically* that of the live brother. It is interesting that Chrysostom later mentions some of the problems of harmony in the Gospels and claims that the genealogy of Matthew refers to three generations of fourteen, but in the third section Matthew only lists thirteen (see Matt 1:12–17). Chrysostom writes, "And this again is another question: why, after having spoken of fourteen generations, he has not in the third division maintained the number" (*Hom. Matt.* 1.14; *NPNF*). Licona acknowledges some of the strained and

fanciful attempts in antiquity to harmonize the Gospels—the genealogies in particular—and approvingly cites Jonathan T. Pennington, who concluded that "if Jesus did not appear as the named figure in both of these accounts [of Matthew and Luke], one would never suspect they were stories about the same person."[22]

6. Augustine (354–430 CE), in his *Harmony of the Gospels* (*De consensus evangelistarum*) books 1–4, offered explanations for some 150 variants and seeming errors or contradictions in the Gospels that he called "apparent discrepancies." Augustine argued that the LXX and the Hebrew text of the Scriptures were both inspired by the Holy Spirit, and both are true in all of their details! (PL 41:603-4; see his *Harmony of the Gospels* 2.21.52 in PL 34:1102). While dealing with Peter's denial of Jesus and the number of times the cock crowed, he concluded, "If, however, the demand is to get at the very words [that Jesus said and the number of times the cock crowed], literally and completely, which the Lord addressed to Peter, *we answer that it is impossible to discover these; and further, that it is simply superfluous to ask them*, in as much as the speaker's meaning—to intimate which was the object he had in view in uttering the words—*admits of being understood with the utmost plainness*, even under the diverse terms employed by the evangelists" (*Cons.* 3.2.5-8). Elsewhere he acknowledges in his letter to Jerome that even if there are mistakes in the surviving scriptural manuscripts, nonetheless the authors of the Scriptures were "completely free from error" and he explains that if there is anything perplexing in the Scriptures that appears to be "opposed to the truth, I do not hesitate to suppose *that either the manuscript is faulty, or the translator has not caught the meaning of what was said, or I myself have failed to understand it*" (*Letters of St. Augustine* 82.34; *NPNF*. Emphasis added).

Augustine also insisted on the authentic authorship of the biblical books and recognized that there were two kinds of writings, namely "those written by authors and those

---

22. Pennington, *Reading the Gospels Wisely*, 55; cf. Licona, *Why Are There Differences*, 263.

ascribed to God speaking through them" (*Civ.* 18.38). He likely thought he was following the rationale of the Jews, who agreed that those writings whose authorship could not properly be ascribed prior to the time of Moses should be rejected. He adds in reference to books like Enoch that "many writings are presented by heretics under the names of apostles, but all these too have been excluded from canonical authority and regularly are passed on under the name of apocrypha" (*Civ.*15.23). Wyrick has shown that Augustine's notion of canonicity depended significantly on the ability to ascribe correct authorship (or a text was determined to be a forgery). He goes on to argue that the attribution analysis of Plato and Hellenism was eventually picked up by Tertullian, Origen, and especially Augustine, and that Western Christianity was influenced by author attribution and the early focus on divine authorship. In this way, the anonymous authors who produced those biblical manuscripts eventually gave way to author attribution analysis, especially following in fourth-century Christianity.[23]

Later, when speaking about Jerome's translation of the Old Testament manuscripts, Augustine adds that supposed errors in the Old Testament Greek manuscripts were likely mutilated or corrupted by the Jews "in order to prevent themselves from being unable to answer the evidence given by these concerning the Christian faith." He then suggests that Jerome send him a copy of his translation of the Septuagint so that "we may be delivered, so far as is possible, from the consequences of the notable incompetency of those who, whether qualified or not, have attempted a Latin translation [of the Septuagint]" produced earlier by Jews or other persons incapable of producing a careful translation of the church's Scriptures (Augustine, *Letters*, 82.34–35; *NPNF*). Clearly, he has little or no confidence in the translators or copiers of the church's Scriptures and assumes that any errors are to be found in the surviving manuscripts rather than in the autographs of those Scriptures.[24]

---

23. Wyrick, *Ascension of Authorship*, 353–67.

24. For more examples of this, see also his *Conf.* 12.36, PL 32:840–41; *Serm.* 82.9, PL 38:510; and *Civ.* 18.23.1–2, PL 41:579–80 in reference to the "bad Latin" of a text concerning Christ.

7. John Chrysostom (347–407), in his commentary on the *Gospel of Matthew* (1.6–8), acknowledged the difficulties in the biblical texts and concluded that when corrections or explanations could not be found to resolve them we must conclude that *God condescended* (*sygkatabasis*; or, with Origen "accommodation," *symperifora*) to humanity and human language. This is similar to Philo and later Clement of Alexandria (see above). He claimed that God employed the language of humans to communicate the divine will to humanity and this was like the incarnation in which God condescended to humanity through his Son, who communicated the divine message of God to humanity (see *Hom. Jer.* 19.3; PG 13:504–5). Chrysostom, writing about the content of Hebrews, says that Paul wrote, not of his own mind and he did not acquire the wisdom to write Hebrews on his own, but it was by the "grace of the Spirit who shows his power by whomever he wills" (*Heb. hom.* 1.2; PG 63:15–16).

8. Jerome (late fourth/early fifth century) was aware of classical scholars notion of divine dictation and claimed the same for the book of Romans saying that Paul's Epistle to the Romans "had been dictated by the Holy Spirit through the Apostle Paul" (*Ep. Rom.* 120.10).

5. Summary:

Historically Christians have not articulated a *universally acknowledged* doctrine of inspiration and most of their discussions of such teachings occurred after the time of the Reformation. Since then, there continues to be little agreement among churches whether in the East or West on what inspiration means and especially how to understand the divine and human elements present in the Scriptures. Many churches come close to holding a dictation perspective, justified by several Old Testament texts (Jer 36:1–9 = dictation; cf. e.g., Lev 12:1; 13:1; 15:1; 18:1–23; Num 1:1–4; 3:5, 14; 6:1–2, 22–27; 10:1; *passim*; over four hundred times the Old Testament Scriptures say the equivalent of "The word of the LORD came to me, saying" or something similar). This suggests to some that the divine words were dictated to the prophetic agent. When does the divine influence begin to focus on texts and less on individuals?

Conclusion

IN THE FORGOING I have listed many of the common questions asked about the Bible, but also several that the casual reader may not have considered yet that are important for understanding the Christian Scriptures. I have tried to respond to some of the most important questions related to the formation of the Bible.

Readers will quickly recognize that there are areas of considerable debate among contemporary biblical scholars but there is also now considerably more agreement on many of them than was possible earlier. Occasionally I have cited other scholars who examine the same ancient texts and arrive at the same or even different conclusions to show why I have taken the positions expressed throughout this volume. Those who examine the ancient texts that I often refer to will also see that I did not address all questions related to the formation of the Bible, but only the most important ones. Those wanting to pursue the subject in much more detail might want to see my 2017 and 2020 publications on these and related topics.

While I am sympathetic to many of the positions on canon formation and inspiration that were at one time a part of my own journey of faith and inquiry, I tried generally *not* to begin with my assumptions about my earlier positions and rather let the evidence we now have before us address the questions we bring to the subjects in question. Hopefully this book will have made clearer what the major challenges are in understanding the complex history of the formation of the Bible and how readers might better understand them.

I have offered a list of many of the key ancient texts for those wanting to pursue their own research on this topic and hopefully those sources, along with the select bibliography, will be helpful for those wishing to continue in their study of the fascinating questions surrounding the formation of the Bible.

Appendix

Photos of Ancient Jewish and Christian Manuscripts (Biblical and Nonbiblical)

THE FOLLOWING COLLECTION OF photos illustrates the origin and quality of ancient religious and biblical texts and incipits, or introductions to ancient scriptural texts, in Hebrew and Greek as well as other languages. They reflect the diverse means of transmitting the ancient Christian Scriptures and other ancient texts showing the variable quality of each text and reflecting the competency of the copiers (or lack thereof). Some of the following texts are not included in the Bible but they are examples of the transmission of ancient manuscripts noted above in questions 61 and 62 and they reflect the varying quality of the surviving ancient manuscripts.

The forthcoming photos include some fragmented ancient texts and some that are more complete and better copied than others; they range from the early stages of transmission to the more recent printed texts of the church's Scriptures.

Several of the following photos and their captions are provided with permissions by Craig A. Evans and Ginny Evans and the Houston Dunham Bible Museum at Houston Christian University.

Cairo Hebrew Exodus Scroll. Although dating to the medieval period, the Cairo Hebrew Exodus Scroll is a fair representation of what Torah Scrolls would have looked like in the time of Jesus and the early church. Courtesy of the Dunham Bible Museum, Houston Christian University. Photo: Ginny Evans.

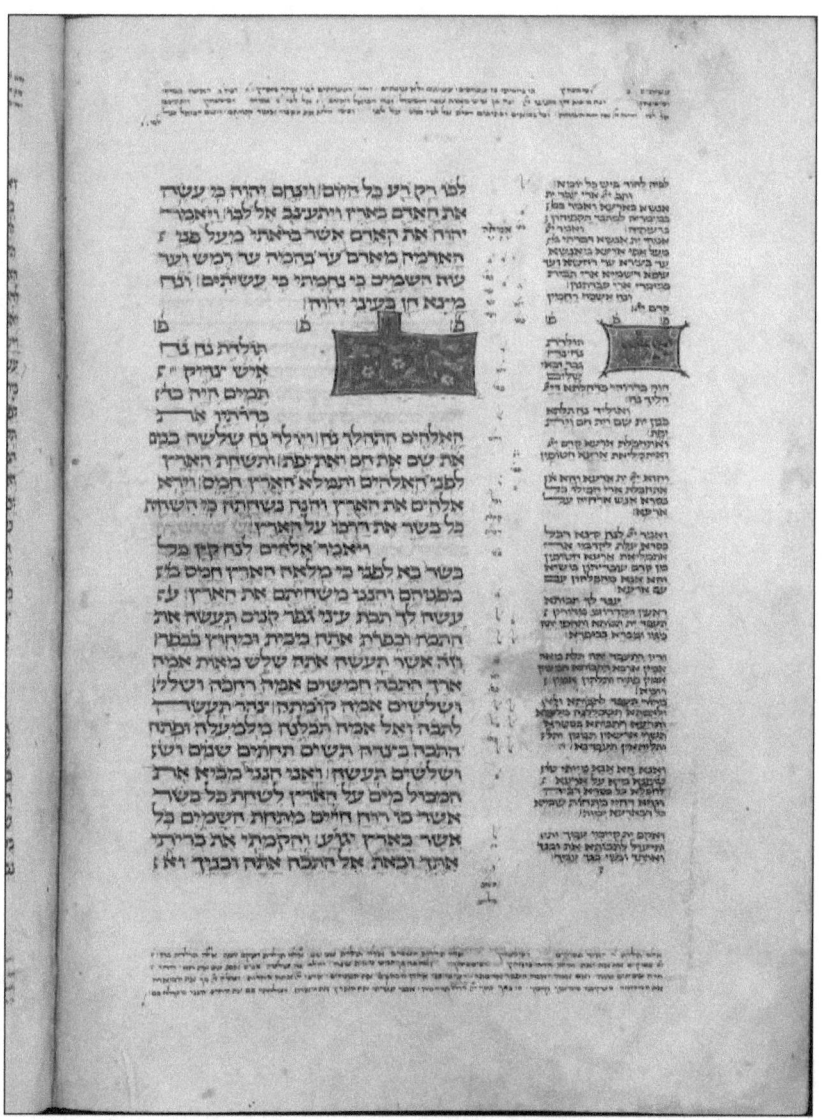

Kennicott Bible. Hebrew scholar Benjamin Kennicott (1718–1783) owned a number of old Hebrew and Aramaic Bibles. Depicted here is the so-called Kennicott Bible (fol. 6v.), which dates to December 1298. It is a Hebrew Bible that includes the Targum. Photo: Public domain.

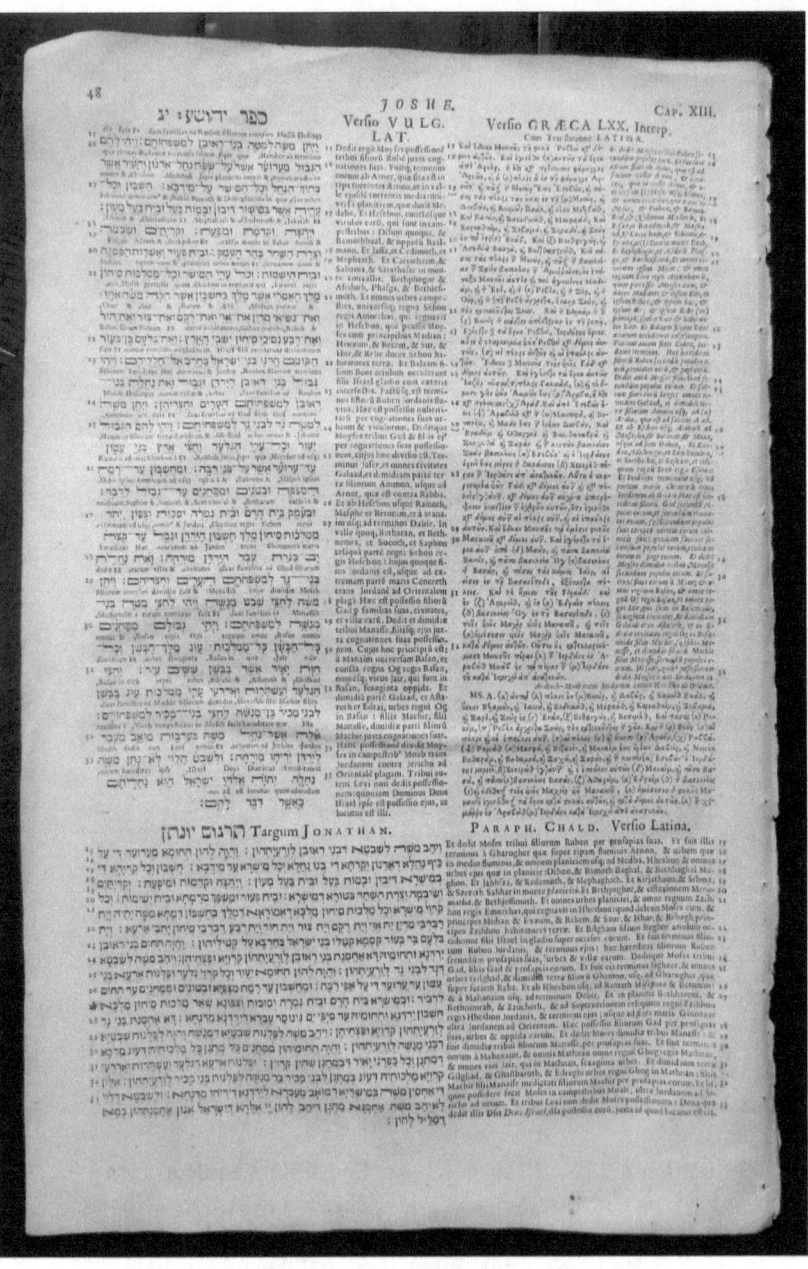

London Polyglot. The *Polyglot* (1657) by Brian Walton (1600–1661), or the London Polyglot, as it became known, exhibited the Hebrew, Greek, and Aramaic texts of the Bible. It was probably the best of its kind in the emerging age of the printing press. Courtesy of Craig A. Evans. Photo: Ginny Evans.

APPENDIX: PHOTOS OF ANCIENT JEWISH AND CHRISTIAN MANUSCRIPTS   215

Grenfell and Hunt at Oxyrhynchus. Local Egyptians worked for B. P. Grenfell and A. S. Hunt in excavating the trash mounds at Oxyrhynchus. Depicted here are workers placing finds in baskets. Photo ca. 1903. Public domain.

Grenfell and Hunt Digging at Oxyrhynchus. One can see in this photo two trenches, which permitted stratigraphical analysis, which in turn made it possible to determine how long manuscripts remained in use before being discarded. Photo ca. 1903. Public domain.

Shem Tov's Hebrew Matthew. Shem Tov ("Good Name") ben Isaac ben Shaprut made a Hebrew translation of the Gospel of Matthew and then wrote mostly negative commentary on the text. Depicted is the first page, with commentary on Matt 1:1. Photo: public domain.

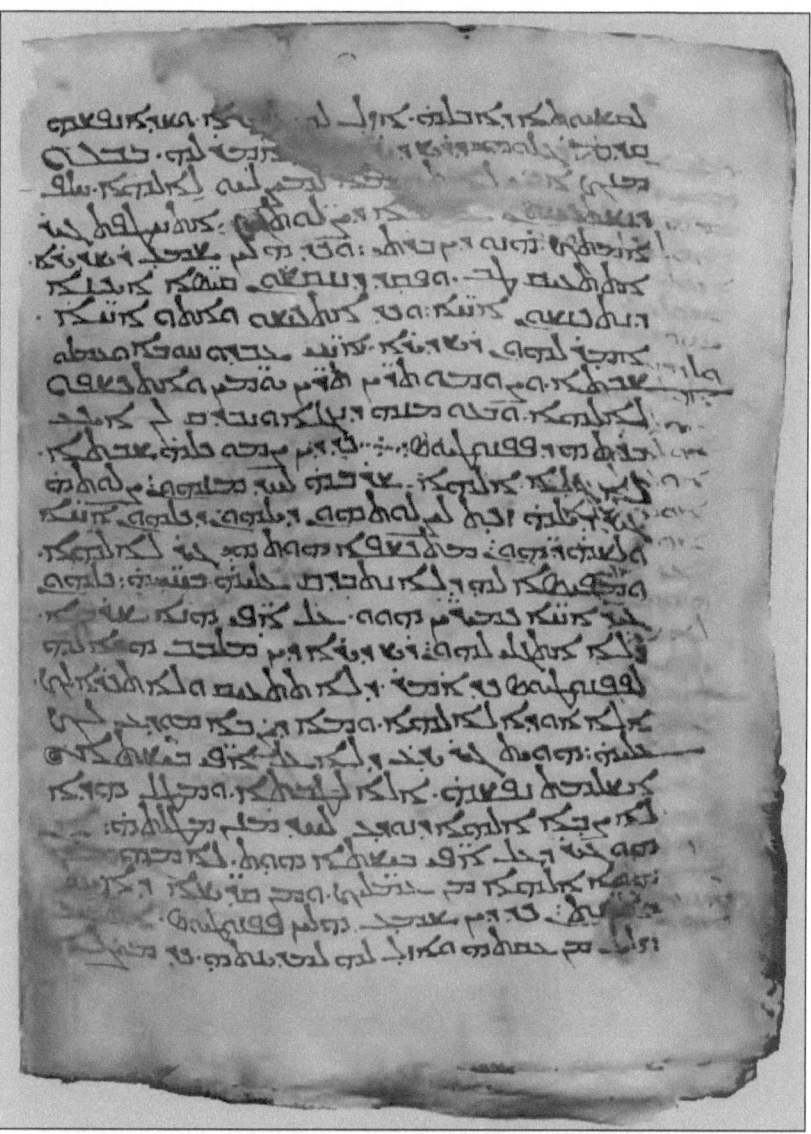

Syriac Sinaiticus Matthew. The Syriac Sinaiticus version of the New Testament Gospels may have appeared at the end of the second century. It is debated whether the Syriac Gospels influenced Tatian, who produced the *Diatessaron*, or if the *Diatessaron* influenced the Syriac Gospels. Depicted is fol. 82b (Matt 1:1–17). Photo: public domain.

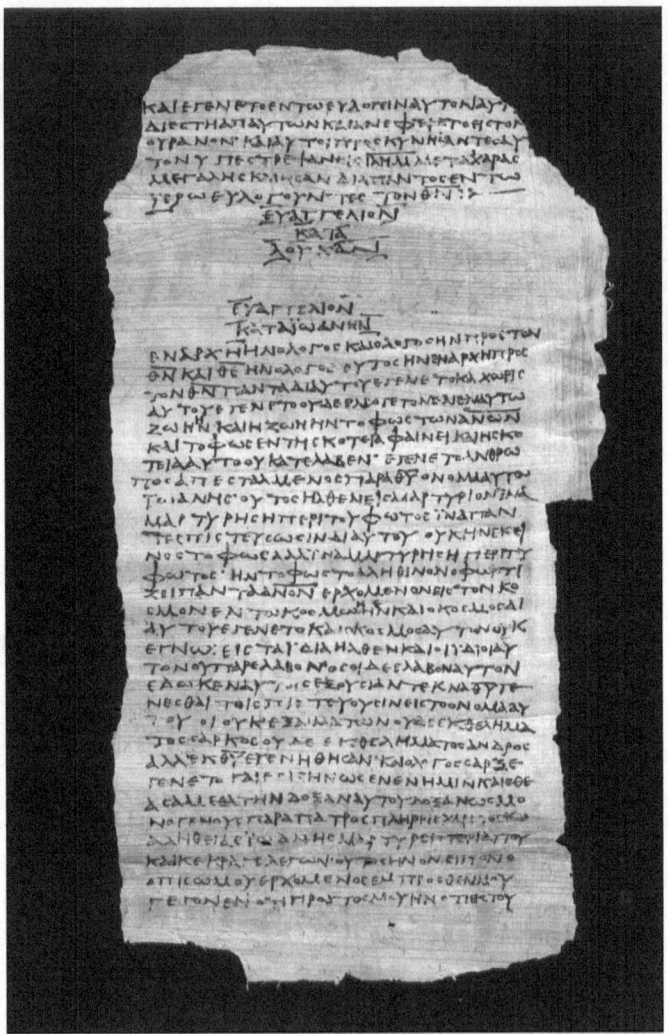

𝔓⁷⁵. Papyrus 75, formerly housed in the Foundation Martin Bodmer Bibliothèque et Musée, Geneva, and now housed in the Vatican, preserves portions of the Gospels of Luke and John. This papyrus codex, possibly one of a set of two (the other containing the Gospels of Matthew and Mark), probably dates to the third century. Depicted here is the end of the Gospel of Luke and the beginning of the Gospel of John. Photo: public domain.

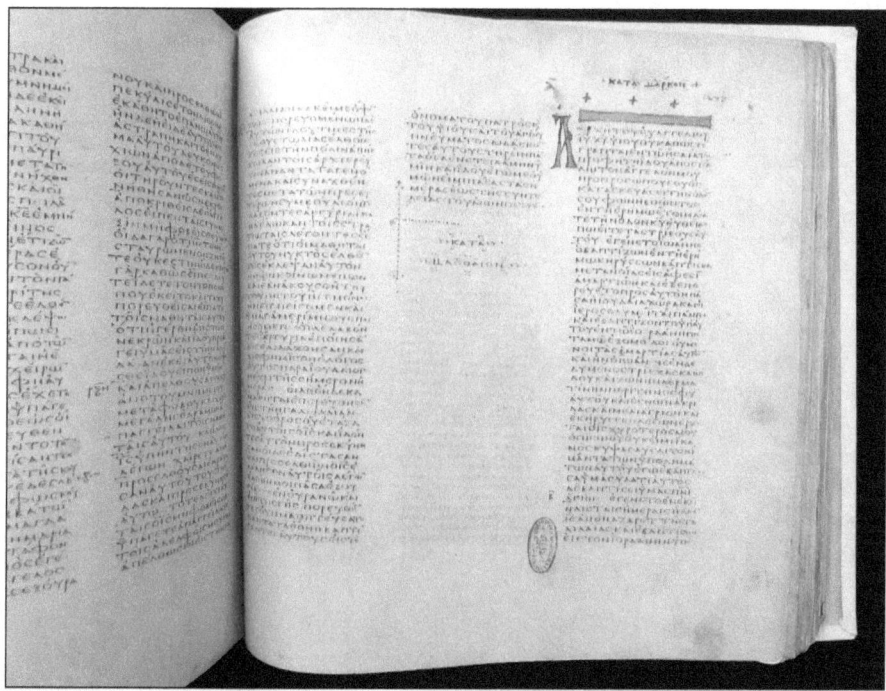

Codex Vaticanus. Codex Vaticanus, made up of three columns per page, is identified by the sigla B and 03. It dates to about the middle of the fourth century. According to Vaticanus, Mark 1:1 (the incipit of Mark) reads, "The beginning of the gospel of Jesus Christ, the Son of God." Textual critics think the last two words (in Greek), "Son of God," were accidentally omitted because of *parablepsis*. One will notice at the bottom of the middle column, where the Gospel of Matthew ends, the words *kata matthaion*, "according to Matthew." Courtesy of the Dunham Bible Museum of Houston Christian University. Photo: Ginny Evans.

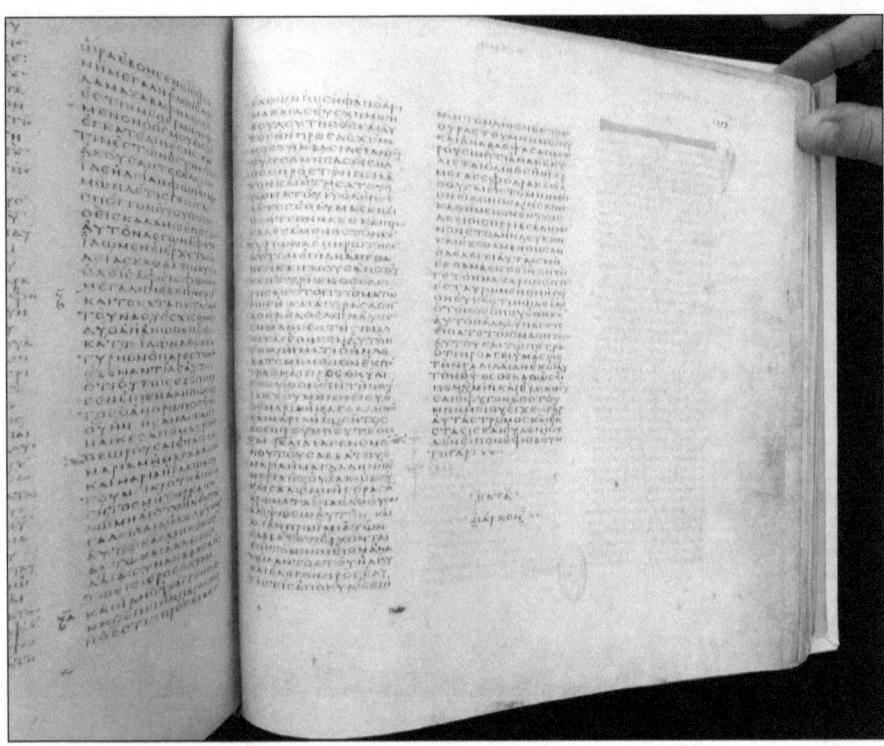

Codex Vaticanus. As in Codex Sinaiticus, Mark 16 in Codex Vaticanus ends with verse 8 about two-thirds down, with the column to the right-hand side left blank. Courtesy of the Dunham Bible Museum of Houston Christian University. Photo: Ginny Evans.

APPENDIX: PHOTOS OF ANCIENT JEWISH AND CHRISTIAN MANUSCRIPTS 221

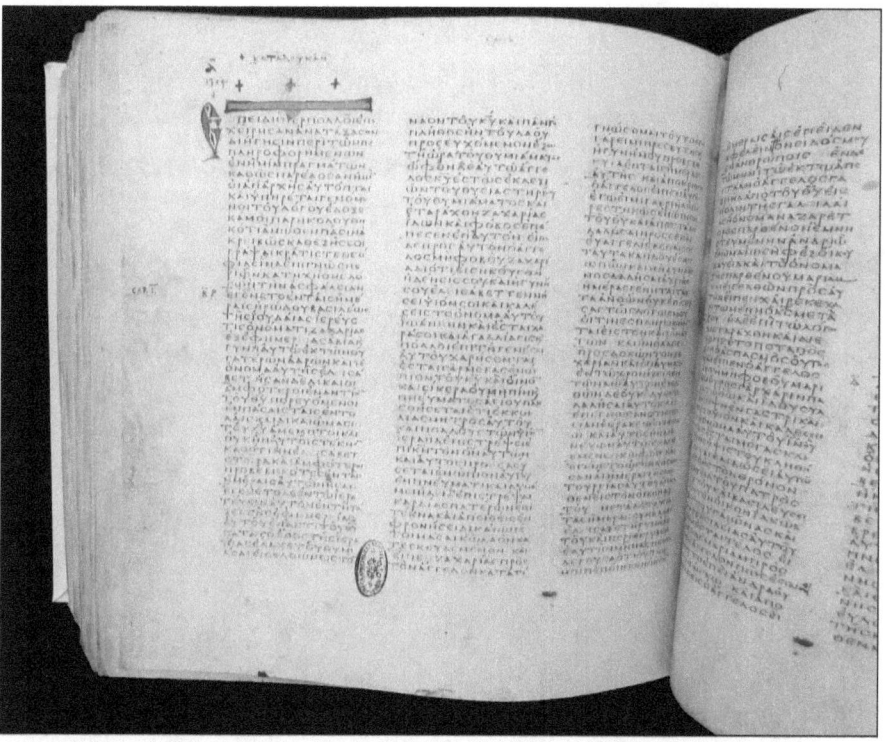

Codex Vaticanus (ca. 375 CE). Luke 1 in Codex Vaticanus begins on page "1304," in the far left-hand column. The opening verse is preceded by a green horizontal bar with three red crosses. The first letter in Luke 1:1, the letter epsilon, is oversized and colored with blue and red ink. One will also note the Biblioteca Apostolica Vaticana stamp near the bottom of the page, between the first and second columns of text. The left side of the stamp obscures the last letter in the last line of the first column. Courtesy of the Dunham Bible Museum of Houston Christian University. Photo: Ginny Evans.

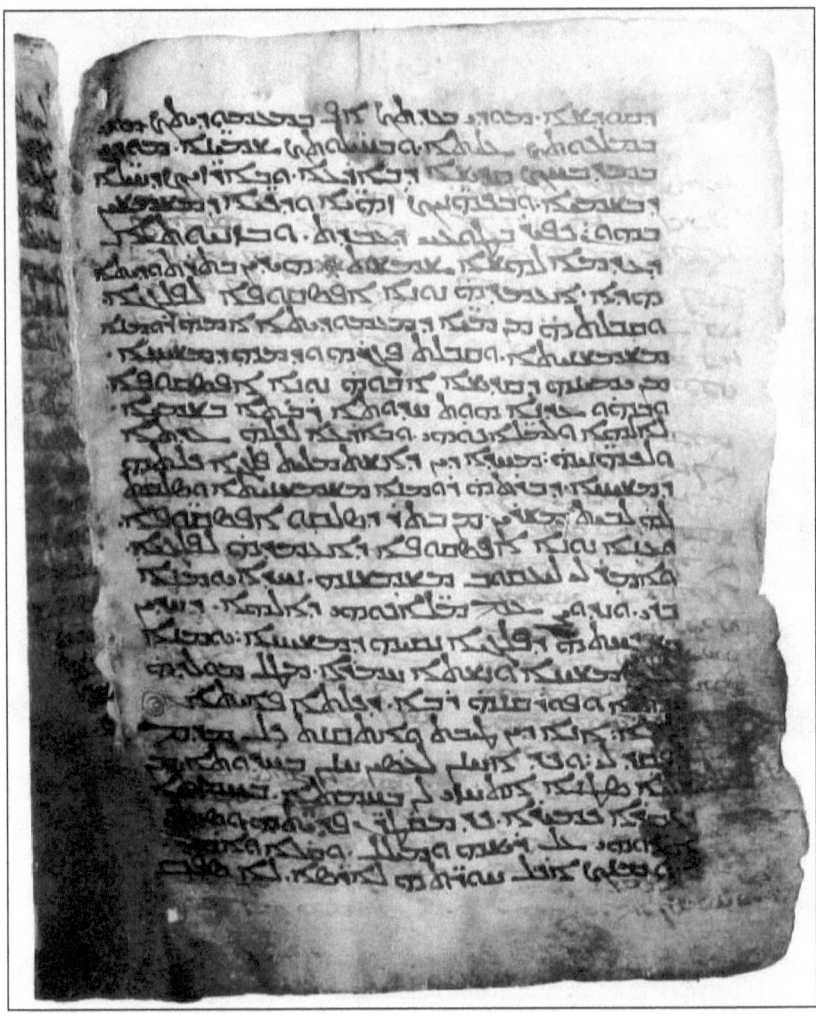

Syriac Sinaiticus John. Depicted is fol. 129r (John 5:46—6:11). Photo: public domain.

APPENDIX: PHOTOS OF ANCIENT JEWISH AND CHRISTIAN MANUSCRIPTS

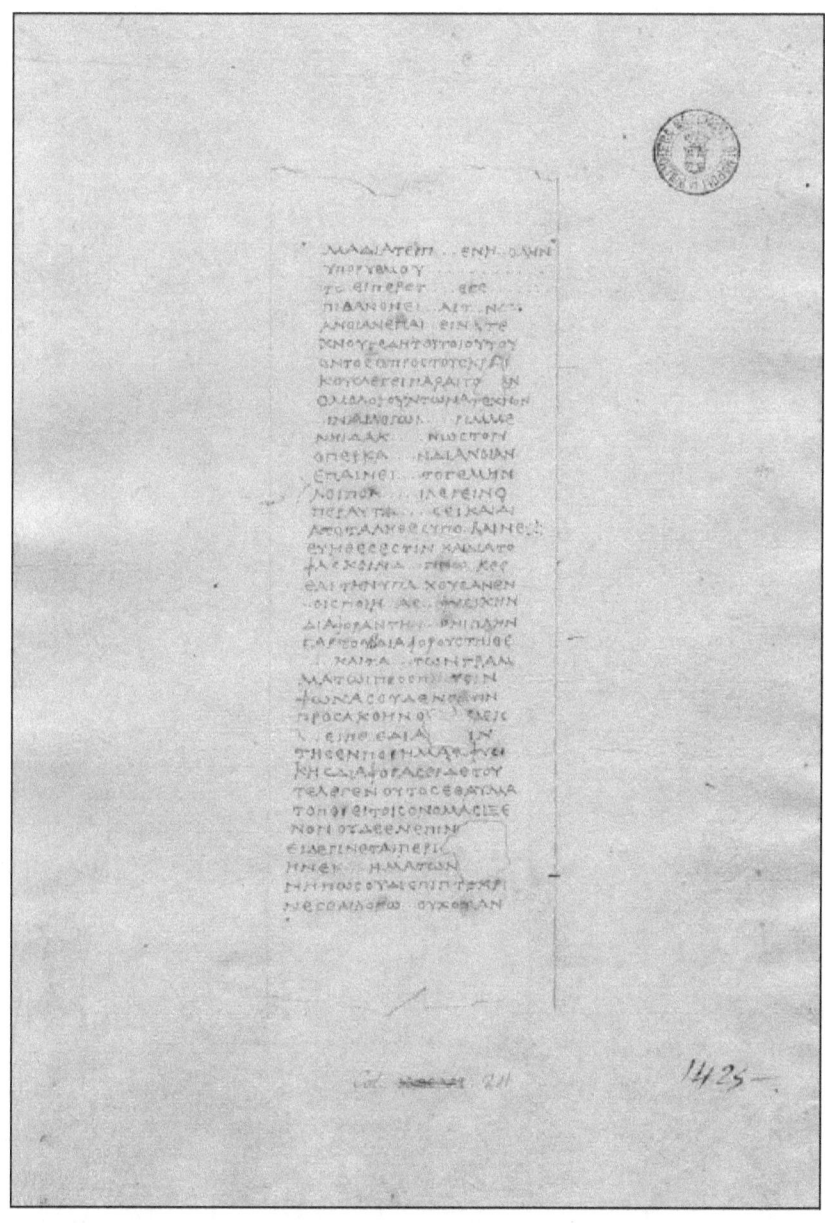

Herculaneum Papyrus 1425 facsimile. Drawn by Giuseppe Casanova ca. 1807. Photo: public domain.

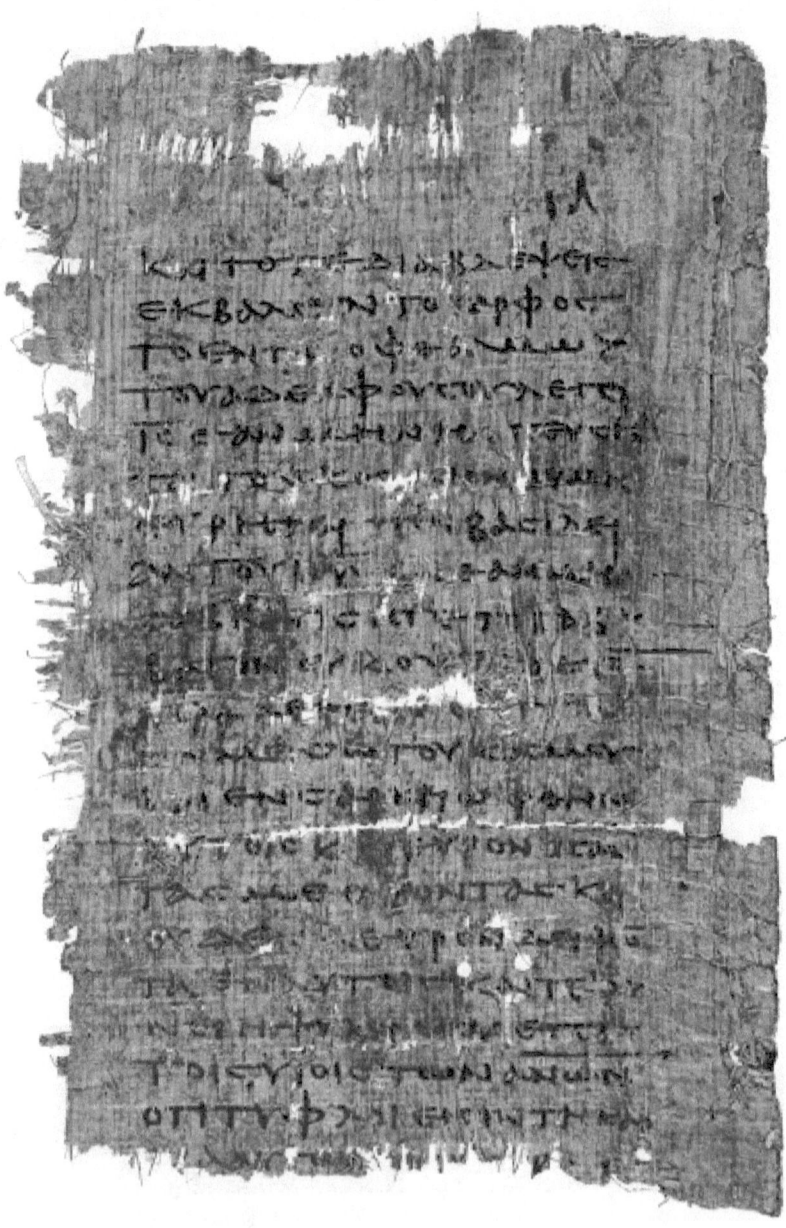

Greek fragment of the *Gospel of Thomas*. Three Greek fragments of unknown "Sayings of Jesus" were recovered from Oxyrhynchus. In 1945 a complete Coptic translation was recovered from Nag Hammadi. It was then that scholars realized that the Greek fragments were from the *Gospel of Thomas*. Depicted is P.Oxy 1. Photo: public domain.

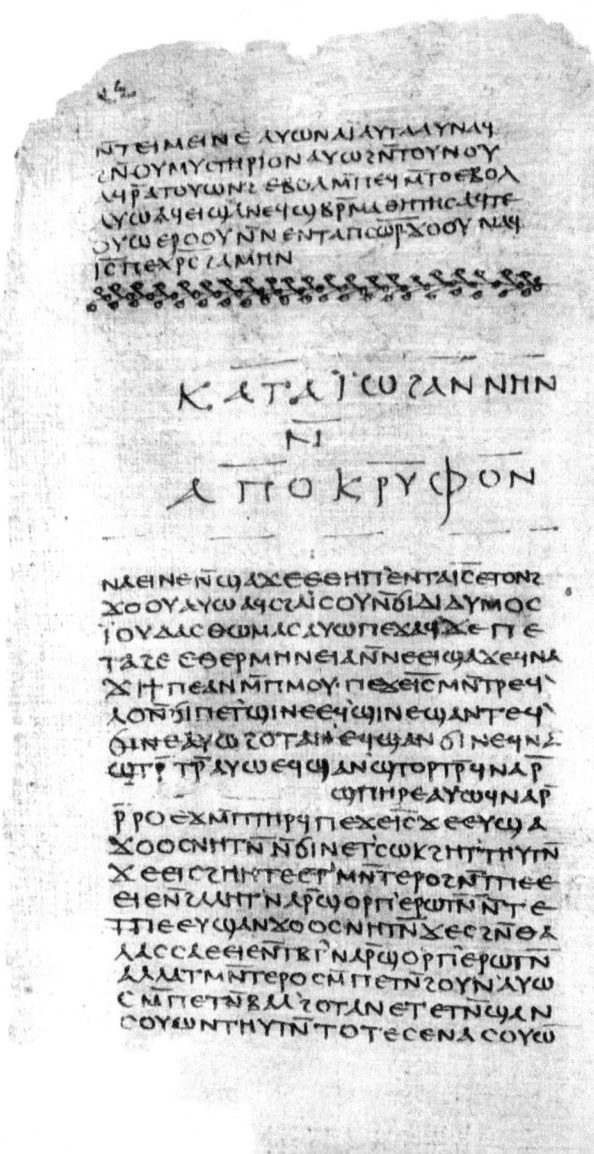

First page of Coptic *Gospel of Thomas*. A complete Coptic version of the *Gospel of Thomas* was found in 1945. It is now designated as tractate 2 in Nag Hammadi Codex II (i.e., NHC II,2). Photo: public domain.

226 APPENDIX: PHOTOS OF ANCIENT JEWISH AND CHRISTIAN MANUSCRIPTS

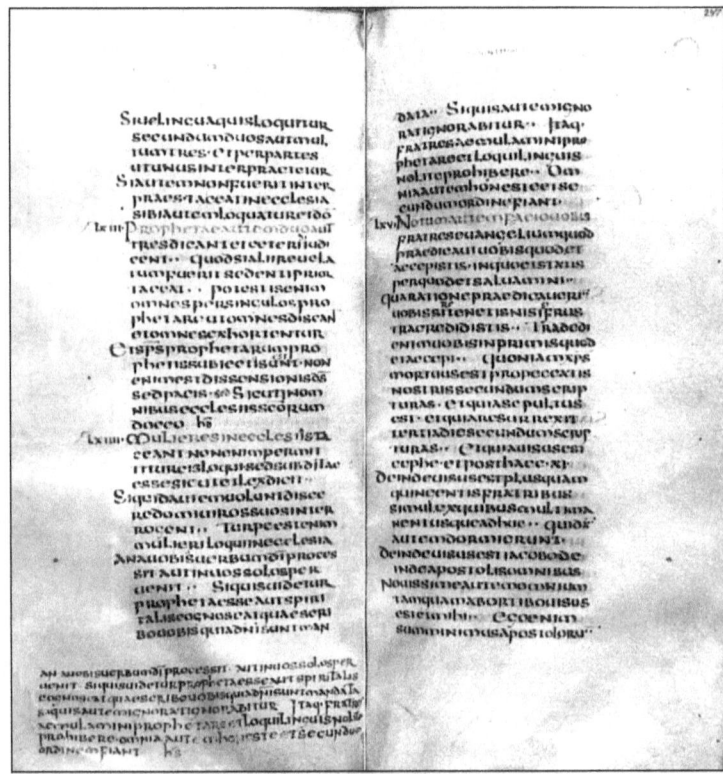

Codex Fuldensis 296–297. The sixth-century Codex Fuldensis 296–297 is an early and important witness to the text of Tatian's *Diatessaron*. Photo: public domain.

Leaf of the Akhmîm Codex, *Gospel of Peter*. A large part of the Passion narrative was recovered from Akhmîm in 1887. The text was eventually identified as belonging to the *Gospel of Peter*, an elaboration of the earlier canonical Gospels, especially Matthew. The *Gospel of Peter* describes a very tall Jesus emerging from the tomb, followed by a walking, talking cross. Photo: public domain.

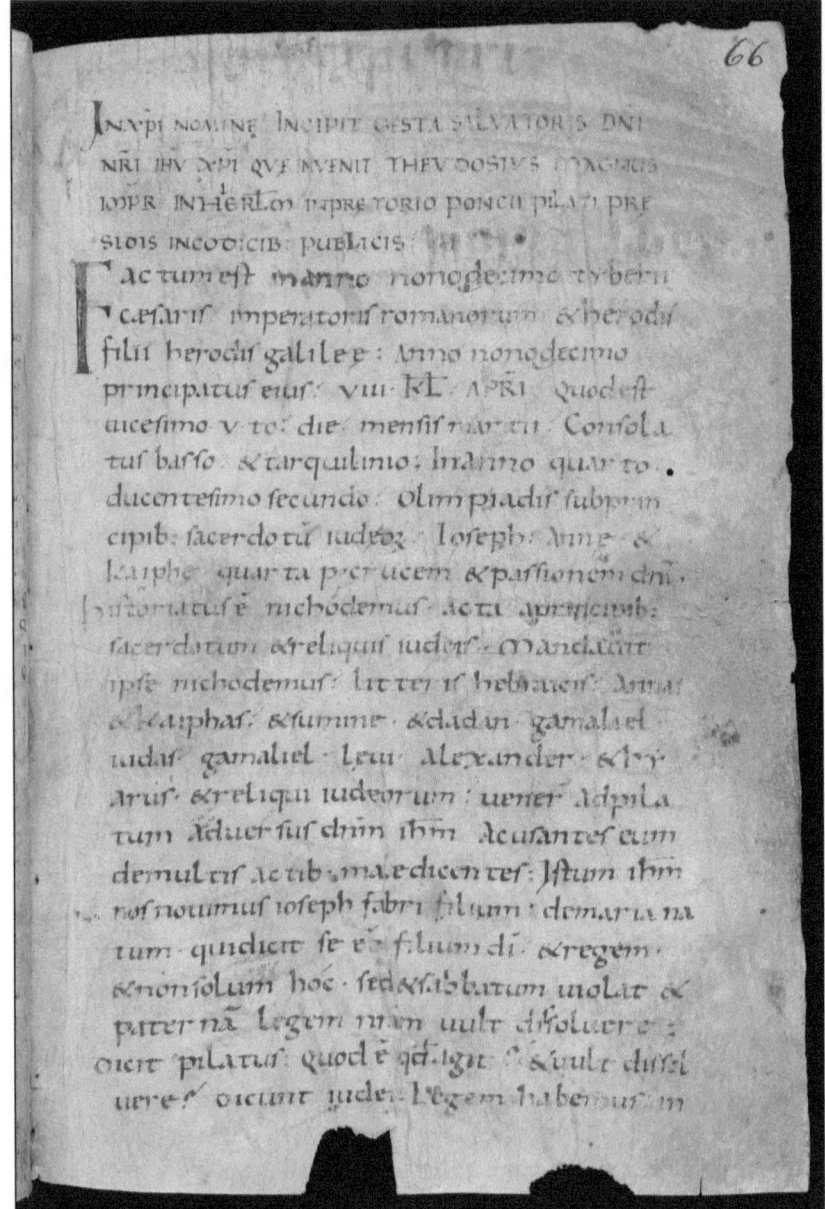

Acts of Pilate / Gospel of Nicodemus. The *Acts of Pilate* (also called the *Gospel of Nicodemus*) narrates a greatly embellished account of the trial, execution, and resurrection of Jesus. Depicted is a page of a ninth- or tenth-century parchment version of this work. Photo: public domain.

APPENDIX: PHOTOS OF ANCIENT JEWISH AND CHRISTIAN MANUSCRIPTS   229

Gospel of Judas. The 2006 publication of the *Gospel of Judas*, one of the tractates found in Codex Tchacos, created a public sensation. The initial interpretation that the *Gospel of Judas* portrays Judas Iscariot, the disciple who betrayed Jesus, as a hero has been largely abandoned. Depicted is leaf 33, the first page of the *Gospel of Judas*. Photo: public domain.

Mar Saba Clementine letter. At the 1960 annual meeting of the Society of Biblical Literature, Columbia University professor Morton Smith announced that he had found a letter of Clement of Alexandria in which mention is made of a mystical or secret version of the Gospel of Mark. Scholars today are sharply divided on the question of the authenticity of this document and Smith's account of its discovery. Depicted is the second of the three pages of Greek penned in the back of an old book found in the Mar Saba Monastery in the Judean Desert. Photo: public domain.

APPENDIX: PHOTOS OF ANCIENT JEWISH AND CHRISTIAN MANUSCRIPTS   231

Jesus in the Infancy Gospel. The fourteenth-century Klosterneuburger *Evangelienwerk* contains some of the Infancy Gospel, in which the youthful Jesus performs astounding feats. Depicted (fol. 28r) is Jesus making birds from clay. Photo: public domain.

P. Egerton 2. The Egerton Papyrus 2 is made up of fragments of what may have been a Gospel harmony. The papyrus dates to the middle of the second century and may actually be an autograph. Depicted are fragments 2–3. Photo: public domain.

APPENDIX: PHOTOS OF ANCIENT JEWISH AND CHRISTIAN MANUSCRIPTS 233

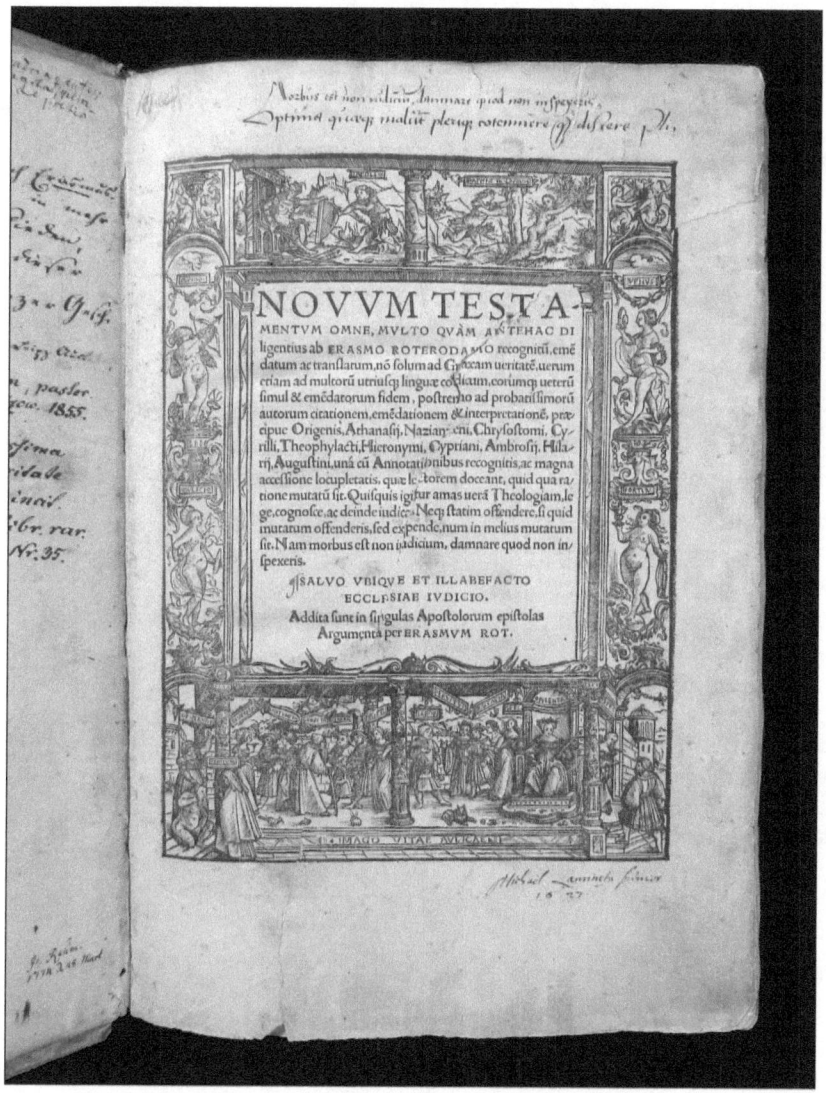

***Novum Testamentum omne* (1519).** Erasmus brought out a second edition of his Greek New Testament in 1519, this time under the title *Novum Testamentum omne*, "The Complete New Testament." Depicted here is the title page. Courtesy of the Dunham Bible Museum, Houston Christian University. Photo: Ginny Evans.

234 APPENDIX: PHOTOS OF ANCIENT JEWISH AND CHRISTIAN MANUSCRIPTS

***Novum Testamentum omne*, Mark's incipit**. The incipit of the Gospel of Mark in the 1519 edition of the *Novum Testamentum omne*. Courtesy of the Dunham Bible Museum, Houston Christian University. Photo: Ginny Evans.

***Novum Testamentum omne* (1519) with error.** The printing press reduced the number of errors in the second edition, but it did not eliminate them. On page 119 of this edition, the running header over the Latin column reads *secundum Marcum*, "according to Mark," instead of *secundum Lucam*, "according to Luke." The running header over the Greek column on the left is correct, however. Courtesy of the Dunham Bible Museum, Houston Christian University. Photo: Ginny Evans.

Martin Luther's *Das Neue Testament* (1524). Depicted is the title page of Martin Luther's 1524 German translation of the New Testament. The page is illustrated with a number of scenes, mostly from the Gospels. Courtesy of the Dunham Bible Museum, Houston Christian University. Photo: Ginny Evans.

APPENDIX: PHOTOS OF ANCIENT JEWISH AND CHRISTIAN MANUSCRIPTS 237

Bishops' Bible, Matthew's incipit. The title of Matthew is given as *"The Gospell by Saint Matthew."* Courtesy of the Dunham Bible Museum, Houston Christian University. Photo: Ginny Evans.

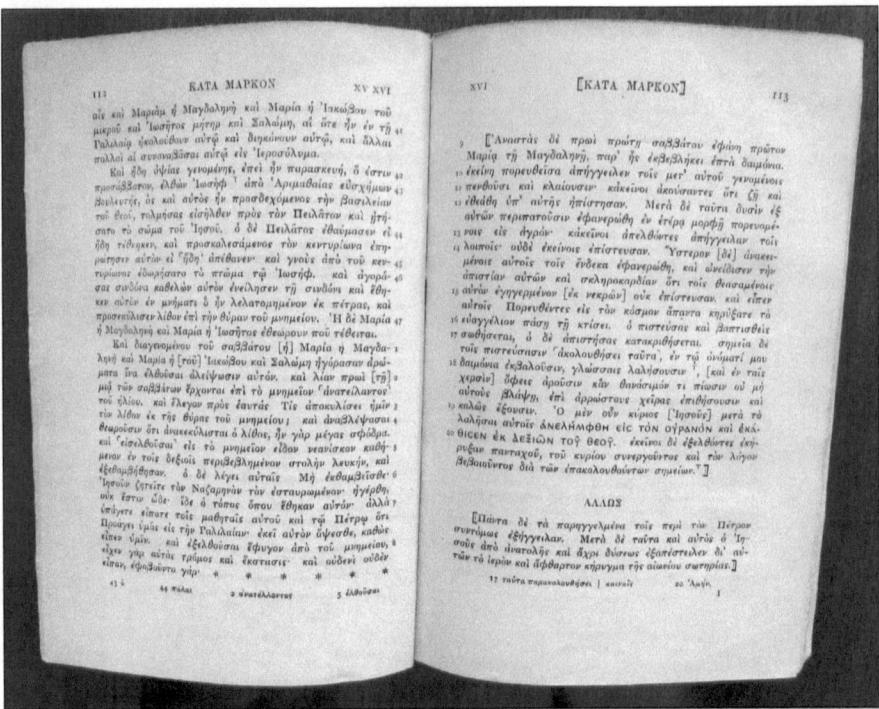

The New Testament in the Original Greek (1881). B. F. Westcott and F. J. A. Hort's *The New Testament in the Original Greek* (1881; American ed., 1882) was controversial because it represented a break from the Textus Receptus, the Greek text based on the Majority Text tradition (the so-called Byzantine mss). Depicted are the last two pages of the Gospel of Mark. On the left (p. 112), Mark 16 ends with verse 8. On the right (p. 113), Westcott and Hort provide the Long Ending (Mark 16:9–20) and the so-called Short Ending. Courtesy of Craig Evans. Photo: Ginny Evans.

Select Bibliography on the Biblical Canon and Inspiration of Scripture

The following sources do not draw the same conclusions, but they all are significant resources on the biblical canon, non-canonical writings, and the notion of inspiration of Scripture in antiquity.

Achtemeier, Paul J. *Inspiration and Authority: Nature and Function of Christian Scripture*. Peabody, MA: Hendrickson, 1999.
Allert, Craig D. *A High View of Scripture? The Authority of the Bible and the Formation of the New Testament Canon*. Grand Rapids: Baker Academic, 2007.
———. "Is Translation Inspired? The Problem of Verbal Inspiration for a Translation and a Proposed Solution." In *Translating the Bible: Problems and Prospect*, edited by S. E. Porter and R. S. Hess, 85–113. London: Sheffield Academic, 1999.
Anderson, G. W. "Canonical and Non-Canonical." In *The Cambridge History of the Bible: From the Beginnings to Jerome*, edited by P. R. Ackroyd and C. F. Evans, 1:113–59. Cambridge: Cambridge University Press, 1970.
Barr, James. *Holy Scripture: Canon, Authority, Criticism*. Philadelphia: Westminster, 1983.
Barton, John. *Holy Writings, Sacred Text: The Canon in Early Christianity*. Louisville: Westminster John Knox, 1997.
———. *Oracles of God: Perceptions of Ancient Prophecy in Israel after the Exile*. Rev. ed. Oxford: Oxford University Press, 2007.
Bauckham, R. J., et al., eds. *Old Testament Pseudepigrapha: More Noncanonical Scriptures*. Vol. 1. Grand Rapids: Eerdmans, 2013.
Beckwith, Roger T. *The Old Testament Canon of the New Testament Church*. Grand Rapids: Eerdmans, 1985.
Beegle, Dewey M. *Scripture, Tradition, and Infallibility*. 2nd ed. Grand Rapids: Eerdmans, 1973.
Berkouwer, G. C. *Holy Scripture: Studies in Dogmatics*. Grand Rapids: Eerdmans, 1975.
Bokedal, Tomas. *The Formation and Significance of the Christian Biblical Canon: A Study in Text, Ritual and Interpretation*. London: T&T Clark, 2014.

Brakke, David. "Canon Formation and Social Conflict in Fourth-Century Egypt: Athanasius of Alexandria's Thirty-Ninth Festal Letter." *Harvard Theological Review* 8 (1994) 395–419.

Brogan, John J. "Can I Have Your Autograph: Uses and Abuses of Textual Criticism in Formulating an Evangelical Doctrine of Inerrancy." In *Evangelicals and Scripture: Tradition, Authority, and Hermeneutics*, edited by V. Bacote et al., 93–111. Downers Grove, IL: InterVarsity, 2004.

Bromiley, G. W. "Inspiration, History of the Doctrine of." In *The International Standard Bible Encyclopedia*, edited by G.W. Bromiley at al., 2:849–54. Rev. ed. Grand Rapids: Eerdmans, 1982.

Brown, Michelle P. "Spreading the Word: The Single-Volume Bible." In *In the Beginning: Bibles Before the Year 1000*, edited by Michelle P. Brown, 176–203. Washington, DC: Smithsonian, 2006.

Brown, Raymond E. *An Introduction to the New Testament.* New York: Doubleday, 1997.

Bruce, F. F. *The Books and the Parchments: How We Got Our English Bible.* 5th ed. London: Marshall Pickering, 1991.

———. *The Canon of Scripture.* Downers Grove, IL: InterVarsity, 1998.

———. *In Retrospect: Autobiographical Remembrances.* Nashville: Kingsley, 2007 (originally published as F. F. Bruce, *In Retrospect: Remembrance of Things Past.* London: Marshall Pickering, 1980).

———. *Paul: Apostle of the Heart Set Free.* Grand Rapids: Eerdmans, 1994.

Burke, Tony, and Brent Landau, eds. *New Testament Apocrypha: More Noncanonical Scriptures.* 2 vols. Grand Rapids: Eerdmans, 2016–2020.

Campenhausen, Hans von. *The Formation of the Christian Bible.* Minneapolis: Fortress, 1977.

Carr, David M. *The Formation of the Hebrew Bible: A New Reconstruction.* Oxford: Oxford University Press, 2011.

———. *Writing on the Tablet of the Heart: Origins of Scripture and Literature.* Oxford: Oxford University Press, 2005.

Chapman, Stephen B. "Canon, Old Testament." In *The Oxford Encyclopedia of the Books of the Bible*, edited by M. D. Coogan, 1:97–109. Oxford: Oxford University Press, 2011.

Charlesworth, J. H., ed. *The Old Testament Pseudepigrapha.* 2 vols. Garden City, NY: Doubleday, 1983, 1985.

Collins, John J. *Apocalypse, Prophecy, and Pseudepigraphy: On Jewish Apocalyptic Literature.* Grand Rapids: Eerdmans, 2015.

———. *The Apocalyptic Imagination: An Introduction to Jewish Apocalyptic Literature.* 3rd ed. Grand Rapids: Eerdmans, 2016.

———. "The 'Apocryphal' Old Testament." In *The New Cambridge History of the Bible: From the Beginnings to 600*, edited by J. C. Paget and J. Schaper, 165–89. Cambridge: Cambridge University Press, 2013.

———. "Before the Canon: Scriptures in Second Temple Judaism." In *Old Testament Interpretation: Past, Present, and Future*, edited by James Luther Mays et al., 225–41. Nashville: Abingdon, 1995.

———. *Beyond the Qumran Community. The Sectarian Movement of the Dead Sea Scrolls.* Grand Rapids: Eerdmans, 2010.

———. *The Invention of Judaism: Torah and Jewish Identity from Deuteronomy to Paul.* Oakland: University of California Press, 2017.

———. "The Penumbra of the Canon. What do the Deuterocanonical Books Represent?" In *Canonicity, Setting, Wisdom in the Deuterocanonicals*, edited by Géza G. Xeravits et al., 1–17. Deuterocanonical and Cognate Literature Studies 22. Berlin: de Gruyter, 2014.

Collins, John J., et al. *Ancient Jewish and Christian Scriptures: New Developments in Canon Controversy*. Louisville: Westminster John Knox, 2020.

Collins, Raymond F. *Letters That Paul Did Not Write: The Epistle to the Hebrews and the Pauline Pseudepigrapha*. Eugene, OR: Wipf and Stock, 2006.

Cowe, S. Peter. "The Bible in Armenian." In *The New Cambridge History of The Bible: From 600–1450*, edited by Richard Marsden and E. Ann Matter, 143–61. Cambridge: Cambridge University Press, 2012.

Craig, William Lane. "'Men Moved by the Holy Spirit Spoke From God' (2 Peter 1.21): A Middle Knowledge Perspective on Biblical Inspiration." *Philosophia Christi* 1 (1999) 45–82. https://www.reasonablefaith.org/writings/scholarly-writings/divine-omniscience/men-moved-by-the-holy-spirit-spoke-from-god-2-peter-1.21-a-middle-knowledge/.

Crawford, Lorin L. "Inspiration." In *Encyclopedia of Early Christianity*, edited by Everett Ferguson 1:576–79. 2nd ed. New York: Garland, 1997.

Cross, Frank Moore. *From Epic to Canon*. History and Literature in Ancient Israel. Baltimore: Johns Hopkins University Press, 1998.

Davila, James R. "Questions from Lost Books in the Hebrew Bible: A New Translation and Introduction with an Excursus on Quotations from Lost Books in the New Testament." In *Old Testament Pseudepigrapha: More Noncanonical Scriptures*, edited by R. Baucham, J. Davila, and A. Panayotov, 1:673–98. Grand Rapids: Eerdmans, 2013.

De Troyer, Kristin. *Rewriting the Sacred Text: What the Old Greek Texts Tell Us About the Literary Growth of the Bible*. Text Critical Studies 4. Atlanta: Society of Biblical Literature, 2003.

deSilva, David A. *The Jewish Teachers of Jesus, James, and Jude: What Earliest Christianity Learned from the Apocrypha and Pseudepigrapha*. Oxford: Oxford University Press, 2014.

Dobrovolny, Mary Kay. "Inspiration and Revelation." In *The Interpreter's Dictionary of the Bible*, edited by Katharine D. Sakenfeld, 3:57–63. Nashville: Abingdon, 2008.

Dunn, J. D. G. "Has the Canon a Continuing Function?" In *The Canon Debate*, edited by Lee Martin McDonald and James A. Sanders, 558–79. Peabody, MA: Hendrickson, 2002.

———. *Jesus Remembered*. Christianity in the Making 1. Grand Rapids: Eerdmans, 2003.

Edrei, Arye, and Doran Mendels. "A Split Jewish Diaspora: Its Dramatic Consequences." *Journal for the Study of Pseudepigrapha* 16 (2007) 91–137.

———. "Why Did Paul Succeed Where the Rabbis Failed? The Reluctance of the Rabbis to Translate Their Teachings in Greek and Latin and the Split Jewish Diaspora." In *Jesus Research: New Methodologies and Perceptions*, edited by J. H. Charlesworth, 361–96. Grand Rapids: Eerdmans, 2014.

Edwards, James R. *The Hebrew Gospel and the Formation of the Synoptic Tradition*. Grand Rapids: Eerdmans, 2009.

Ehrman, Bart D. *Forged: Writing in the Name of God—Why the Bible's Authors Are Not Who We Think They Are*. New York: Harper Collins, 2011.

Elliott, J. K., ed. *The Apocryphal New Testament: A Collection of Apocryphal Christian Literature in an English Translation Based on M. R. James*. Oxford: Clarendon, 1993.

Enns, Peter. *Inspiration and Incarnation: Evangelicals and the Problem of the Old Testament*. Grand Rapids: Baker Academic, 2005.

Epp, Eldon Jay. "Issues in the Interrelation of New Testament Textual Criticism and Canon." In *The Canon Debate*, edited by Lee Martin McDonald and James A. Sanders, 485–515. Peabody, MA: Hendrickson, 2002.

———. *Perspectives on New Testament Textual Criticism: Collected Essays, 1962–2004*. NovTSup 116. Leiden: Brill, 2005.

Evans, Craig A. *Jesus and the Manuscripts: What We Can Learn from the Oldest Texts*. Peabody, MA: Hendrickson, 2020.

———. "Textual Criticism and Textual Confidence: How Reliable Is Scripture?" In *Textual Reliability of the New Testament: Bart D. Ehrman and Daniel B. Wallace in Dialogue*, edited by Robert B. Stewart, 162–72. Minneapolis: Fortress, 2011.

Ferguson, Everett. "Inspiration." In *Encyclopedia of Early Christianity*, edited by Everett Ferguson, 1:576–79. 2nd ed. New York: Garland, 1997.

Flint, Peter W., ed. *The Bible at Qumran: Text Shape and Interpretation*. Grand Rapids: Eerdmans, 2001.

———. "Noncanonical Writings in the Dead Sea Scrolls." In *The Bible at Qumran: Text, Shape, and Interpretation*, edited by P. W. Flint, 80–126. Grand Rapids: Eerdmans, 2001.

Frey, Jörg, and John R. Levinson, eds. *The Holy Spirit, Inspiration, and the Cultures of Antiquity: Multidisciplinary Perspectives*. Ekstasis 5. Berlin: de Gruyter, 2014.

Frey, Jörg, and Kathleen Ess. *The Letter of Jude and Second Letter of Peter: A Theological Commentary*. Waco, TX: Baylor University Press, 2018.

Gallagher, Edmon L. "The Blood from Abel to Zechariah in the History of Interpretation." *New Testament Studies* 60 (2014) 121–38.

———. "The End of the Bible? The Position of Chronicles in the Canon." *Tyndale Bulletin* 65 (2014) 181–99.

Gallagher, Edmon L., and John Meade. *The Biblical Canon Lists from Early Christianity: Texts and Analysis*. Oxford: Oxford University Press, 2017.

Gamble, Harry Y. *Books and Readers in the Early Church: A History of Early Christian Texts*. New Haven, CT: Yale University Press, 1995.

Gerstner, John. *A Bible Inerrancy Primer*. Winona Lake, IN: Alpha, 1985.

Gnuse, Robert. *The Authority of the Bible: Theories of Inspiration, Revelation, and the Canon of Scripture*. Mahwah, NJ: Paulist, 1985.

Grant, Robert M. "The New Testament Canon." Pages 284–307 in *From the Beginnings to Jerome*. Edited by P. R. Ackroyd and C. F. Evans. Vol. 1 of *Cambridge History of the Bible*. Cambridge: Cambridge University Press, 1970.

Graves, Michael. *The Inspiration and Interpretation of Scripture: What the Early Church Can Teach Us*. Grand Rapids: Eerdmans, 2014.

Goodacre, Mark. "Fatigue in the Synoptics." *New Testament Studies* 44 (1998) 45–58. http://www.markgoodacre.org/Q/fatigue.htm.

Gregory, Andrew W., and Christopher Tuckett, eds. *The Oxford Handbook of Early Christian Apocrypha*. Oxford: Oxford University Press, 2015.

Gunkel, Heidrun, et al. "Plutarch and Pentecost: An Exploration in Interdisciplinary Collaboration." In *The Holy Spirit, Inspiration, and the Cultures of Antiquity:*

Multidisciplinary Perspectives, edited by J. Frey and John R. Levinson, 63–95. Ekstasis 5. Berlin: de Gruyter, 2014.

Hill, C. E. "The Truth Above All Demonstration: Scripture in the Patriotic Period to Augustine." In *The Enduring Authority of the Christian Scriptures*, edited by D. A. Carson, 43–88. Grand Rapids: Eerdmans, 2016.

———. *Who Chose the Gospels? Probing the Great Conspiracy*. New York: Oxford University Press, 2010.

Holladay, Carl R. *A Critical Introduction to the New Testament: Interpreting the Message and Meaning of Jesus Christ*. Nashville: Abingdon, 2005.

Hovhanessian, Vahan S. "New Testament Apocrypha and the Armenian Version of the Bible." In *The Canon of the Bible and the Apocrypha in the Churches of the East*, edited by V. Hovhanessian, 63–87. Bible in the Christian Orthodox Tradition 2. New York: Lang, 2012.

Hubbard, David A. "The Current Tensions: Is There a Way Out?" In *Biblical Authority*, edited by Jack Rogers, 149–81. Waco, TX: Word, 1997.

Hurtado, Larry W. *The Earliest Christian Artifacts: Manuscripts and Christian Origins*. Grand Rapids: Eerdmans, 2006.

———. "The Origins of the Nomina Sacra." *Journal of Biblical Literature* 117 (1998) 655–73.

James, M. R. *The Apocryphal New Testament*. Corrected ed. Oxford: Clarendon, 1953.

Johnson, Luke Timothy. *Religious Experience in Earliest Christianity: A Missing Dimension in New Testament Study*. Minneapolis: Fortress, 1998.

Johnston, Robert K. *Evangelicals at an Impasse: Biblical Authority in Practice*. Atlanta: John Knox, 1979.

Kalin, Everett R. "Argument from Inspiration in the Canonization of the New Testament." ThD diss., Harvard University, 1967.

———. The Inspired Community: A Glance at Canon History." *Concordia Theological Monthly* 42 (1971) 541–49.

Keener, Craig S. *Acts: An Exegetical Commentary. Introduction and 1:1—2:47*. Grand Rapids: Baker Academic, 2012.

———. *Acts: An Exegetical Commentary. 15:1—23:35*. Grand Rapids: Baker Academic, 2014.

Keener, Craig. S., and L. William Oliverio Jr., eds. *The Spirit Throughout the Canon: Pentecostal Pneumatology*. Leiden: Brill, 2022.

Kelly, J. N. D. *Early Christian Doctrines*. Rev. ed. New York: Harper & Row, 1978.

Kelsey, David H. *The Uses of Scripture in Recent Theology*. Philadelphia: Fortress, 1975.

Koester, Helmut. *Ancient Christian Gospels: Their History and Development*. London: SCM, 1990.

Kruger, Michael J. "Early Christian Attitudes Toward the Reproduction of Texts." In *The Early Text of the New Testament*, edited by Charles E. Hill and Michael J. Kruger, 63–80. New York: Oxford University Press, 2014.

———. *The Question of Canon: Challenging the Status Quo in the New Testament Debate*. Downers Grove, IL: InterVarsity, 2013.

Lampe, G. W. H. "Inspiration and Revelation." In *The Interpreter's Dictionary of the Bible*, edited by G. A. Buttrick, 2:713–18. Nashville: Abingdon, 1962.

Levine, A.-J. "Bearing False Witness: Common Errors Made About Early Judaism." In *The Jewish New Testament*, edited by A.-J. Levine and M. Z. Brettler, 118–19, 249–50, and 759–63. 2nd ed. Oxford: Oxford University Press, 2017.

Levine, L. I. *The Ancient Synagogue: The First Thousand Years.* 2nd ed. New Haven, CT: Yale University Press, 2005.

Lewis, Jack P. "Jamnia Revisited." In *The Canon Debate*, edited by L. M. McDonald and J. A. Sanders, 146–62. Peabody MA: Hendrickson, 2002.

———. "What Do We Mean by Jabneh." *Journal of Bible and Religion* 32 (1964) 125–32.

Licona, Michael R. *Jesus, Contradicted: Why the Gospels Tell the Same Story Differently.* Grand Rapids: Zondervan, 2024.

———. *Why Are There Differences in The Gospels? What We Can Lean from Ancient Biography.* New York: Oxford University Press, 2017.

Liere, Frans van. *An Introduction to the Medieval Bible.* New York: Cambridge University Press, 2014.

Light, Laura. "The Thirteenth Century and the Paris Bible." In *The New Cambridge History of the Bible from 600–1450*, edited by Richard Marsden and E. Ann Matter, 2:380–91. Cambridge: Cambridge University Press, 2012.

Lim, Timothy H. *The Formation of the Jewish Canon.* AYBRL. New Haven, CT: Yale University Press, 2013.

Lindsell, Harold. *The Battle for the Bible.* Grand Rapids: Zondervan, 1976.

Marshall, I. Howard. *The Pastoral Epistles.* ICC. Edinburgh: T&T Clark, 1999.

Martens, Peter W. *Origen and Scripture: The Contours of the Exegetical Life.* Oxford: Oxford University Press, 2012.

McDonald, Lee Martin. "Ancient Manuscripts and Translations: What They Tell Us About the Status of the Church's Scriptures." In *Christian Origins and the Formation of the Early Church*, edited by S. E. Porter and Andrew W. P. Pitts. ECHC 5. Leiden: Brill, forthcoming.

———. *Before There Was a Bible: Authorities in Early Christianity.* London: T&T Clark, 2022.

———. "Bible, 04: Formation of Canons." *Brill Encyclopedia of Early Christianity Online.* http://dx.doi.org/10.1163/2589-7993_EECO_COM_036540.

———. *The Biblical Canon: Its Origin, Transmission, and Authority.* 3rd ed. Peabody, MA: Hendrickson, 2011.

———. "The Burial of Jesus in Light of Jewish Burial Practices and Roman Crucifixions." In *The Tomb of Jesus and His Family? Exploring Ancient Jewish Tombs Near Jerusalem's Walls*, edited by J. H. Charlesworth, 447–76. Grand Rapids: Eerdmans, 2013.

———. "The Canonical History of the Old Testament Apocrypha." In *Oxford Handbook of the Apocrypha*, edited by Gerbern Oegema, 24–51. Oxford: Oxford University Press, 2021.

———. "The Emergence of the Biblical Canons in Orthodox Christianity." In *The Oxford Handbook of the Bible in Orthodox Christianity*, edited by Eugen Pentiuc, 149–63. Oxford: Oxford University Press, 2022.

———. "Fluidity in the Early Formation of the Hebrew Bible/Tanakh." *Hebrew Studies Journal* 61 (2020) 201–23.

———. *Forgotten Scriptures: The Selection and Rejection of Early Religious Writings.* Louisville: Westminster John Knox, 2009.

———. *The Formation of the Bible: The Story of the Church's Canon.* Peabody, MA: Hendrickson, 2012.

———. *The Formation of the Biblical Canon.* 2 vols. London: T&T Clark, 2017.

———. *The Formation of the Christian Biblical Canon.* Nashville: Abingdon, 1998.

———. *The Formation of the Christian Biblical Canon.* Rev. and exp. ed. Peabody, MA: Hendrickson, 1995.

———. "Forming Christian Scriptures as a Biblical Canon." In *Ancient Jewish and Christian Scriptures: New Developments in Canon Controversy*, edited by John J. Collins et al., 133-40. Louisville: Westminster John Knox, 2020.

———. "The Gospels in Early Christianity: Their Origin, Use, and Authority." In *Reading the Gospels Today*, edited by S. E. Porter, 150-78. Grand Rapids: Eerdmans, 2004.

———. "Hellenism and the Biblical Canons: Is There a Connection?" In *Christian Origins and Hellenistic Judaism: Social and Literary Contexts for the New Testament*, edited by Stanley E. Porter and Andrew W. Pitts, 2:13-49. Texts and Editions for New Testament Study 10, Christianity in Its Hellenistic Context. Leiden: Brill, 2013.

———. "Jesus Tradition, Christian Creeds, and the New Testament Canon." In *Fountains of Wisdom: In Conversation with James H. Charlesworth*, edited by Gerbern S. Oegema et al., 185-97. London: T&T Clark, 2022.

———. "Lost Books." In *The Oxford Encyclopedia of the Books of the Bible*, edited by M. D. Coogan, 1:581-87. New York: Oxford University Press, 2011.

———. *The New Testament: Its Authority and Canonicity.* Volume 2 of *The Formation of the Biblical Canon.* London: T&T Clark, 2017.

———. "The Odes of Solomon in Early Christianity." In *Sacra Scriptura: How "Non-Canonical" Texts Functioned in Early Judaism and Early Christianity*, edited by J. H. Charlesworth and Lee M. McDonald, 108-36. T&T Clark Jewish and Christian Texts Series 20. London: T&T Clark, 2013.

———. *The Old Testament: Its Authority and Canonicity.* Vol. 1 of *The Formation of the Biblical Canon.* London: T&T Clark, 2017.

———. *The Origin of the Bible.* Guides for the Perplexed Series. New York: T&T Clark International/Continuum, 2011.

———. "The Parables of Enoch in Early Christianity." In *Parables of Enoch: A Paradigm Shift*, edited by D. L. Bock and J. H. Charlesworth, 329-63. T&T Clark Jewish and Christian Texts Series 11. London: Bloomsbury, 2011.

———. "Primary Authorities in Early Christianity: Canons and Rules of Faith." In *Essays in Honor of Craig A. Evans*, edited by Thomas Hatina and Stanley E. Porter, 296-332. Leiden: Brill, 2022.

———. "Pseudepigrapha in Early Christianity." In *The New Testament Canon in Contemporary Research*, edited by S. E. Porter and B. P. Laird. Leiden: Brill, forthcoming.

———. "The Reception of the Writings and Their Place in the Biblical Canon." In *The Oxford Handbook of the Writings of the Hebrew Bible*, edited by Donn Morgan 397-413. Oxford: Oxford University Press, 2018.

———. Review of *The Formation and Significance of the Christian Biblical Canon*, by Tomas Bokedal. *Review of Biblical Literature*, Feb. 8, 2016. http://www.bookreviews.org/BookDetail.asp?TitleId=9700.

———. "The Scriptures of Jesus: Did He Have a Biblical Canon?" In *Jesus Research: New Methodologies and Perceptions—The Second Princeton-Prague Symposium on Jesus Research, Princeton 2007*, edited by James H. Charlesworth, 827-62. Grand Rapids: Eerdmans, 2014.

———. *The Story of Jesus in History and Faith: An Introduction.* Grand Rapids: Baker Academic, 2013.

McDonald, Lee Martin, and James H. Charlesworth, eds. *Jewish and Christian Scriptures: The Function of "Canonical" and "Non-Canonical" Religious Texts.* Jewish and Christian Texts in Contexts and Related Studies Series 7. London: T&T Clark, 2010.

———. *"Non-Canonical" Religious Texts in Early Judaism and Early Christianity.* Jewish and Christian Texts in Contexts and Related Studies 14. London: T&T Clark, 2012.

McDonald, Lee Martin, and Joel B. Green, eds. *The World of the New Testament: An Examination of the Context of Early Christianity.* Grand Rapids: Baker Academic, 2013.

McDonald, Lee Martin, and Charles Hedrick. "Is the Bible the Word of God?" *Fourth 4* 29 (2016) 3–11.

McDonald, Lee Martin, and James A. Sanders, eds. *The Canon Debate.* Peabody, MA: Hendrickson, 2002.

McDonald, Lee Martin, and S. E. Porter. *Early Christianity and Its Sacred Literature.* Peabody, MA: Hendrickson, 2000.

———. *New Testament Introduction.* IBR Bibliographies 12. Grand Rapids: Baker Book House, 1996.

McDonald, Lee Martin, et al., eds. *Sacra Scriptura: How "Non-Canonical" Texts Function in Early Judaism and Early Christianity.* London: T&T Clark, 2013.

Metzger, B. M. *The Bible in Translation: Ancient and English Versions.* Grand Rapids: Baker, 2001.

———. *The Canon of the New Testament: Its Origin, Development, and Significance.* Oxford: Clarendon, 1987.

———. "Introduction to Apocryphal/Deuterocanonical Books." In *The New Oxford Annotated Bible with the Apocryphal/Deuterocanonical Books*, edited by B. M. Metzger and R. E. Murphy, iii–xv. New York: Oxford University Press, 1991.

Metzger, B. M., and Bart Ehrman. *The Text of the New Testament: Its Transmission, Corruption, and Restoration.* 3rd ed. New York: Oxford University Press, 1992.

Miller, J. W. "The Prophetologion: The Old Testament of Byzantine Christianity." In *The Old Testament in Byzantium*, edited by P. Magdalino and R. S. Nelson, 55–75. Washington, DC: Dumbarton Oaks Research Library and Collection, 2010.

Moore, George Foot. "Christian Writers on Judaism." *Harvard Theological Review* 14 (1921) 197–254.

———. *Judaism in the First Centuries of the Christian Era: The Age of the Tannaim.* 3 vols. Cambridge: Harvard University Press, 1927–1930.

Morgan, Donn F. *Between Text and Community: The "Writings" in Canonical Interpretation.* Minneapolis: Fortress, 1990.

Mroczek, Eva. *The Literary Imagination in Jewish Antiquity.* Oxford: Oxford University Press, 2016.

Neusner, Jacob. "Inspiration." In *Dictionary of Judaism in the Biblical Period*, edited by J. Neusner and W. S. Green, 316–17. Peabody, MA: Hendrickson, 1999.

Neusner, Jacob, and W. S. Green. *Writing with Scripture: The Authority and Uses of the Hebrew Bible in the Torah of Formative Judaism.* Minneapolis: Fortress, 1989.

Nickelsburg, George W. E. *1 Enoch 1.* Hermeneia. Minneapolis: Fortress, 2001.

———. *Resurrection, Immortality, and Eternal Life in Intertestamental Judaism and Early Christianity*. 2nd ed. Harvard Theological Studies 66. Cambridge: Harvard University Press, 2006.

Nickelsburg, George W. E., and James C. VanderKam. *1 Enoch 2*. Hermeneia. Minneapolis: Fortress, 2012.

Nongbri, Brent. *God's Library: The Archaeology of the Earliest Christian Manuscripts*. Translation Edition. New Haven, CT: Yale University Press, 2020.

Origen. *Commentary on Gospel of John*. Cambridge: Cambridge University Press, 2019.

Orr, James. *Revelation and Inspiration*. Grand Rapids: Eerdmans, 2015.

Osiek, C. *The Shepherd of Hermas*. Hermeneia. Minneapolis: Fortress, 1999.

Pennington, Jonathan T. *Reading the Gospels Wisely: A Narrative and Theological Introduction*. Grand Rapids: Baker Academic, 2012.

Pentiuc, Eugen J. *The Old Testament in Eastern Orthodox Tradition*. Oxford: Oxford University Press, 2014.

Poirier, John C. *The Invention of the Inspired Text: Philological Windows on the Theopneustia of Scripture*. LNTS 640. London: T&T Clark, 2021.

Porter, S. E., and Andrew W. Pitts. *Fundamentals of New Testament Criticism*. Grand Rapids: Eerdmans, 2015.

Quinn, Jerome D., and William C. Walker. *The First and Second Letters to Timothy*. Eerdmans Critical Commentary. Grand Rapids: Eerdmans, 2000.

Rajak, Tess. *Translation and Survival: The Greek Bible of the Ancient Jewish Diaspora*. Oxford: Oxford University Press, 2009.

Reed, Annette Yoshiko. "The Modern Invention of 'Old Testament Pseudepigrapha.'" *Journal of Theological Studies* 60 (2009) 403–36.

Reuss, E. W. *History of the Canon of the Holy Scriptures in the Christian Church*. Translated by D. Hunter. Edinburgh: Hunter, 1891.

Richards, E. Randolph. *Paul and First Century Letter Writing: Secretaries, Composition, and Collection*. Downers Grove, IL: IVP Academic, 2004.

Robinson, H. Wheeler. *Inspiration and Revelation in the Old Testament*. Oxford: Clarendon, 1946.

Rogers, Jack. *Biblical Authority*. Waco, TX: Word, 1977.

Rompay, Lucas Van. "1.1.3. The Syriac Canon." In *The Textual History of the Bible: The Deuterocanonical Scriptures*, edited by Armin Lange and Matthias Henze, 2A:136–65. Leiden: Brill, 2020.

Rothschild, Clare K. *The Muratorian Fragment*. WUNT I. Tübingen: Mohr Siebeck, 2022.

———. "The Muratorian Fragment as Roman Fake." *Novum Testamentum* 60 (2018) 55–82.

———, ed. *New Essays on the Apostolic Fathers*. WUNT 375. Tübingen: Mohr Siebeck, 2017.

Rouwhorst, Gerald. "The Bible in Liturgy." In *The New Cambridge History of the Bible from the Beginnings to 600*, edited by A. Lange, 822–42. Cambridge: Cambridge University Press, 2012.

Sanders, James A. "Canon: Hebrew Bible." In *Anchor Bible Dictionary*, edited by D. N. Freedman, 1:837–52. New York: Doubleday, 1992.

———. *The Monotheizing Process: Its Origins and Development*. Eugene OR: Cascade, 2014.

———. "'Spinning' the Bible." *Bible Review* 14 (1998) 22–29, 44–45.

———. "The Scrolls and the Canonical Process." In *The Dead Sea Scrolls After Fifty Years: A Comprehensive Assessment*, edited by P. W. Flint and J. C. VanderKam, 2:1–23. Leiden: Brill, 1999.

———. *Torah and Canon*. Philadelphia: Fortress, 1972.

Scanlin, Harold P. "The Old Testament Canon in the Orthodox Churches." In *New Perspectives on Historical Theology: Essays in Memory of John Meyendorf*, edited by Bradkey Nassif, 300–312. Grand Rapids: Eerdmans, 1996.

Schmidt, Daryl D. "The Greek New Testament as a Codex." In *The Canon Debate*, edited by L. M. McDonald and J. A. Sanders, 469–84. Peabody MA: Hendrickson, 2002.

Schneemelcher, Wilhelm, ed. *New Testament Apocrypha*. Rev. ed. 2 vols. Translated by R. McL. Wilson. Louisville: Westminster/John Knox, 1991.

Schneiders, Sandra M. "Inspiration and Revelation." In *The New Interpreter's Dictionary of the Bible*, edited by Katharine Doob Sakenfeld, 3:57–63. Nashville: Abingdon, 2008.

Schweizer, Eduard. "θεόπνευστος." In *The Theological Dictionary of the New Testament*, edited by Gerhard Kittel and Gerhard Friedrick, translated and edited by Geoffrey W. Bromiley, 6:453–55. Grand Rapids: Eerdmans, 1977.

Stendahl, Krister. "Apocalypse of John and the Epistles of Paul in the Muratorian Fragment." In *Current Issues in New Testament Interpretation: Essays in Honor of Otto A. Piper*, edited by W. Klassen and G. F. Snyder, 239–45. London: SCM, 1962.

Stuckenbruck, Loren T. *1 Enoch 91–108*. CEJL. Berlin: de Gruyter, 2007.

———. "Apocrypha and Pseudepigrapha." In *Early Judaism: A Comprehensive Overview*, edited by John J. Collins and Daniel C. Harlow, 179–203. Grand Rapids: Eerdmans, 2012.

———. "Daniel and the Early Enoch Traditions." In *The Book of Daniel: Composition and Reception*, edited by John J. Collins and Peter W. Flint, 368–86. VTSup 83. FIOTL 2. Leiden: Brill, 2001.

Talmon, S. *Text and Canon of the Hebrew Bible: Collected Essays*. Winona Lake, IN: Eisenbrauns, 2010.

Taussig, H., ed. *A New New Testament: A Bible for the Twenty-First Century*. New York: Houghton Mifflin Harcourt, 2013.

Tertullian. *Apologetical Works*. Translated by Rudolph Arbesmann et al. The Fathers of the Church 10. Washington, DC: Catholic University of America, 1985.

Tuckett, C. M. "Nomina Sacra: Yes or No?" In *The Biblical Canons*, edited by J.-M. Auwers and H. J. de Jonge, 431–58. Bibliotheca Ephemeridum Theologicarum Lovaniensium 163. Leuven: Leuven University Press, 2003.

Ulrich, Eugene C. *The Dead Sea Scrolls and the Developmental Composition of the Bible*. VTSup 169. Leiden: Brill, 1997.

———. "The Jewish Scriptures: Texts, Versions, Canons." In *Early Judaism: A Comprehensive Overview*, edited by J. J. Collins and Daniel C. Harlow, 97–119. Grand Rapids: Eerdmans, 2012.

———. "The Non-Attestation of a Tripartite Canon in 4QMMT." *Catholic Biblical Quarterly* 65 (2003) 202–14.

———. "The Notion and Definition of Canon." In *The Canon Debate*, edited by L. M. McDonald and J. A. Sanders, 21–52. Peabody MA: Hendrickson, 2002.

VanderKam, James C. *Enoch and the Growth of an Apocalyptic Tradition*. CBQMS 16. Washington, DC: Catholic Biblical Association of America, 1984.

———. "Questions of Canon Viewed Through the Dead Sea Scrolls." In *The Canon Debate*, edited by L. M. McDonald and J. A. Sanders, 91–109. Peabody MA: Hendrickson, 2002.

Vawter, Bruce. *Biblical Inspiration*. Theological Resources. Philadelphia: Westminster, 1972.

Verheyden, Joseph. "The Canon Muratori: A Matter of Dispute." In *The Biblical Canons*, edited by J.-M. Auwers and H. J. de Jonge, 487–556. BETL 163. Leuven: Peeters, 2003.

Vermes, Geza. *The Complete Dead Sea Scrolls in English*. Rev. ed. London: Penguin, 2004.

Warfield, B. B. *The Inspiration and Authority of the Bible*. Grand Rapids: Baker, 1964.

———. "Inspiration." In *The International Standard Bible Encyclopedia*, edited by G. W. Bromiley, 2:839–49. Grand Rapids: Eerdmans, 1982.

Wayment, T. A. *The Text of the New Testament Apocrypha (100-400 C.E.)*. London: T&T Clark, 2013.

Weitzman, M. P. *The Syriac Version of the Old Testament: An Introduction*. Cambridge: Cambridge University Press, 1999.

Witherington, Ben, III. *Invitation to the New Testament: First Things*. New York: Oxford University Press, 2013.

Witterreider, Annette. "The Infusion of the Spirit: The Meaning of ἐμφυσάω in John 20:22-23." In *The Holy Spirit, Inspiration, and the Cultures of Antiquity: Multidisciplinary Perspectives*, edited by Jörg Frey and John R. Levinson, 119–52. Ekstasis 5. Berlin: de Gruyter, 2014.

Wyrick, Jed. *The Ascension of Authorship: Attribution and Canon Formation in Jewish, Hellenistic, and Christian Traditions*. Cambridge: Harvard University Press, 2004.

Young, Francis. "Rethinking the Alexandrian–Antiochene Hermeneutical Antithesis." In *The Oxford Handbook of Origen*, edited by Ronald E. Heine and Karen Jo Torjesen, 175–91. Oxford: Oxford University Press, 2022.

www.ingramcontent.com/pod-product-compliance
Lightning Source LLC
Chambersburg PA
CBHW030822230426
43667CB00008B/1335